EXTRA INNINGS

BASEBALL

All-Star Stories, Stats, Lore & Legends

Publications International, Ltd.

Contributing Writers: Paul Adomites, Bruce Markusen, Matthew Silverman, Jon Springer, Marty Strasen, Jodi Webb, Saul Wisnia

Contributing Illustrator: Elizabeth Traynor

Facts verified by: Marci McGrath and Chris Smith

Contents

Seventh Inning

Eighth Inning

Ninth Inning

Batter Up!

Hey, baseball fans! Welcome to *Armchair Digest™: Extra Innings Baseball*.

Baseball has a long and colorful history, with fascinating personalities, long-standing traditions, spirited rivalries, and generation after generation of devoted fans. Sure, the uniforms and equipment have changed, and the players now earn a lot more money than they once did, but baseball today retains much of its vintage style.

Over the years, baseball has remained steeped in tradition and true to its original principles. It still has six outs per inning, nine innings per game. Take ball four and walk to first base; hit it fair over the fence and trot around the bases. The positions on the field haven't changed for more than 100 years, and even many of the teams are the same. The Pirates still play in Pittsburgh; the Cubs still suit up in Chicago; and even though they moved from Brooklyn to Los Angeles, the Dodgers still boast the same name. This uniformity and consistency is one of baseball's greatest traits. Throughout all the challenges it has faced (the Black Sox scandal, the Great Depression, segregation, World Wars I and II, the strikes of 1981 and 1994, the steroid controversy), the game's essence has endured.

With hundreds of entertaining anecdotes, memorable moments, and fascinating facts, baseball comes alive in *Armchair Digest™: Extra Innings Baseball*. The book pays tribute to the game's rich traditions with a treasure trove of eye-opening and compelling information, including the greatest moments, the unique and colorful personalities, the tension and the thrills, the joy of victory, and the heartbreak of loss. This is certainly one of the most entertaining compendiums on baseball you'll ever read.

Here are just a few of the many great stories you'll find inside:
- The biggest blunders and bloopers in baseball
- The history of baseball cards, Little League, and team mascots
- The nasty antics of baseball's bad boys
- The scrappiest on-field brawls
- The best—and quirkiest—ballparks, and what makes them so special
- The teams that earn the dubious honor of "worst of all time"

Once you start reading *Armchair Digest™: Extra Innings Baseball,* you'll find it hard to stop. There's no need to start at the beginning, either—you can open up to any page you like and begin your journey into the past.

After you've savored the stories, been fascinated by the facts, and learned about the greats of yesterday and today, you'll conclude that America's favorite pastime is still the same grand game it has always been— perhaps now it's even better.

The Oddest Homers in History

*Not every home run is a cut-and-dried event;
some are downright weird.*

Sometimes it is obvious that a home run has been hit the second the ball leaves the bat. Other times fans anxiously wait to see whether the ball sneaks over the wall or collides with the foul pole before they are able to celebrate a home run. And then there are those times when the ball takes an entirely different route and does something downright strange.

In the Doghouse

One of the oddest homers in history took place at American League Park, which was the home of the Washington Senators from 1904 to 1910. In this ballpark there was a doghouse near the outfield flagpole. The groundskeeper stored the flag inside the doghouse between games. One afternoon the doghouse door was left open, and a member of the Senators hit the ball inside of it. Philadelphia A's center fielder Socks Seybold crawled inside to retrieve the ball and got stuck, allowing the batter to circle the bases for an "inside-the-doghouse" home run.

Not a Stolen Base—A Stolen Ball!

That wasn't the first time an open door figured into a homer. On May 3, 1899, the Louisville Colonels were enjoying a comfortable lead over the home-team Pittsburgh Pirates until the Bucs staged a rally in the bottom of the ninth. Jack McCarthy had already homered when teammate Tom McCreery drove a ball to the right-field fence. A Pirates employee opened the right-field gate, picked up the ball, and ran off with it. McCreery circled the bases, and despite protests from the Louisville players, the umpire allowed the play to stand. The outcome was a 7–6 Pittsburgh victory. However, later that season at a league meeting, the game was thrown out and was replayed. It did not count in the final National League standings.

Feeling Heat from the Warm-Ups

In 1911, American League President Ban Johnson attempted to speed up games by eliminating warm-up pitches between innings. On June 27, at the Huntington Avenue Baseball Grounds, the Athletics' Stuffy McInnis capitalized on the rule change when he noticed Boston pitcher Ed Karger tossing warm-ups. McInnis hurried to the plate and drilled a ball that center fielder Tris Speaker refused to chase because he thought it was hit during warm-ups. McInnis rounded the bases for a home run. Umpire Ben Egan had no choice but to allow the homer to count because Johnson was sitting in the stands.

Oddities at Ebbets

In 1940 at Ebbets Field, Lonnie Frey of the Cincinnati Reds hit a ball to right field. It bounced off the screen and landed on top of the wall that extended between the scoreboard and foul pole. The ball bounced up and down but never fell back to the field of play, allowing Frey to complete an inside-the-park home run. Brooklyn's Pee Wee Reese duplicated the feat in the final game of the 1950 season.

Another home run that occurred at Ebbets Field seemed to defy the laws of gravity. George Cutshaw, who played for the Dodgers from 1912 to 1917, hit a line drive to the left-field wall. Apparently the ball had a lot of topspin on it; when it hit the wall, the ball rolled up and over the fence for a home run.

It Is! Or Is It?

One of the most memorable homers of George Brett's career was disallowed for a brief period of time. Brett's two-out, two-run, ninth-inning homer off Yankees relief ace Goose Gossage was a majestic drive. The game took place on July 24, 1983, at Yankee Stadium, and the blast gave the Royals a 5–4 lead over the Yanks. But after Brett circled the bases, New York manager Billy Martin came out of the dugout and asked the home plate umpire to examine Brett's bat. It was determined that the pine tar on Brett's bat exceeded the legal limit of 18 inches. Brett was called out, and the home run was nullified. The umpire was later overruled by American League President Lee MacPhail; the home run counted, and the game was picked up at that point and finished three weeks later despite Martin's furious protests. The Royals held on to their lead to claim the victory.

Just a Hop, Skip, and a Jump

Sometimes the opposition actually helps the hitter. In May 1993, Cleveland's Carlos Martinez hit a fly ball to right field that bounced off Jose Canseco's head and over the fence for a home run. The gift round-tripper gave the Tribe a 7–6 win over the Rangers.

While that was embarrassing for Canseco, it was at least less frustrating than what happened to Dick Cordell during a minor-league game on August 9, 1952. In the seventh inning of a scoreless game between Denver and Omaha in the Western League, Cordell ran down a long drive off the bat of Denver's Bill Pinckard. Cordell caught the ball before crashing into the left-field wall. The ball was jarred from his glove on impact, ricocheted off the wall, then bounced off his head and over the fence. After a lengthy discussion, the umpires ruled that Pinckard's drive was indeed a homer. It turned out to be the only run of the game.

Only the Best of Intentions

For Jim Bottomley, one home run wasn't worth all of the grief. Bottomley, who spent 16 seasons in the majors and led the NL with 31 homers in 1928, was once sued after one of his home runs hit a spectator in the face. The suit stated that Bottomley "swung on that ball deliberately and with the intention of creating a situation commonly known as a home run."

During questioning at a deposition, an attorney suggested that a skilled contact hitter could place the ball to whichever part of the field he determined. He then asked Bottomley, "Did you deliberately intend to hit anyone when you batted that ball?"

"No sir," replied Bottomley. "There is no malice in any of my home runs."

All-Time Great

Walter Johnson

The game's first true power pitcher rocketed wicked fastballs that approached 100 miles per hour with regularity.

Born: November 6, 1887; Humboldt, KS

MLB Career: Washington Senators, 1907–27

Hall of Fame Resume: Retired as the all-time strikeout king • His 110 career shutouts are 20 more than second-best • Pitched more than 300 innings nine years in a row • Led league in complete games six times • Averaged nearly 30 wins per season over a five-year period (1912–16)

Inside Pitch: Johnson also holds the record for shutouts lost (65), with 26 of them being to scores of 1–0.

The Cy Young Award is given annually to the best pitcher in each league, which is ironic considering it isn't even named for the finest pitcher of all time. Sure, Young had more wins than any other major-leaguer, with 511. But while Cy's time was winding down around 1910, another transcendent hurler was just getting started with the Washington Senators. And before he was through 21 years later, Walter Perry Johnson would be heralded as one of the game's grandest gentlemen—and the greatest pitcher of them all.

The son of Kansas farmers, Johnson was discovered playing for a semipro team in Idaho and was dispatched on a train to Washington—and the major leagues. A long-limbed right-hander with an easygoing sidearm motion, the 19-year-old could throw a blazing fastball but struggled to learn on the job, going 32–48 during his first three years with teams that never rose above seventh place.

In 1910, Johnson started to become more comfortable with his role as Washington's ace and turned in his first spectacular season with a 25–17 record, 1.36 ERA, and 313 strikeouts for the seventh-place Senators. In a pattern that would repeat itself many times, the man nicknamed "Big Train" was a frequent victim of nonsupport from his light-hitting mates; he would eventually lock up a record 64 contests decided by a 1–0 score—winning 38 of them.

The Senators improved dramatically over the next few years, and Johnson anchored second-place finishes in 1912 and '13 with records of 33–12 and 36–7, respectively. The latter may have been the finest performance ever by a major-league hurler, as it included such glittering numbers as a 1.14 ERA, 11 shutouts, and five one-hitters. Those who claim Sandy Koufax's 1962–66 binge was the finest five-year stretch in history should view Johnson's work from 1912 to '16: a 149–70 record, an ERA below 1.90 each season, 1,202 strikeouts, and just 326 walks over 1,794 innings. Eventually, he would pace the AL 12 times in strikeouts, six times in wins, and five times in ERA.

Washington slipped back to the second division as the years wore on; from 1914 to '23, Johnson finished with a winning record only four times. He still put together six straight 20-win campaigns, and then, in 1924, enjoyed the most satisfying year of his career—leading the league with 23 wins, a 2.72 ERA, 158 strikeouts, and six shutouts, and winning the seventh game of the only victorious World Series in Senators history.

Three more seasons and another World Series appearance followed before a broken leg derailed Johnson's career, but by then he had racked up 417 wins (second only to Young), a 2.17 ERA, and 3,509 strikeouts (a record that stood for more than 50 years). Shutouts? The charter Hall of Famer had a record 110 of them, 34 more than a guy named Young.

⚾ ⚾ ⚾

"You can't hit what you can't see."

> —John Daley after pinch-hitting against Walter Johnson

⚾ ⚾ ⚾

"You can have it. It wouldn't do me any good."

> —Ray Chapman to umpire Billy Evans after taking two strikes from Walter Johnson in 1915; he had already been on his way to the dugout when Evans informed him he still had one strike left

What Might Have Been

A great deal of luck is needed to sustain a productive major-league career. Sometimes that luck eludes a young superstar.

One of the heartbreaking elements of sport is that a player on his way to greatness can be derailed by something entirely out of his control. Three promising baseball stars who debuted between 1970 and '80 were struck down by illness or injury, leaving their sad and disappointed fans to wonder what might have been.

J. R. Richard

At 6'8", J. R. Richard possessed the size of an NBA star. He chose baseball instead—a good choice, given that he possessed a right arm that could unleash fastballs at nearly 100 miles per hour and sliders almost as fast. In his major-league debut for the Houston Astros, on September 5, 1971, Richard dominated the potent attack of the San Francisco Giants, striking out 15 batters.

Despite his record-tying debut, Richard's success was not a given. He struggled with his control, three times leading the National League in walks. He also suffered from a lack of stamina, the result of throwing too hard too early in each game. By 1978, Richard had addressed some of those weaknesses: He still walked too many batters, but he led the league in strikeouts, becoming the first right-hander in NL history to reach 300 Ks in a single season. The following year, Richard led all NL starters with a tidy 2.71 ERA. Richard's high-powered pitching not only intimidated opposing hitters; it also frightened his own teammates. "I've never taken batting practice against him," Astros first baseman Bob Watson told *The Sporting News*, "and I never would. I have a family to think about."

Richard continued his march toward stardom in 1980. While winning ten of his first 14 decisions, he posted an ERA of 1.90. It seemed as though Richard's career was on a Hall of Fame track. But in early July, Richard started complaining of a tired arm and said he wasn't feeling well. Some critics charged Richard with being lazy and unprofessional. Some fans and teammates even thought he had underlying motives for not wanting to play. But on July 30,

Richard felt so nauseated during a light workout with former teammate Wilbur Howard that he had to lay down on the field. Within moments, he was rushed to the hospital.

Doctors had previously determined that Richard had developed a blood clot in his pitching shoulder that was blocking the flow of blood in a vessel near his ribs. When another clot formed in Richard's right carotid artery, a major stroke ensued. The stroke completely paralyzed the left side of his body.

Richard did his best to recuperate. He ran four miles a day and regained some of the zip on his fastball. In 1982, he attempted a comeback in the minor leagues, but he was hit hard and struggled badly with his control. Richard would never make it back to the major leagues.

Mark "The Bird" Fidrych

While Richard struck an intimidating pose, Mark "The Bird" Fidrych looked more like a character from *Sesame Street*. As a rookie with the Detroit Tigers in 1976, Fidrych brought a whole new attitude to the lagging team. When one of his infielders made a great defensive play, Fidrych openly applauded. After recording the third out of each inning, The Bird didn't walk off the mound—he *ran*, usually in full sprint. He liked to "landscape" the mound with his cleats. And then there was his most distinctive habit: Fidrych actually talked to the baseball. By doing so, he felt he could make his pitches move in the ways that he wanted. Although not quite sure what to make of his antics at first, observers and players soon realized that Fidrych was a genuinely joyful (and talented) person, and his goofy style of play won The Bird a large flock of fans.

Showing excellent control of his above-average fastball, the 22-year-old Fidrych won 19 games in 1976 and sported the American League's best ERA (2.34). After Fidrych's amazingly successful debut season (for which he earned the AL's Rookie of the Year Award), the Tigers eagerly awaited his encore. But during a spring training game in 1977, Fidrych hurt his knee chasing a pop-up. He also tore his rotator cuff, but the injury went undiagnosed until 1985. He tried to keep playing, but he never regained the brilliance he displayed in his debut year.

Joe Charboneau

Big, bad Joe Charboneau was just as colorful as Fidrych but without the down-home innocence. His ride to the majors was rocky. After being signed by the Philadelphia Phillies in 1976, Charboneau quit playing ball in his second minor-league season because of a dispute with management. He took up slow-pitch softball for a while before returning to the Phillies. He hit well in the California League, but his habit of barroom brawling led the Phillies to trade him to the Cleveland Indians organization. After hitting .352 at Double-A in 1979, Charboneau finally earned a promotion to the major leagues, where he promptly won the 1980 American League Rookie of the Year Award.

Charboneau became enormously popular in Cleveland—and not just for his lusty hitting. Nicknamed "Super Joe," Charboneau emerged as a cult figure because of his unusual habits. He ate cigarettes, opened beer bottles with his eye sockets (and drank the brew through a straw in his nose), and once rid himself of an unwanted tattoo by cutting it out with a razor blade. He even tried to fix his own broken nose by twisting it back into place with pliers. Apparently his penchant for pain rubbed off on his fans: In March 1980, one of them stabbed him with a pen as he waited for the team bus. But Charboneau's crazy behavior didn't keep him from shining on the field, where he had a .289 batting average and knocked out a team-leading 23 home runs, along with 87 RBI.

However, Charboneau's reckless ways seemed to foreshadow a short career; his intensity was bound to catch up with him. In 1981, he slumped so badly that the Indians demoted him to the minor leagues (making him the first-ever Rookie of the Year to play in the minors the following year). A back injury only made his situation worse, necessitating two operations, neither of which helped. By 1983, Charboneau was playing minor-league ball for Cleveland's affiliate in Buffalo. Struggling with a .200 batting average, he decided to give the hometown fans an "obscene salute." The gesture angered Indians management, which gave him his release. Only four years after it had begun, the legend of Super Joe had reached its final chapter.

No-Hitter—No?

*Harvey Haddix pitches a game that will
go down in history—but not in the record books.*

On May 26, 1959, on a cool, damp night in Milwaukee, Pittsburgh Pirates lefty Harvey Haddix, while battling a powerful Braves lineup, pitched what is probably the greatest game in history, retiring 36 batters in a row before one reached base. Yet he lost the game. And then, years later, Major League Baseball said he hadn't pitched a no-hitter at all. You had to wonder what Harvey had done in a previous life to merit this kind of treatment.

The Braves had won back-to-back NL pennants and even toppled the legendary Yankees in the World Series two years before. The pitching star of that Series was Lew Burdette, the rangy right-hander who may or may not have thrown a spitball but made sure everyone thought he did. Harvey was up against Lew on May 26, 1959. That night Harvey was perfect, while Lew defined the notion of "good enough." The Pirates managed 12 singles and two walks, but the Braves turned three double plays and erased a baserunner at third on an overaggressive move.

Harvey's perfect game continued into extra innings, but the Pirates kept failing to score. Then, in the last of the 13th, Braves leadoff hitter Felix Mantilla reached on an error. There was a sacrifice bunt and an intentional walk before Joe Adcock hit the ball to deep right center. In the dismal conditions it was hard to tell if it cleared the fence—but it did. Amid the confusion, the runner on first, Hank Aaron, was passed by Adcock, turning the home run into a double. But it didn't matter. The run had scored, and Haddix's near-perfect masterpiece had ended.

In 1991, after a few questionable "no-hit" efforts began to clog the record books, MLB ruled that a pitcher had to finish the game, win, and not allow a hit in order to be credited with a no-hitter. Harvey was out of the record books despite what many consider the finest pitching performance in the history of the game.

Turning It Around

*Every so often, a team manages to turn their fortunes around,
digging themselves out from a huge deficit.*

When all is said and done, baseball is a game of streaks. Even the
worst hitter gets hot for a game or two; even the best puts together
a 2-for-30 at some point. What separates the champion from the
others is that the latter has more "up" streaks than "down" and
keeps them going longer.

Here are the tales of four teams that traveled a long way during
the course of one season to finish first, including some that fought
back from the verge of elimination to become world champs.

The Team: 1914 Boston Braves
The Deficit: 15 games behind first-place Giants on July 4
The Comeback: 68–19 after July 4

The Braves had lost 100 games or more four years in a row
when George Stallings was hired as manager for the 1913 season.
Their fifth-place finish that year was a welcome delight, but the
team started 1914 back in the cellar and was languishing there as
late as the Fourth of July.

Traveling home after a road trip, the Braves stopped for an
exhibition game against the minor-league Buffalo team. They got
trounced 10–2, which was a serious wake-up call for Stallings's
crew. They made their move, thanks in part to near-perfect pitching by 27-year-old Dick Rudolph (who
went 18–1 the sec-
ond half of
the season)
and 22-year-old
Bill James (17–1) and
great infield defense from new
kid Rabbit Maranville at short and old
hand Johnny Evers at second. Manager Stallings
relied on platooning to maximize his offensive strength, and his
team roared from last place to first in just 37 days.

In early September, Stallings conjured up another marvel by starting an inexperienced hurler (who had made only 21 big-league appearances through 1914) named George Davis against the Phils. The spitballer twirled a no-hitter. And once the Braves moved past the Giants, there was no stopping them. They finished the season 10½ games ahead of John McGraw's men. Then they jumped into the World Series and swept Connie Mack's Philadelphia A's in four games. No wonder they became known as "The Miracle Braves."

The Team: 1951 New York Giants
The Deficit: 13½ games back on August 11
The Comeback: 37–7 in the final 44 regular-season games

By 1951, the Giants and the Dodgers had been adversaries for decades. So when the Dodgers swept a three-game series at Ebbets Field from their rivals to take a huge 12½-game lead on August 9, they were in a celebratory mood. Knowing they could be heard in the visiting clubhouse, they began to sing, "Roll out the barrel! We've got the Giants on the run!" Jackie Robinson used a bat to bang out the beat on the door between the clubhouses.

Then Leo Durocher's Giants kicked it up a notch. The Dodgers didn't play badly, but the Giants played amazingly well. At one point, they won 16 games in a row. The Dodgers still had a seven-game lead on September 1, but the relentless Giants squeezed into first place on the next-to-last day of the season, and the Dodgers had to win a 14-inning nail-biter against the Phillies to set up the three-game playoff.

In the first game, Giants third baseman Bobby Thomson hit a home run off Dodger pitcher Ralph Branca to give his team a 2–1 lead and eventual 3–1 win. Game 2 was a 10–0 Dodger cakewalk. In Game 3, Branca returned to the mound to face Thomson again, trying to hold a 4–2 Dodger lead with two men on—but Thomson attacked a Branca fastball and lined it into the lower deck of the Polo Grounds' left-field seats. The sensational Giants' two-month upswing was capped by this incredible comeback. Thomson and Branca are forever linked in myth and memory, and Thomson's homer became known as "The Shot Heard 'Round the World." (See pages 78–79 for more about this game.)

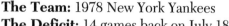

The Team: 1978 New York Yankees
The Deficit: 14 games back on July 18
The Comeback: The Yanks beat the Boston Red Sox in a one-game playoff to advance to the postseason

The 1978 Red Sox were a force to be reckoned with. Led by slugger Jim Rice, who would finish the season leading the league in hits, triples, homers, total bases, and RBI, they pounded the ball. By mid-July they were more than 30 games over .500, leading Milwaukee by 9 games and the Yankees by 14.

Yankee owner George Steinbrenner couldn't abide scurrilous comments by Yank manager Billy Martin, who resigned midseason and was replaced by the mellow Bob Lemon. The effect on the team was immediate. By mid-August the Yanks had taken 10 out of 12. Then they won 12 out of 14. As the Sox fell prey to an assortment of injuries, the Yankees kept up the pressure, capped off by a four-game September sweep in Fenway Park in which the Yanks outscored the Sox 42–9. The Boston press dubbed it "The Boston Massacre."

In only about seven weeks, the Yankees had chewed up the 14-game difference and moved into a 3½-game lead. But the Red Sox fought back, winning their final eight regular-season games to force a one-game playoff at Fenway. Yankees shortstop Bucky Dent, who had belted a total of five home runs all year, stepped up to the plate in the seventh and slugged a three-run shot over the Green Monster in Fenway's left field. The Yankees' huge comeback was complete. To this day Boston fans consider "Bucky Dent" a vile epithet.

The Team: 2004 Boston Red Sox
The Deficit: Down three games to none in the American League Championship Series
The Comeback: Four straight wins, including two in extra innings

The Red Sox seemed to be a team trapped by history. Many a rabid Bostonian believed in "The Curse of the Bambino," which claimed that the Sox were doomed never to win the World Series because they had the gall to sell the greatest player of all time,

Babe Ruth. So when the team began the 2004 American League Championship Series by dropping three in a row to their archrivals, the New York Yankees, few expected them to overturn history's applecart.

To get an idea of the scale of the mountain the Sox had to climb, consider that in 36 League Championship Series and 95 World Series, no team had ever come back from a 3–0 deficit to win a best-of-seven series. In fact, in the 20 times a team had taken a 3–0 lead, only three times did their opponents even win Game 4.

But these Red Sox called themselves "the idiots," because their all-out style of play didn't leave time for fretting over historical matters. The Sox were competitive in Games 1 and 2, although they wound up with losses in both, but they got absolutely clobbered in Game 3 (19–8).

Game 4 should have been the clincher for the Yanks. In fact, they were three outs away from sweeping the Series when suddenly the Sox roared back. Boston rallied against their longtime nemesis, Yank reliever Mariano Rivera, in the ninth inning and won on a David Ortiz homer in the 12th. The next night it took 14 innings for the Bostonians to eke out another win, this time also on an Ortiz RBI. He fouled off six pitches in a ten-pitch at-bat before he got the one he could knock out of the park. In Game 6, Curt Schilling rose to the occasion on a surgically patchworked right ankle (his tendon was temporarily sewn into place) and delivered seven heroic innings as the Sox tied the Series at three in what is now known as the "Blood on the Sock" game. Then Boston blew out the Yanks and rewrote history with a 10–3 victory in Game 7. They kept it rolling, sweeping the World Series in four games over the St. Louis Cardinals.

◖ ◖ ◖

"You've just got to keep the faith. The game is not over until the last out."

—David Ortiz

Larger than Life

The big and tall who made the other guys look small.

Monsters

Walter "Jumbo" Brown: 6'4", 295 lbs.
He led the National League in saves in 1940 and '41. Enos Slaughter called him the toughest pitcher he ever faced.

Garland Buckeye: 6'0", 260 lbs.
In the 1920s, "Gar" wasn't just a threat on the baseball field—he played professional football, too.

Frank Howard: 6'7", 275 lbs.
In 1968, a year known for dominant pitching, "The Capital Punisher" slugged ten home runs over a stretch of 20 at-bats.

Ted Kluszewski: 6'2", 225 lbs.
In the early 1950s he cut the sleeves off his Reds uniform because they were so tight on his massive arms they impeded his swing.

Boog Powell: 6'4", 270 lbs.
He won the 1970 AL MVP Award and formed a slugging power-house duo with Orioles teammate Frank Robinson.

Dick Radatz: 6'5", 235 lbs.
Known as "The Monster," this powerhouse holds the single-season record for most strikeouts by a relief pitcher: 181 in 1964.

Stocky Guys

Steve Bilko: 6'1", 240 lbs.
While in the minors in 1956 and '57, "Stout Steve" hit 55 and 56 home runs, respectively.

Tony Gwynn: 5'11", 199 lbs.
In 1997, this lifelong Padre tied Honus Wagner's record of eight NL batting titles.

Harry Lumley: 5′10″, 183 lbs.
He led the National League in triples and homers as a rookie for the Brooklyn Superbas in 1904.

Kirby Puckett: 5′8″, 210 lbs.
This career-long Twin was the first player born in the 1960s to be elected to the Hall of Fame.

Tall Pitchers
John Candelaria: 6′7″
The "Candy Man" was a quality pitcher, winning 177 games in 19 big-league seasons.

Randy Johnson: 6′10″
"The Big Unit's" size (and glare) has kept batters in line since he first took the mound in 1988 for the Expos.

Jon Rauch: 6′11″
When he debuted with the Chicago White Sox in 2002, he surpassed Randy Johnson as Major League Baseball's tallest player ever.

Rick Sutcliffe: 6′7″
One of the greatest midseason pickups ever. In 1984, he hurled the Cubs to the NL East Division pennant.

Bob Veale: 6′6″
In 1965, he had a career-high 276 strikeouts.

Tallest Non-Pitcher
Richie Sexson: 6′8″, 237 lbs.
"Big Sexy" has hit 29 homers or more in seven seasons of major-league play.

Tallest Champs
The 1979 world champion Pittsburgh Pirates had five pitchers who stood 6′4″ or taller: Bruce Kison (6′4″), Don Robinson (6′4″), Kent Tekulve (6′4″), Jim Bibby (6′5″), and John Candelaria (6′7″).

Learning the Lingo

To live in the world of baseball, one must speak the language.
Below, common slang terms and their origins.

Accordion act: To choke, often as a team. **Origin:** Descriptive of the bellows of the instrument, which collapse.

Apple: A generic term for a baseball. Other food-related words for baseballs include onion, bun, and egg. **Origin:** Descriptive.

Backdoor: A pitch, often a slider or curveball, that curves from outside the batter to inside. **Origin:** Descriptive.

Banana stick: A bat of inferior quality. **Origin:** Descriptive of weak or wobbly wood.

Bingle: A single. **Origin:** A combination of the exclamation "bingo!" and single.

Broadway: A pitch over the middle of the plate. **Origin:** A wide street often in the center of a town.

Cadillac: To showboat; also, a home run hitter. **Origin:** Ralph Kiner's remark: "Home run hitters drive Cadillacs."

Crooked number: A score greater than one, usually in one inning. **Origin:** Describes the shape of any number but one.

Dying quail: A batted fly ball that drops in front of a fielder, seemingly suddenly. **Origin:** Hunting.

Eephus: A slow, high-arching pitch usually delivered to disturb a batter's timing. **Origin:** Rip Sewell's name for such a delivery.

Fan: To strike out swinging. Also, a baseball supporter. **Origins:** A swinging strikeout fans the air. Also, a variation on the word "fanatic" or the British term "fancy," meaning "admire."

Gardener: An outfielder. **Origin:** Descriptive of someone who works in an open field. A center fielder is often called the middle gardener.

Glass arm: A pitcher susceptible to injury. **Origin:** Descriptive of fragility.

Hoover: A good infielder. **Origin:** The vacuum cleaner brand.

Makeup: A player's overall attitude and aptitude. **Origin:** Baseball scouting term.

Moxie: Vigor, pep. **Origin:** Descriptive qualities of the acquired taste of a New England soft drink endorsed by Ted Williams.

On deck: The next batter in the lineup. **Origin:** Nautical, probably from the expression of preparedness, "all hands on deck."

Punch-and-Judy hitter: A batter with little power who frequently slaps the ball for singles. **Origin:** Refers to the "Punch and Judy" puppet show; in this case "punch" is descriptive of how such a hitter meets the ball.

Red: A fastball. A batter "looking dead red" is expecting a fastball. **Origin:** Descriptive. Red symbolizes heat.

Sayonara home run: A home run that ends a game. **Origin:** Japanese word meaning "good-bye."

Small ball: A strategy where a team plays to manufacture runs using sacrifice bunts, steals, and other plays that generally don't require extra-base hits. **Origin:** Play on the term "long ball," or home run.

Through the wickets: A ball that goes between the legs of a fielder for an error. **Origin:** Cricket, in which the batsman stands on guard in front of a set of three upright stumps called a wicket.

Ruth by the Numbers

The numbers prove that Babe Ruth was one of a kind.

• In the American League in 1920, 14.6 percent of all home runs—54 of 369—were hit by Ruth. To match that percentage today, a slugger would have to belt close to 400 homers in a season.

• After being sold by the Red Sox to New York, Ruth out-homered the entire Boston team in ten of the next 12 seasons.

• From 1920 through 1932, there were only two seasons in which Ruth didn't knock out at least 40 home runs. He had totals as high as 60, 59, and 54 (two times).

• Babe led the American League in dingers 12 times (1918–21, 1923, 1924, 1926–31).

• Of Babe's 714 home runs, ten were inside-the-park shots (although not one ever bounced out of the park, even when that was a legal homer). Sixteen were hit in extra innings, and one was as a pinch-hitter.

• Ruth's record of 457 total bases in 1921 has never been equaled.

• Babe's career .690 slugging percentage (total bases divided by at-bats) is the highest ever. The next-highest is more than 50 points back (Ted Williams, .634). Ruth led the AL in slugging 13 times.

• Babe batted over .370 six times, with a high of .393 in 1923. His .342 batting average is the tenth-best in major-league history.

• As a pitcher, Ruth had a career record of 94–46 and a 2.28 ERA. He is universally regarded as the greatest hitting pitcher, the best pitching hitter, and because of that parlay, the greatest player *period* in baseball history.

Bill Veeck: Man of the People

One man seemed to have the magic touch when it came to boosting attendance, and doing it fast. That man was Bill Veeck, and he kept fans in stitches with gimmicks and goofiness for years.

Bill Veeck was literally born into baseball. His father was president of the Chicago Cubs. The junior Veeck grew up in the ballpark, working as everything from a soda-pop vendor and ticket taker to groundskeeper (he claimed to have planted the ivy on the outfield walls of Wrigley Field) before moving up to club treasurer while he took night courses in business, accounting, and engineering.

A Man of the People

In 1941, Veeck bought the American Association Milwaukee Brewers. He was just 27 years old, but he was already exploding with ideas. He never announced his promotions ahead of time, so folks would show up at the park with no idea what to expect. What they received were giveaways such as live lobsters, buckets of nails, or hosiery. They also got fireworks, live bands, and ballet. Anything could happen, and the fans loved it.

Veeck was unlike any other owner. While the other big-league moguls still wore steamed shirts and stickpins, Veeck never—ever—wore a tie. He much preferred the company of the bleacher fans to that of millionaires and movie stars. He spent his time during the games out in the stands, chatting with the fans, joining them for a beer, talking baseball. He asked the fans what they wanted, and he listened to their answers.

Taking Chances

As owner of the Cleveland Indians, Veeck had his greatest success. He integrated the American League by signing Larry Doby in 1947. (Veeck allegedly received 20,000 pieces of hate mail about the signing and replied to each one by hand.) When he persuaded living legend Satchel Paige to join his team in '48, many called it a ridiculous publicity stunt. But it turned out to be anything but when Paige (at age 42, the oldest rookie in major-league history), went 6–1 in 72.2 innings, recorded an ERA of 2.48, and threw three complete games and two shutouts in his seven starts. The Indians won the pennant and the World Series in 1948, and fans came out in record numbers.

Make 'em Laugh

Veeck bought the St. Louis Browns in 1951, and that year he engineered a stunt designed to send the fans home chuckling and the baseball powers huffing and puffing in dismay. The fans were there to help celebrate the 50th anniversary of the American League; everyone received a slice of birthday cake as they entered the gate. Between games of the doubleheader, a fake birthday cake was rolled onto the field, and out of it jumped 3'7" Eddie Gaedel, wearing a Browns uniform with number ⅛ on the back. His job was to crouch down and ensure he'd get a walk. He did, and the fans went crazy.

The Fans Have Their Say

Another memorable Veeck promotion was "Grandstand Managers' Day" on August 24, 1951, in which more than 1,000 St. Louis Browns fans decided on the game strategy while manager Zack Taylor sat alongside the dugout, propped up his feet, and drank an orange soda while he counted the fans' votes. The fans were given signs that said "YES" or "NO." Before the game, they held up these cards to select the Browns' starting lineup. During the game, they used these cards to vote on such questions as "Infield In?" or "Bunt?" The lineup choice was probably the fans' best decision. They replaced the regular starting catcher and first baseman with bench-sitters Sherm Lollar and Hank "Bow Wow" Arft. Each wound up with two RBI; Lollar had a homer and a double. The Browns, who had lost four of their previous five games, snapped the streak with a 5–3 crowd-managed win. Then they lost their next five.

In 1959, Veeck bought the Chicago White Sox and continued his fun-filled promotions. He created the exploding scoreboard that set off fireworks when a Sox player homered. And it was Veeck's idea to have Harry Caray lead the crowd in singing "Take Me Out to the Ball Game" during the seventh-inning stretch, a tradition that moved with Harry from Comiskey Park to Wrigley Field in 1982.

Versatile Veeck

Any attempt to categorize Bill Veeck will inevitably result in slamming into a few walls of contradictions. Was he simply a ruthless (self) promoter who delighted in blowing the buttons off stuffed shirts? Was he truly the fans' owner, the man who cared for them more than anything? Was he merely a hustler, a Barnum, primarily a con man? Was he a savvy baseball intellect, or was he just lucky?

The answer to the final question is probably easiest. From 1947 through 1964, the New York Yankees were toppled from their habitual perch atop the American League just three times— twice by a team Veeck owned (1948 Indians, 1959 White Sox) and once by a team he had built (1954 Indians). If Veeck didn't always know how to make money running a team, he knew how to make money selling it. Every deal he made showed substantial profits. His teams set attendance records in Cleveland and Chicago, and he quintupled attendance in St. Louis.

Even when Bill Veeck made a mistake, he turned it into good publicity (or at least a good laugh). But perhaps the trait that most clearly defined the huge and paradoxical style of Bill Veeck was his sheer lust for life. Despite living in severe pain (he was said to have had 36 different operations), he never let it hold him back. After he died, one of his obituaries noted that if a life is measured not by how long it is, but by how full it is, "the old rapscallion [Veeck] must have turned over the odometer a few times."

Notable Nicknames

Back in the day, a ballplayer's nickname told you something about him and—occasionally—how he played the game.

Throughout baseball history, nicknames have been the name of the game. Colorful or descriptive, humorous or just plain fitting, creative monikers have added flavor to the game. Today, nicknames are more often than not the effortless shortening of a name: A-Rod (Alex Rodriguez)...Jetes (Derek Jeter)...Junior (Ken Griffey, Jr.).... These nicknames could apply to anyone, anywhere. Looking at some of the best from years past—"The Sultan of Swat" (Babe Ruth) and "Death to Flying Things" (Bob Ferguson)—might help conjure up a few creative names for today's players.

Jay Hanna "Dizzy" Dean and Paul "Daffy" Dean
In some cases, nicknames fit the player; in other cases, they're contrived to make headlines or accommodate a story line. Jay Hanna "Dizzy" Dean acquired his nickname while pitching in a 1928 exhibition game for the U.S. Army against the Chicago White Sox. When Dean started mowing down opposing batters, White Sox manager Lena Blackburne reportedly yelled to his players, "Don't let that dizzy rookie fool ya'." In 1930, Dean cemented the nickname when he joined the St. Louis Cardinals and exhibited the unusual behavior and speech patterns that would stamp him as one of the game's most colorful characters. After games, he liked to say to the press, "If you can do it, it ain't braggin'."

Four years later, younger brother Paul Dean made the Cardinals roster. St. Louis sportswriters gave him the nickname "Daffy" because it worked in combination with Dizzy. In reality, Paul was nowhere near as colorful as his brother. Quiet and serious, Daffy was actually called "Harpo" in certain company because he reminded people of the Marx brother who never spoke.

Ralph "The Road Runner" Garr
Major-league outfielder Ralph "The Road Runner" Garr became almost as well-known for the nickname as the original Looney

Tunes cartoon figure created by Chuck Jones. The Atlanta Braves public relations department gave Garr the nickname after he arrived in the big leagues; in fact, the Braves so wanted to market Garr that they wrote to Warner Brothers, Inc., to receive official permission to use the nickname and the catchphrase "Beep! Beep!" in promotional efforts. Warner Brothers came to a historic agreement with the Braves. "Our contract with the Braves makes Ralph the first licensed nickname to our knowledge anywhere in the world," said Licensing Corporation of America chairman Jay Emmett. The unusual agreement also made it illegal for any other athlete to use the nickname.

"Shoeless Joe" Jackson

Sometimes a nickname becomes so synonymous with a player that it becomes attached to the front end of his or her real name. "Shoeless Joe" Jackson acquired his handle early in his professional career while playing for Greenville of the Carolina Association. During the 1908 season, Jackson tried to break in a new pair of shoes. The next game, his feet hurt so badly that he switched back to his old pair, but the pain persisted, prompting his decision to play the game without wearing any shoes at all. One fan noticed and called out to the rest of the crowd: "Look at Shoeless Joe!"

Brooks "Vacuum Cleaner" Robinson

Even nice guys are given nicknames. Hall of Fame third baseman Brooks Robinson, a consummate gentleman among the game's greats, acquired two of the best nicknames of the expansion era (1961–1976)—one that is well known and one that is a bit more obscure. Robinson's ability to inhale ground balls with his soft hands earned him the title "Vacuum Cleaner," a nickname that seemed all the more appropriate when artificial turf came into vogue in the late 1960s. And then there was the handle that his Oriole teammates preferred, one that might be considered a little less flattering. Some enjoyed calling Brooksie "The Head," since his receding hairline made his skull appear larger than it actually was.

Ted "The Splendid Splinter" Williams

Early in Williams's career, the Boston press dubbed him "The Splendid Splinter." The nickname made sense, given his spindly frame as a younger player. At 6'3", he weighed only 168 pounds, yet he could still crank out the hits. Williams actually preferred two other nicknames: "The Kid," which is how he began referring to himself early in his Red Sox career, and "Teddy Ballgame," which was started rather inadvertently by the young son of a Boston photographer. When asked to name the ballplayer he most wanted to meet, the boy responded by saying, "Teddy... Teddy Ballgame."

With all of the above players long since retired, nicknames have become far less commonplace. However, a couple of contemporary players have acquired descriptive monikers.

Roger "The Rocket" Clemens

Possessing a high, riding fastball that approached the upper 90s in velocity, Clemens became known as "The Rocket." With his launchpad heater revving at its peak on April 29, 1986, Clemens struck out 20 Seattle Mariners, setting a nine-inning record and solidifying the nickname. After the handle took hold, most baseball fans didn't realize that Clemens had earned another nickname during his college days. A star at the University of Texas, he was sometimes referred to as "Big Tex."

Frank "The Big Hurt" Thomas

At 6'5" and 275 pounds, Frank Thomas is one of the largest men to ever pick up a major-league bat. His enormous size (which helped him play football as a tight end in college), combined with his ability to hit searing line drives and gargantuan home runs, led Chicago White Sox broadcaster Ken "Hawk" Harrelson to dub Thomas "The Big Hurt." The moniker perfectly captures his immensity in the batter's box and his ability to strike the ball with unusual force.

Keeping Score and Hawking Dogs

You can thank 19th-century entrepeneur Harry M. Stevens for many of the staples found nationwide at ballparks today.

In 1885, Ohio entrepreneur Harry M. Stevens invented scorecards as a way to keep track of the players and the action (and to sell some advertising space). He sold them at various ballparks for five cents each. By the turn of the century he was also selling ice cream and sodas to baseball fans. When sales proved slow on cold, early-season days at New York's Polo Grounds, he sent out some of his salespeople to buy "dachshund" sausages and buns, then encouraged them to yell, "Get 'em while they're red hot!" Thus the term "hot dog" was popularized. Even today, when fans can find everything from nachos to sushi at the ballpark, people still line up for the staples that have been sold for more than a century, including bags of peanuts and soda that is drunk through a straw (both of which were also Stevens's ideas).

Prices for everything at the ballpark have increased by leaps and bounds through the years, but this has become especially true in the past two decades as the corporate culture has provided a base of customers willing to pay more for better seats and fancier eats. A brief history of a few of the staples:

Some selected ballpark prices from selected seasons (not adjusted for inflation):

	1920	1942	1962	1980	2006
Program/Scorecard	$.10	$.10	$.25	$.50	$4.00
Hot Dog	$.10	$.15	$.35	$1.00	$4.50
Soda	$.05	$.10	$.25	$.55	$4.75

All-Time Great

Ty Cobb

Not just one of the greatest hitters ever, he was also one of the toughest and probably the nastiest.

Born: December 18, 1886; Narrows, GA
MLB Career: Detroit Tigers, 1905–26; Philadelphia A's, 1927–28
Hall of Fame Resume: .367 BA (first) • 4,189 hits (second) • 724 doubles (fourth) • 295 triples (second) • 3,053 singles (second) • 892 steals (fourth) • 2,246 runs (second) • 12 batting titles
Inside Pitch: The famous incident of Cobb challenging Honus Wagner in the 1909 World Series ("I'm coming down, Krauthead") never happened.

A movie about the life of Babe Ruth drew hordes to the theaters despite being a critical flop a few years back, but when a similar picture about Ty Cobb debuted a while later, it was gone in a matter of weeks. Most folks had little interest in paying tribute to the greatest hitter for average (.367) in major-league history. Nearly 70 years after Cobb's career ended, the reputation of "The Georgia Peach" apparently hasn't changed much. He might have hit and run better than anyone else in baseball, but he was still one mean SOB.

Cobb's vicious streak seemed at times to engulf him: He used a brutal ferocity to attack the game and beat down opponents. Harassed as a scrawny 18-year-old with the Tigers in 1905, he

quickly added weight and muscle along with a philosophy of playing hard and trusting no one. He never hit below .316 after his rookie season, and with his .350 mark in 1907 (at the age of 20), he became the youngest player in history to win a batting title. He led the American League with 119 RBI, 212 hits, a .468 slugging mark, and 49 stolen bases to boot.

The left-handed hitter with the split-handed grip could bash line drives and bunt with equal skill and take an extra base seemingly at will. In the field, he used his speed and a solid arm to cut down runners, and he registered 20 or more assists on ten occasions.

But what he did best was hit—and run the bases. His 1907 batting title was the first of nine straight and 12 overall (although two of the batting titles are disputed). Cobb led the Tigers to three consecutive pennants, from 1907 to '09, and remained the key to Detroit's attack for 20 years. Perennially among American League leaders in slugging and steals (he won six stolen base crowns), he was also the team's most reliable RBI man for many years—averaging 106 a season from 1907 to '12 en route to 1,937 for his career. He was rumored to slide with his spikes high, and he liked that intimidating image of himself.

Cobb won the Triple Crown in 1909 with nine homers, 107 RBI, and a .377 average, and two years later he had perhaps his finest season with a career-high .420 average and league-leading totals in hits (248), doubles (47), triples (24), runs (147), RBI (127), and steals (83). In 1915, he set a stolen base record of 96 that stood for nearly 50 years, and in 1922, at the age of 35, he hit .400 for the third and final time. After serving as player/manager his final six years with the Tigers, he joined Connie Mack's Athletics in 1927 to finish his career. He retired rich from wise investments—but virtually devoid of friends. His major-league marks for hits (4,189) and steals (892) have since been topped, but his .367 mark will likely endure—along with the sordid reputation of the man who achieved it.

🏀 🏀 🏀

"There probably have been players in the game who had as much natural ability and as good a physique as [Ty] Cobb; there may also have been some—although I doubt it—who could think as fast. But there certainly never was another athlete who combined Cobb's ability and his smartness—or even came close."

—Fred Haney

Negro League Greats

*Real or exaggerated, the great Negro League performers
are surrounded by a legendary aura.*

Most of the numbers can't be found in record books. The documentation simply doesn't exist. Many of the tales cannot be read in newspaper or magazine clippings. Negro League baseball games were not covered with the same media blanket as their major-league counterparts, leaving many of the best stories to be passed from one generation to the next by word of mouth.

This is both the curse and the blessing of the Negro Leagues. While it's a shame the records and statistics, in many cases, don't hold up to encyclopedic accuracy, there's a certain charm and reverence in the way these remarkable stories have been told and retold.

The Black Babe Ruth

Josh Gibson would undoubtedly have challenged major-league home run records had he been given the chance to swing his mighty bat against white contemporaries. The "Black Babe Ruth" is said to have hit as many as 962 home runs in his career, though some came against semipro competition.

In Negro League games, the number is agreed to be in the vicinity of 800—nearly 40 more than Barry Bonds's major-league record of 762. In 1936, one year before he traded his Pittsburgh Crawfords jersey for the Homestead Grays, Gibson is said to have hit 84 round-trippers, 11 more than Bonds's big-league record.

It was not only the frequency of Gibson's home runs that stood out. One story holds that he once hit a ball right out of Yankee Stadium, although this has been disputed by news accounts, and Gibson himself never made the claim. A taller tale has him hitting a ball so far in Pittsburgh that it dropped into an outfielder's glove in Philadelphia the next day, prompting an umpire to declare, "You're out! Yesterday in Pittsburgh."

Said Hall of Famer Monte Irvin, "I played with Willie Mays and against Hank Aaron. They were tremendous players, but they were no Josh Gibson."

Speaking of Home Runs...

Dale Long, Don Mattingly, and Ken Griffey, Jr., share the major-league record of belting home runs in eight consecutive games. Had any of them extended their streaks by three more games, they would merit mention with John Miles's feat of 1948. Stated Negro League historian Dean Lollis, "You can take the greatest home-run hitters in baseball history—Babe Ruth, Hank Aaron, Willie Mays, Mark McGwire, Sammy Sosa, Barry Bonds—and even in their greatest years, they never came close to that streak."

Miles, a tall man with long arms and big, strong wrists, could not recall the locations of those 11 consecutive games. His team, the Chicago American Giants, played almost all of their games in major-league parks, such as Comiskey Park, the Polo Grounds, and Yankee Stadium, so the legitimacy of the accomplishment is seldom questioned.

Super Speedy

By his own count, James "Cool Papa" Bell once stole 175 bases in a 200-game season. The dazzling leadoff man, baserunner, and center fielder hit .400 or better several times. He once forfeited a Negro League batting title to Monte Irvin to increase Irvin's chances of being allowed to play in the majors.

Two tall tales were Bell's most lasting legacies. Fellow Negro Leaguers liked to say that this Mississippi native was so fast he could turn out the light and be tucked in bed before the room got dark. They also said that he once hit a ball up the middle and was called out because it hit him as he was sliding into second base.

Tales from the Mound

Satchel Paige is widely considered to be the greatest pitcher of the Negro League era. He dominated major-league hitters in exhibition games, fared well against them when he finally got his big-league chance at age 42, and made a career out of entertaining fans, not only with his deep repertoire of first-rate "stuff" and crazy trick pitches, but also as a showman.

Bell once said Paige "made his living by throwing the ball to a spot over the plate the size of a matchbook." Satch, as he was called, threw so many no-hitters in his 1,500 (or more)-game career that somewhere along the line the count was lost. He is said to have tossed more than 300 shutouts, but that, too, is a number that will never be verified.

Smokey Joe

Paige was hardly the only Negro League pitcher with an amazing tale. "Smokey" Joe Williams, pitching for the Homestead Grays at age 44 in 1930, struck out 27 Kansas City Monarchs in a 12-inning, 1–0 victory. He is said to have pitched dozens of no-hitters himself. "If you have ever witnessed the speed of a pebble in a storm," Leland Giants owner Frank Leland once said of Williams, "you have not seen the equal of the speed possessed by this wonderful Texan."

The Unsung Iron Man

One of the Negro Leagues' most amazing accomplishments came from a man who stood only 5'8" and weighed 160 pounds. Larry Brown arrived from Pratt City, Alabama, as a 17-year-old catcher for the Birmingham Black Barons and gained acclaim as one of the greatest defensive backstops of all time.

If Lou Gehrig was the "Iron Horse" and Cal Ripken, Jr., was baseball's record-setting "Iron Man," Brown deserves a metallic nickname as well. In 1930, he reportedly caught 234 games in one season. No one knows how many consecutive games he played during a career that spanned more than four decades and ten teams, but it would likely compare with the well-documented streaks of Gehrig (2,130) and Ripken (2,632).

And, like his durable white counterparts, it was not only the number of games played by Brown that was impressive, but also the quality of his performance. He led his clubs to three championships and played in six East-West All-Star Classics while calling games for the likes of Paige, Willie Foster, and Ted "Double Duty" Radcliffe. "He was strong as an ox and could throw bullets to catch stealing baserunners," Radcliffe said of Brown.

Although we'll never know the exact numbers racked up by these legends of the Negro Leagues, their talent can never be disputed.

Blast from the Past

"[Harry Wright] eats baseball, breathes baseball, thinks baseball, dreams baseball, and incorporates baseball in his prayers."

—Cincinnati Enquirer, 1869

"Never change a decision, never stop to talk to a man. Make 'em play ball and keep their mouths shut, and...people will be on your side and you'll be called the king of umpires."

—Player and manager-turned-umpire Bob Ferguson, circa 1890

"The tradition of professional baseball always has been agreeably free of chivalry. The rule is: Do anything you can get away with."

—Heywood Broun, circa 1900

"This should prove the leather is mightier than the wood."

—White Sox manager Fielder Allison Jones after his 1906 "Hitless Wonders" won the World Series with a .228 club batting average

"I was not able to understand how it could be right to pay an actor, or a singer, or an instrumentalist for entertaining the public, and wrong to pay a ball player for doing exactly the same thing."

—Albert Spalding, circa 1900

"It depends on the length of the game."

—King Kelly's response to a reporter asking if he ever drank while playing, late 19th century

"A surge of joy flooded over me that I shall never forget. I felt like shouting out that I had made a ball curve; I wanted to tell everybody; it was too good to keep to myself."

—Candy Cummings, who claimed to have invented the first curveball around 1864, *How I Curved the First Ball*

All-Star Game Classics

From the moment Babe Ruth swatted the first All-Star Game home run to MLB's recent decision to award the winning league home-field advantage in the World Series, baseball's All-Star Game has held an appeal unmatched in other sports.

In 1933, *Chicago Tribune* sports editor Arch Ward set the Midsummer Classic in motion when, with much prodding, he convinced owners to stage an exhibition between the best of the American and National Leagues. Commissioner Landis wasn't too keen on the idea until Ward suggested all proceeds be used to augment the pension fund for needy ex-players. The first game, planned to coincide with the Chicago World's Fair, was held on July 6, 1933, in Chicago's Comiskey Park.

Via a newspaper poll, fans from all over the country selected the players to represent the two leagues. The top vote-getter was the A's Al Simmons, followed by Chuck Klein of the Phils. Babe Ruth finished sixth overall. But the Babe didn't let that bother him. In the third inning, with the American League leading 1–0 and Charlie Gehringer on base, Ruth lined a homer to right that opened up the game for good. Baseball's first All-Star Game had been decided by its greatest player.

The game caught on instantly. Over the years, fans have played a large part in choosing the participants, and managers have racked their brains trying to concoct ways to get all their big bats and strong arms into the lineup.

Between 1965 and '85, the National League won 19 All-Star Games while losing just twice. Through 2008, however, the American League was unbeaten over a stretch of 12 years, narrowing the Senior Circuit's overall lead to 41–36–2. The All-Star Game has provided more than its share of drama along the way.

1933: The Babe Gets It Started

It could not have been scripted better. Babe Ruth, 38 years old and in his next-to-last season with the Yankees, socked the first home run in All-Star Game history. But the Babe was not finished.

Though not known for his fielding—and certainly not at this stage of his career—Ruth made a fabulous leaping catch in right field to rob Chick Hafey of a hit in the eighth inning. The defensive gem helped preserve the first All-Star Game pitching victory for Ruth's teammate, Lefty Grove.

1934: K–K–K–K–K

"I can recall walking out to the hill in the Polo Grounds that day," National League starter Carl Hubbell recalled, "and looking around the stands and thinking to myself, 'Hub, they want to see what you've got.'"

One by one, future Hall of Famers stepped to the plate for the American League: Babe Ruth. Lou Gehrig. Jimmie Foxx. Al Simmons. Joe Cronin. And one by one, Hubbell struck them out in the single greatest performance in All-Star Game history.

Hubbell's five consecutive Ks did not keep the American League from rallying for a 9–7 win. It did, however, leave some of the greatest hitters in the history of the game scratching their heads as they failed to make contact with Hubbell's devastating screwball.

1946: A Splintered Eephus

Back home from the war, which had prompted cancellation of the 1945 All-Star Game, Ted Williams treated his Fenway Park faithful to a classic performance. His 4-for-4, two-homer game remains one of the greatest, and most unusual, in All-Star history.

By the time the Splendid Splinter strode to the plate in the eighth inning, he was 3-for-3 with a home run and an RBI single for the American League, which held a 9–0 cushion. National League pitcher Rip Sewell was on the mound. Williams had warned Sewell not to throw his zany "eephus" pitch—a ball that was lobbed some 25 feet in the air before it fell on a sharp downward plane, often through the strike zone—in a showcase as grand as the All-Star Game. But Sewell, smiling, warned Williams that it was coming. And when the eephus crossed the plate, Williams attacked it, stepping up in the box and hammering it over the right-field fence. "He hit it right out of there," Sewell described. "And I mean he hit it."

1949: No More Barriers

The 1949 All-Star Game was not about the score, but the circumstance. Two years earlier, Jackie Robinson had broken baseball's color barrier. Now, for the first time, black players would stand in their rightful place in the game's showcase of its best players.

Robinson, Roy Campanella, and Don Newcombe took the field for the National League, and Larry Doby suited up for the American League. Robinson, the first African American to start an All-Star Game, crossed the plate three times, but it was not enough to keep Joe DiMaggio from leading the AL to an 11–7 win.

"The 1949 All-Star Game was a huge step because it proved to baseball and all the naysayers that we were in fact here to stay," said Newcombe 50 years after the milestone day. "By us being chosen to play in that game, it affirmed that African American players were stars and would continue to be stars and there was nothing anybody could do to stop it."

1955: Stan the Comeback Man

It was the greatest comeback in All-Star Game history. By the time the National League erased a 5–0 deficit to win 6–5, however, it wasn't so much the comeback that people were talking about, but the dramatic blow that ended the game.

Before Stan Musial stepped to the plate to lead off the bottom of the 12th inning in Milwaukee, NL manager Harry Walker pulled the Cardinals star aside and said, "Let's end this now. I'm hungry." Musial made sure it was dinnertime when Boston's Frank Sullivan threw him a mouthwatering fastball, and Stan the Man launched it into the right-field seats to end the game in dramatic fashion.

1970: Playing to Win

In 1970, Ray Fosse was one of baseball's best young catchers, and Pete Rose was on his way to becoming the majors' career hits king.

When their paths collided, literally, in one of the most debated plays in the history of the All-Star Game, fate was knocked on its heels.

In the bottom of the 12th inning, Rose came charging home as third-base coach Leo Durocher waved him on. When Amos Otis's throw from center went a few feet up the third base line, Fosse moved up to field it. As he did, Rose, rather than leaping into one of his patented head-first dives, dropped his shoulder and sent Fosse flying, separating the catcher from his glove while Rose tumbled across the plate with the winning run in a 5–4 decision.

Many people chalked it up to Charlie Hustle's aggressive style of play. Others were appalled by the violent contact, particularly in an exhibition game. Fosse sustained a fractured and separated left shoulder that was not diagnosed until the following year, and his career was never the same.

1971: Power Play

Six future Hall of Famers—Hank Aaron, Johnny Bench, Roberto Clemente, Reggie Jackson, Harmon Killebrew, and Frank Robinson—homered to account for every run in the 1971 All-Star Game, a 6–4 American League victory.

Although the AL snapped an eight-year losing streak with the power-fueled triumph, one home run stood out above all others. With one runner on in the third inning, Reggie Jackson laced a Dock Ellis offering high into the Detroit sky for a home run that hit off the Tiger Stadium roof's light tower some 520 feet from home plate. "To this day, I can still see Reggie hit that ball," said National League manager Sparky Anderson of Cincinnati. "It was incredible. I don't know where the ball would have went if the light tower had not been there."

1983: Slammin' Freddy

The 50th anniversary of the All-Star Game was celebrated where it all began—Comiskey Park. And just as the very first edition featured a memorable home run by Babe Ruth, the golden anniversary was marked with a milestone blast. Hard to believe, but there had never been a grand slam hit in All-Star Game play until the California Angels' Fred Lynn cleared the bases in the third inning.

Lynn's blast off Atlee Hammaker followed an intentional walk to Robin Yount. "I take it personally," Lynn said. It also helped the American League snap an 11-game losing streak with a 13–3 romp.

1984: King Carl Would Be Proud

If the All-Star Game's 50th birthday was a bash, the golden anniversary of Carl Hubbell's memorable five-strikeout run may have been even more remarkable. Fifty years after Hubbell fanned five straight hitting legends, National League aces Fernando Valenzuela and Dwight Gooden did one better, combining to set down six in a row on strikes.

The Dodgers' Valenzuela started the streak in the fourth inning, whiffing future Hall of Famers Dave Winfield, Reggie Jackson, and George Brett consecutively. Gooden, at age 19 the youngest player in All-Star history, relieved Valenzuela in the fifth and used his heat to handcuff the next three hitters: Lance Parrish, Chet Lemon, and Alvin Davis. Their performances helped the NL to a 3–1 win in San Francisco.

1999: For Starters, None Better than Pedro

Great pitching performances are nothing new to the All-Star Game. In hitter-friendly Fenway Park, however, Pedro Martinez's efforts in the 1999 edition were a cut above. The Red Sox ace, who entered the game with 15 wins on the season, was surrounded by history on this night. Ted Williams teared up as he threw out the ceremonial first pitch, and baseball's All-Century Team pregame celebration brought out the likes of Bob Feller, Warren Spahn, Stan Musial, Hank Aaron, and Willie Mays.

And then there was Pedro. He struck out the first three NL batters—Barry Larkin, Larry Walker, and Sammy Sosa—and then fanned Mark McGwire to lead off the second inning. The four consecutive strikeouts to start a game set an All-Star Game record, garnering Martinez MVP honors in the 4–1 AL win.

2001: Farewell, Cal

Cal Ripken, Jr., will be remembered for what he did over the long haul—playing in a major-league-record 2,632 consecutive games and providing Baltimore with All-Star shortstop play for the better part of two decades. But this Iron Man will also be remembered for a tremendous one-night performance in the last of his 18 All-Star Games.

The 40-year-old received a long standing ovation when he came to bat for the first time in the bottom of the third inning and another when he sent Chan Ho Park's first offering over the left-field fence, becoming the oldest player in All-Star Game history to hit a home run. His efforts led the AL to a 4–1 win, earned game MVP honors for Ripken, and prompted one of the most emotional curtain calls ever for a man who had taken many of them in his career. "I tried to acknowledge [the fans] very quickly because I didn't want the game to be delayed for that," Ripken said.

2002: The Tie Goes to the . . . Well, Who Wants It?

It was an amazing game with an anticlimactic outcome. In fact, calling the outcome anticlimactic is an understatement. After 11 innings and some terrific baseball, with both teams out of players on their 30-man rosters and the bullpens depleted, commissioner Bud Selig and managers Bob Brenly and Joe Torre decided to call the game. With that, the 2002 All-Star Game was declared a 7–7 draw, prompting chants of "Let them play!" from the capacity crowd at Milwaukee's Miller Park.

The decision was the subject of fan debate and disappointment in the coming days. It also put a damper on an otherwise spectacular showcase that featured 25 hits, home runs by Barry Bonds and Alfonso Soriano, and one memorable deep fly to center by Bonds that was headed over the wall until Twins star Torii Hunter leaped up and pulled it back for an out.

🏀 🏀 🏀

"The fans got to see stars, they got to see good pitching, good hitting, great plays. The only thing they didn't get to see was a winner."

—Pitcher Eddie Guardado on the 2002 All-Star Game

Double No-No's

*With luck and force of will,
Johnny Vander Meer made lightning strike twice.*

The Setting: Ebbets Field, Brooklyn; June 15, 1938
The Magic: Johnny Vander Meer reaches the stars with his unprecedented—and unmatched—second consecutive no-hitter.

It's a record that is highly unlikely to be tied and almost certain never to be broken: no-hitters in back-to-back performances. Cincinnati Red Johnny Vander Meer was just 23 years old when he faced the Boston Bees on June 11 and notched a 3–0 victory without allowing a hit. It was the 48th no-hitter since the National League had been founded in 1876. Four days later, he faced the Brooklyn Dodgers at Ebbets Field. The game was already historic—it was the first night game ever played there. In fact, some claim that the poor lighting had as much to do with Vandy's success as his furious fastball did. Vander Meer was a notoriously hard-throwing wild lefty. Sometimes the ball went where it was supposed to, and plenty of times it didn't.

In his first no-hitter, on June 11, Vander Meer had walked just three. Things were different the night of June 15. He had already given free passes to five Dodgers when the ninth inning started. One out came quickly. Then the torture began. He walked Babe Phelps, Cookie Lavagetto, and Dolph Camilli in succession to load the bases. A ground ball forced one man out at home. The next batter was the veteran Leo Durocher. On a 2–2 count, Durocher tagged a Texas Leaguer into center that Harry Craft nabbed at the knees. Thanks to his own skill and the help of his teammates, Vandy had claimed a new spot in the record books—one that will probably never be matched.

Your MVP or Mine?

What attributes are most *valuable in an MVP?*
Do stats count more than character? Should a player from
a second-division team win? Is a pitcher more or less valuable
than a slugger? There are no easy answers.

Baseball's Most Valuable Player Award was established in 1911.
In the century since, there has been more than a little controversy
regarding some of its recipients. In some years, the most valuable
player in the league has been an obvious choice; in others, however, the lines of distinction have blurred.

1925 AL MVP: Roger Peckinpaugh
(.294 BA, 4 HR, 64 RBI, 67 R)
Who Could Have Won: Al Simmons
(.387 BA, 24 HR, 129 RBI, 122 R)
The Controversy: The value of a winning team.
    Veteran shortstop Peckinpaugh won a narrow victory over
Simmons, the hard-hitting sophomore center fielder for the A's,
primarily because he was credited with leading his Washington
Senators to a pennant. Peckinpaugh accepted the award, then
had a nightmarish World Series (eight errors, including a critical
eighth-inning miscue in Game 7 that allowed Pittsburgh to take
the lead and ultimately win the game and the Series). It was no
coincidence that, beginning in 1926, all MVP voting results were
released after the World Series.

1928 AL MVP: Mickey Cochrane
(.293 BA, 10 HR, 57 RBI, 92 R)
Who Could Have Won: Heinie Manush
(.378 BA, 13 HR, 108 RBI, 104 R)
The Controversy: Value relative to position.
    In a magnificent race between two future Hall of Famers in
their prime, Cochrane edged Manush in a vote that rewarded
offensive firepower from the catching position ahead of superior
numbers from a corner outfielder.

1941 AL MVP: Joe DiMaggio
(.357 BA, 30 HR, 125 RBI, 122 R)
Who Could Have Won: Ted Williams
(.406 BA, 37 HR, 120 RBI, 135 R, 147 BB)
The Controversy: The value of writing the record books.

Brilliant years from each of the longtime combatants left voters to ponder the more valuable milestone: DiMaggio's record 56-game hitting streak, or Williams eclipsing the .400 mark?

1942 AL MVP: Joe Gordon
(.322 BA, 18 HR, 103 RBI, 88 R)
Who Could Have Won: Ted Williams
(.356 BA, 36 HR, 137 RBI, 141 R)
The Controversy: The value of relationships.

A frosty relationship with the press couldn't have helped Williams's cause: He led the AL in all Triple Crown categories but saw the hardware go to Gordon, the affable Yankees second baseman.

1952 NL MVP: Hank Sauer
(.270 BA, 37 HR, 121 RBI, 89 R)
Who Could Have Won: Robin Roberts (28–7, 2.59 ERA, 148 SO); or one of five Dodgers
The Controversy: Value relative to teammates. Is a top performer on a second-division club worth more than a solid contributor on a pennant-winner?

The NL-champion Dodgers had five legitimate candidates, including rookie reliever Joe Black, who finished third in the voting, Jackie Robinson, Pee Wee Reese, Duke Snider, and Roy Campanella, who finished seventh through tenth in the voting, respectively. But the powerful Sauer was a shining star with the 5th-place Cubs.

1962 NL MVP: Maury Wills
(.299 BA, 6 HR, 48 RBI, 130 R, 104 SB)
Who Could Have Won: Willie Mays or Frank Robinson
(Mays: .304 BA, 49 HR, 141 RBI, 130 R); (Robinson: .342 BA, 39 HR, 136 RBI, 134 R)
The Controversy: The value of speed.

While Wills's 104 stolen bases more than tripled his next nearest competitor and helped usher in a new emphasis on the running game, there are many who argue the real MVP race that year should have come down to Mays, who finished second, and Robinson, who finished fourth. Robinson actually improved upon his 1961 MVP-winning year and nearly won a Triple Crown. Mays led the league in home runs and led the Giants to the NL pennant. But Wills, true to his talent, stole votes from both.

1988 NL MVP: Kirk Gibson
(.290 BA, 25 HR, 76 RBI, 106 R)
Who Could Have Won: Darryl Strawberry
(.269 BA, 39 HR, 101 RBI, 101 R)
The Controversy: The value of inspiration.

Occasionally, an inspiring player on an overachieving team steals the hearts of voters at the expense of a candidate with comparable (or better) numbers. It happened in 1979 (Willie Stargell's co-MVP honors with Keith Hernandez), in 1991 (Terry Pendleton over Barry Bonds), and in 1988, when Gibson of the surprising Dodgers edged the mighty Mets' Strawberry in a battle of corner outfielders for division winners. Strawberry's cause may also have been hurt by splitting votes with a deserving teammate, Kevin McReynolds, who finished third.

1999 AL MVP: Ivan Rodriguez
(.332 BA, 35 HR, 113 RBI, 116 R)
Who Could Have Won: Pedro Martinez
(23–4, 2.07 ERA, 313 SO)
The Controversy: The values of the voters.

Results this year spotlighted how sportswriters can affect outcomes based on how they interpret the rules of voting. Martinez's astonishing season, in the midst of an explosive offensive era, garnered him more first-place votes than Rodriguez, but Martinez lost the award when one writer left Martinez off his ballot completely, arguing that pitchers should not be eligible for the award since they don't play every day.

It's Bombs Away for the Bronx Bombers

The Yankees have had some not-so-civil wars.

The Enemies: George Steinbrenner and Billy Martin
The Feud: Their intense competitive fires kept tearing them apart—and then bringing them back together.
The Upshot: After losing Martin for the fifth time, it took Steinbrenner eight years to find a manager he could deal with.

Billy Martin seemed an obvious choice for Yankee manager. A former Yank himself, a battler and bruiser and notorious party pal of Mickey Mantle and Whitey Ford, he had managed weaker teams to divisional titles. And George Steinbrenner loved his fire. But every Martin mistake was amplified by his combative comments, and he often let his fists do the talking for him. Martin dug himself plenty of holes over the years, but Steinbrenner's sniping and micromanaging didn't make things easier for the feisty skipper.

In July 1978, as the Yankees were chasing the Red Sox, Martin publicly disparaged team superstar Reggie Jackson and Steinbrenner. "One's a born liar, and the other's convicted," he said, referring to Steinbrenner's convictions for illegal contributions to Richard Nixon's 1972 presidential campaign. The day after making the comment, Martin resigned—perhaps seeing the writing on the wall. He returned in '79, thus beginning years of back-and-forth: He was ousted by Steinbrenner after the season, rehired for 1983, fired before the 1984 season, rehired in '85 and let go once again after that season, after an ugly fight with one of the Yankee pitchers. Steinbrenner tried him once again in 1988, but he lasted only into late June. At the time of his death in 1989, Martin was hopeful of someday managing the Yanks again.

The Enemies: Babe Ruth and Miller Huggins
The Feud: Babe felt his home runs made up for his lack of discipline; Huggins disagreed.
The Upshot: Huggins died while still the Yank manager.

When Babe Ruth joined the Yankees and started slamming home runs all over the American League, he was also leading the league in partying. His diminutive manager, Huggins, tried to get him to settle down, but Babe wouldn't budge. After Huggins berated him during a July 1925 train trip, Babe dangled the little guy over the railing of the train by his ankles. Later that year, when Huggins had finally had enough, he fined the big guy $5,000—a fine ten times larger than any ever before levied in major-league baseball. Babe got the message. But Huggins's health, never rosy, worsened as the years went on, and he struggled to keep his charges in line. He died in 1929 at age 51, and Babe Ruth cried at his funeral.

The Enemies: Billy Martin and Reggie Jackson
The Feud: Martin thought Jackson was Steinbrenner's man; Reggie said of himself that he was "the straw that stirred the drink."
The Upshot: Reggie was gone before Billy returned for a third go-round.

It was a Saturday afternoon in 1977, and the game was being broadcast on national television. When Reggie apparently "loafed" on a play in right field, manager Billy Martin sent Paul Blair out to replace him on the spot. Naturally, Reggie was perturbed, and words between the manager and the player boiled over into a near-brawl in the dugout—and the TV cameras caught it all. The bad blood was there for everyone to see, yet the Yankees pushed the distractions aside and won the pennant and the World Series that year. Jackson led the way with three homers in the clinching game.

By the following July, things were sour again. During a game on the 17th, Jackson tried to bunt after Martin had ordered that he swing away. The result was a five-day suspension for Reggie. A week later, Martin made his "born liar" statement and then resigned. Yet, despite the turmoil, the Yankees went on to win the World Series for the second year in a row.

Martin's return as manager in 1979 stoked the fire once again, though the feud between the men cooled as each moved further from Steinbrenner. Martin lasted only until the end of the season, and Reggie departed the Yanks after two more. Thus ended one of the trickiest triangles in the history of the game.

Hard-Hitting Hack

For a few years, Hack Wilson was the most powerful hitter in baseball this side of Babe Ruth. He was elected to the Hall of Fame on the basis of a five-year stretch in which he hit .331 and averaged 142 RBI.

Lewis Robert "Hack" Wilson looked like a fire hydrant made of muscle. He wasn't tall, but he was thick: Only 5'6", with size-six shoes, he topped the scales at a rock-solid 190 pounds. Hack was power personified; some said his nickname came from his resemblance to a European wrestler named Georg Hackenschmidt, but it's just as much fun to believe it came from the way he approached his job at the plate.

Wilson was as tough as he was sturdy; no one wanted to scrap with him. He proved he had hitting skills with the Cubs, topping .313 in each of his first four years with them (1926–29), knocking home at least 109 runs, and homering 21 times or better. Hack earned three home run titles in these four years. His 159 RBI in 1929 was the National League's all-time high to that point.

But in 1930, Wilson was positively unstoppable: 56 homers, 190 RBI (since changed to 191), and 423 total bases (then fifth-best all time). The homers would remain the NL record until 1998; the RBI are still the most by anyone, ever. Along with all that, Wilson batted .356, and his .723 slugging percentage was second best in NL history and wouldn't be topped for 64 years. In a year when Bill Terry batted .401, Hack was the league's Most Valuable Player.

Wilson's 1930 manager, Joe McCarthy, knew how to get the most from his happy-go-lucky slugger. But late in the season McCarthy was ousted in favor of the tactless Rogers Hornsby, and under Rajah's constant harping and withering criticism, Hack just couldn't hack it. The big little man just seemed to give up. His batting average dropped nearly 100 points in 1931, and his homer total plummeted from 56 to a mere 13. He never batted .300 or hit 25 homers again, and his career was essentially over after just three more seasons.

Who in the Hall?

1) Which two Hall of Famers form the top career home run team-mate tandem in major-league history?

A: Hank Aaron and Eddie Mathews (863 home runs as teammates)

2) Which members of the Hall were born on Christmas Day?

A: Pud Galvin and Nellie Fox

3) Which two Mobile, Alabama–born Hall of Famers both wore No. 44?

A: Hank Aaron and Willie McCovey

4) Which Hall of Fame outfielder was drafted in three pro sports?

A: Dave Winfield (by the San Diego Padres, the NFL's Minnesota Vikings, and the NBA's Atlanta Hawks and the ABA's Utah Stars)

5) Who in the Hall named his son after his Hall of Fame double-play partner?

A: Luis Aparicio named his son Nelson after White Sox teammate Nellie Fox

6) Who was the second African American elected to the Hall?

A: Roy Campanella

7) Who was the youngest player elected to the Hall of Fame?

A: Sandy Koufax, 36

8) Who was the first Latino player elected to the Hall of Fame?

A: Roberto Clemente in 1973

9) Who was the only member of the inaugural Hall of Fame class to receive more votes than Babe Ruth?

A: Ty Cobb

10) Who is the only Hall of Famer to have played for the Rays?

A: Wade Boggs

All-Time Great

Joe DiMaggio

His record of hitting safely in 56 consecutive games is a perfect metaphor for his style of play—quiet, consistent excellence.

Born: November 25, 1914; Martinez, CA
MLB Career: New York Yankees, 1936–42, 1946–51
Hall of Fame Resume: Batted .340 or better five times • Record 56-game hitting streak in 1941 • Hit 30 homers or more seven times • Led league in homers and RBI twice; triples and runs once each
Inside Pitch: Joe could have been a Yankee a year earlier, but the cash-poor San Francisco Seals, who owned his contract, figured they could get more for the sale if he played an extra year for them.

He was the most regal of performers during his career with the New York Yankees, and the quiet, somewhat mysterious way he carried himself outside the game only added to the sense of elegance surrounding Joe DiMaggio. Upon first coming to the Yankees in 1936, DiMaggio was no early candidate for nobility. This poor son of an Italian fisher had what reporters called "squirrel teeth" and the naïveté to ask if a "quote" was some kind of soft drink. After hitting .323 with 44 doubles, 15 triples, 29 home runs, and 125 RBI his rookie season, in his second year he outdid even the great Lou Gehrig, leading the league with 46 homers (15 in the month of July alone), 151 runs, and a .673 slugging average while batting .346.

One of three DiMaggio brothers (along with Vince and Dom) to play in the majors, Joe appeared to have no weaknesses as a ballplayer. A right-handed batter who almost always made contact (he never struck out more than 39 times in a season), he was hurt by the 457-foot "Death Valley" in left-center field of Yankee Stadium but still managed to hit .315 there over his career. As a center fielder, he was fast and graceful but never flashy, making great plays look easy and always delivering strong throws to the

right man. He was seldom called upon to steal bases (he stole 30 in 39 career attempts), but nobody doubted he was one of the fastest players of his generation. Though quiet, he was a leader in the Yankees clubhouse.

After winning batting titles in 1939 (when his .381 mark earned him the MVP Award) and '40 (.352), DiMaggio captured the attention of the entire country in 1941. Beginning with a single off Chicago's Edgar Smith on May 15 and ending with two great stops by Cleveland's Ken Keltner on July 17, Joe compiled a major-league-record 56-game hitting streak—during which he hit .408 with 15 homers. He was the subject of songs, prompted contests and endless media coverage, and beat out Ted Williams (a .406 batter on the season) for his second MVP trophy.

World War II intervened in 1943, and 31-year-old Joe came back three years later slightly below his previous form. His average and power numbers were down (he won a third MVP Award with subpar .315–20–97 totals in 1947), but he still got the job done: After missing the first 65 games of the '49 season because of a heel injury, DiMaggio returned to the lineup in Boston and hit four homers in three games—sparking the Yankees to the seventh of the nine world championships they would win in his 13-year career.

Age and mounting injuries hampered Joe's effectiveness, and he retired after a final World Series win in 1951 to go about marrying Marilyn Monroe, peddling Mr. Coffee, and simply being Joe DiMaggio. His final statistics (361 homers, .325 batting average, and 1,537 RBI) do not approach the all-time greats, but when injuries and military service are factored in, Joe's average season translates into 34 homers, 143 RBI, and a .579 slugging percentage—numbers worthy of his 1969 selection by Major League Baseball as its "greatest living player."

Baseball's Worst Trades

High hopes; bad deals. There's an inherent risk in all trades, and today's GMs know that any swap they make has the potential to backfire—and earn its spot among the worst deals of all time.

Listed below are some of the most one-sided swaps in baseball history. In each, future superstars (noted in bold) with great years ahead of them were dealt for players beyond their prime or on the fast track to mediocrity. General managers and owners had to live with the ramifications—and reminders from fans—for decades. All you have to do is read about them.

The Date: January 1, 1894
The Trade: Brooklyn Grooms send **OF Wee Willie Keeler** and **1B Dan Brouthers** to Baltimore Orioles for 3B Billy Shindle and OF George Treadway.
The Fallout: Keeler (.371) and Brouthers (.347) shined for the Orioles in 1894, with Wee Willie eventually batting above .300 for 13 straight seasons after the trade—including .424 with the Orioles in 1897. Shindle, while productive, never went over .300 for the Grooms. Treadway had one good year but was gone from the majors in three.

The Date: December 15, 1900
The Trade: Cincinnati Reds send **P Christy Mathewson** to New York Giants for P Amos Rusie.
The Fallout: Mathewson shares the NL record for most career wins (tied with Grover Cleveland Alexander at 373)—all but one of which were with the Giants, whom he pitched to five pennants. Rusie had won 246 but went just 0–1 with the Reds before retiring.

The Date: April 12, 1916
The Trade: Boston Red Sox send **OF Tris Speaker** to Cleveland Indians for P Sam Jones, 3B Fred Thomas, and $55,000.
The Fallout: This was the first of many disastrous deals made by Boston. Speaker, a .336 hitter and top-notch fielder with the Sox

over nine years, lasted another 13 stellar seasons (11 with the Indians) and retired with a lifetime .345 batting average and 3,514 hits. Jones helped the Sox to the 1918 World Series title but was a mediocre 64–59 with Boston overall. Thomas, a .225 lifetime hitter, spent just one forgettable year with the Sox.

The Date: January 3, 1920
The Trade: Boston Red Sox send **OF Babe Ruth** to New York Yankees for $425,000 in cash and loans.
The Fallout: The granddaddy of bad swaps shifted baseball's power base from Boston to New York, where Babe hit 659 homers and rewrote the record books while leading the Yanks to seven pennants and four World Series championships in 15 years. The Sox, World Series victors four times from 1912 through 1918, wouldn't win it all again until 2004. Then-Sox owner Harry Frazee is still reviled in New England for this one.

The Date: May 6, 1930
The Trade: Boston Red Sox send **P Red Ruffing** to New York Yankees for OF/1B Cedric Durst and $50,000.
The Fallout: The last in a string of stars sent from cash-poor Boston to New York in one-sided deals, Ruffing rebounded from a 39–96 mark with woeful Sox clubs to a Cooperstown-worthy 231–124 slate with the Yanks—plus a 7–2 mark in ten World Series starts. Durst hit .245 with one homer for Boston during the rest of 1930, his last year in the majors.

The Date: June 15, 1964
The Trade: Chicago Cubs send **OF Lou Brock,** P Jack Spring, and P Paul Toth to St. Louis Cardinals for P Ernie Broglio, P Bobby Shantz, and OF Doug Clemens.
The Fallout: It was essentially a Brock-for-Broglio swap. The Cubs hoped Broglio (having racked up an 18–8 record in 1963) would anchor their staff; instead, he went 7–19 over parts of three seasons. Brock, a .251 hitter with Chicago, caught fire with the Cards, batting .348 with 33 steals the rest of '64 to help St. Louis win the World Series title. He retired in 1979 with 3,023 hits,

a then-record 938 stolen bases, and a .391 average in 21 World Series games.

The Date: December 9, 1965
The Trade: Cincinnati Reds send **OF Frank Robinson** to Baltimore Orioles for P Milt Pappas, P Jack Baldschun, and OF Dick Simpson.
The Fallout: After ten stellar seasons (including 324 home runs), Robinson was deemed "an old 30" by Reds owner Bill DeWitt, architect of the swap. Robinson went on to win the Triple Crown and AL MVP Award in 1966 and led the Orioles to four pennants and two World Series titles through 1971, eventually hitting 586 career homers. Pappas won 209 games in his career but went just 30–29 with the Reds. Throw-ins Baldschun and Simpson gave Cincinnati one win and five homers, respectively.

The Date: April 21, 1966
The Trade: Philadelphia Phillies send **P Ferguson Jenkins,** OF Adolfo Phillips, and OF John Herrnstein to Chicago Cubs for P Larry Jackson and P Bob Buhl.
The Fallout: Jenkins, who went 2–1 in two years with the Phillies, won at least 20 in each of the next six years for Chicago en route to 284 lifetime victories. Phillips (mediocre) and Herrnstein (awful) were soon gone from the scene, while the aging Jackson and Buhl—once very good pitchers—were a combined 47–53 with the Phils.

The Date: December 10, 1971
The Trade: New York Mets send **P Nolan Ryan**, P Don Rose, OF Leroy Stanton, and C Frank Estrada to California Angels for SS Jim Fregosi.
The Fallout: The Mets saw Fregosi, a six-time All-Star shortstop with the Angels, as the long-term key to their third-base woes; instead, he failed to adapt to his new position and hit just .232 in 1972 before he was sent packing in '73. Young fireballer Ryan, 29–38 with New York, was an instant sensation with the Angels, winning 19 with 329 strikeouts in '72 on the way to staggering life-

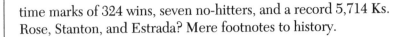

time marks of 324 wins, seven no-hitters, and a record 5,714 Ks. Rose, Stanton, and Estrada? Mere footnotes to history.

The Date: February 25, 1972
The Trade: St. Louis Cardinals send **P Steve Carlton** to Philadelphia Phillies for P Rick Wise.
The Fallout: Wise was a dependable pitcher before and after this trade, going 32–28 in 1972–73 and winning 188 games in his career, but he was no Steve Carlton. "Lefty" went an incredible 27–10 for the last-place Phillies of '72 and, all told, won 241 games and four Cy Youngs for the club en route to 329 lifetime victories.

The Date: January 27, 1982
The Trade: Philadelphia Phillies trade **2B Ryne Sandberg** and SS Larry Bowa to Chicago Cubs for SS Ivan DeJesus.
The Fallout: Sandberg played just 13 games for Philadelphia but became a legend with the Cubs, hitting 282 homers and earning nine Gold Gloves over 15 years. The aging Bowa, a perennial All-Star with the Phils, was Ryne's double-play partner for three years with the Cubs, the same amount of time DeJesus—a .250 hitter with zero power and a so-so glove—lasted in Philadelphia.

The Date: August 31, 1990
The Trade: Boston Red Sox send **1B Jeff Bagwell** to Houston Astros for P Larry Andersen.
The Fallout: It wasn't as bad as Ruth for cash, but it was close. The Sox, seeking a reliever for the stretch drive, got 22 solid innings from Andersen and won the 1990 AL East. He then left as a free agent—while Boston-born Bagwell debuted as '91 Rookie of the Year with Houston and eventually smashed 449 homers and 488 doubles as the greatest hitter in Astros history.

⚾ ⚾ ⚾

"I believe the sale of Babe Ruth will ultimately strengthen the team."

—Red Sox owner Harry Frazee, January 1920

Hall of Fame Talk

"You gotta be a man to play baseball for a living, but you gotta have a lot of little boy in you, too."

—Roy Campanella

"All I want out of life is that when I walk down the street, people will say, 'There goes the greatest hitter who ever lived.'"

—Ted Williams as a rookie

"There is always some kid who may be seeing me for the first or last time. I owe him my best."

—Joe DiMaggio

"...A kind of baseball that none of us had ever seen before— throwing and running and hitting at something close to the level of absolute perfection, playing to win but also playing the game almost as if it were a form of punishment for everyone else on the field."

—Writer Roger Angell on the performance of
Roberto Clemente in the 1971 World Series, *Five Seasons*

"For Lou, the game was almost holy, a religion."

—Sportswriter Stanley Frank on Lou Gehrig

"When they start the game, they don't yell 'Work Ball!' They say 'Play Ball!'"

—Willie Stargell

"To do what he did has got to be the most tremendous thing I've ever seen in sports."

—Pee Wee Reese on the rookie season of Dodger teammate
Jackie Robinson, *The Boys of Summer*

Superstitions and Good-Luck Recipes

No one is more superstitious than a player on a winning streak.

What makes a baseball team successful? Is it a player who can slug dingers over the fence, a fielder who snags the ball with ease, a pitcher who blazes a flame over the plate? Or is there something more? Many players are firm believers in luck, and they aren't satisfied to let it come to them. Instead they participate in elaborate rituals designed to keep their luck from running out.

On-Field Rituals

Many well-known baseball superstitions are practiced by everyone from Little League players to Hall of Famers. Step on one of the bases as you leave the field between innings or spit on your hand before picking up your bat for good luck. If you comment on a pitcher's performance when it looks like he might throw a no-hitter, you're guaranteed to jinx it. These traditions are as much a part of baseball as chewing tobacco, batboys, and the seventh-inning stretch. Said Ralph Kiner, who never stepped on the foul lines, "It didn't help or hurt me. I just didn't want to take any chances."

But other players don't court luck as casually as Kiner. Instead they perform individualized rituals. Some may have evolved from well-known superstitions, but others are, well, out of left field. For instance, Hall of Famer Clark Griffith thought shutouts were unlucky and went through his first 127 starts without one (in the dead-ball era). He once ordered rookie Frank Chance to drop a pop-up to allow a score and break up his own shutout in a one-sided game. He finally completed one in 1897, then went on to tie Cy Young for the

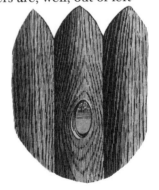

most shutouts in two different leagues in 1900 and 1901. Not so unlucky after all.

Eat, Drink, and Be Lucky

Food can be the key to ensuring a good game. Baltimore Orioles pitcher Jim Palmer ate pancakes before every start, while Wade Boggs stuck to chicken. Pitcher Turk Wendell would chew licorice (and brush his teeth) between innings. After Lou Gehrig's mom sent a jar of pickled eels to the clubhouse, the Yankees went on a hitting streak—and an eel streak. To ensure the streak continued, each team member, including Babe Ruth, would have at least a few bites of eel before every game.

For Denny McLain of the Tigers, Pepsi-Cola was a magic elixir. McLain would sometimes drink more than 20 bottles a day, even taking a bottle to bed so he could sip it when he woke up during the night. Despite drinking himself through 31 victories in the 1968 season, McLain was never appointed an official spokesperson for Pepsi.

Magical Equipment

Bats receive royal treatment because of the luck they hold. Every baseball fan knows you never lend your bat to another player, and if you need an extra shot of luck, you can always try sleeping with your bat. Some players would make an annual trip to Hillerich & Bradsby Company in Louisville, Kentucky, to ensure that their bats were lucky. Both Ted Williams and Al Simmons would roam the warehouse to pick out the perfect pieces of wood for their bats; Williams needed a narrow grain, while Simmons swore by the widest. Apparently they were both on to something: Their lifetime batting averages were .344 and .334, respectively.

For Hugh Duffy, whose average was .324, the wood had to sound just right. Duffy would bounce pieces of wood off the concrete, listening for the sound of success that only he could discern. Orlando Cepeda wasn't that particular about wood or sound, just as long as his bats were "productive." Cepeda would only use bats that had never made an out. Len Dykstra felt the same way about his batting gloves, throwing them away if he failed to get a hit in a single at-bat.

Since Mark "The Bird" Fidrych was a pitcher, it only seems reasonable that he centered his superstitions around the pitcher's mound. In addition to playing with the dirt, Fidrych would talk to his ball before a pitch.

Don't Go Changing...

Routine is the driving force behind many players' superstitions. If you have good luck, you must do everything exactly the same; if you have bad luck, change, change, change! Many of the routines involve clothing. Rafael Palmeiro wore the same T-shirt under his jersey if he was hitting well. Charlie Kerfeld of the Houston Astros was another member of the T-shirt club. He wore the same George Jetson shirt the entire 1986 season and finished with 11 wins and two losses. Former Astros second baseman Craig Biggio kept his luck in his cap: He didn't wash it at all during the season.

For some, their superstitions were their undoings. Blue Jays catcher Rick Cerone wore long johns under his uniform for an April 1979 game and promptly began a hitting streak. He refused to abandon the thermals that he thought were responsible for his good luck even as the season wore on and the temperature climbed. Although he kept his thermals, he didn't keep his luck. His season's batting average was a dismal .239. Cerone could have learned a thing or two from Milwaukee Brewers pitcher Pete Vukovich, who stopped the final game of the 1982 World Series so he could change a shoe. (Mismatched shoes had brought him luck in the past.) Perhaps he should have changed both shoes: The Brewers lost to the St. Louis Cardinals.

Sometimes the rituals work, and sometimes they don't. But that doesn't stop the players from believing in the old ones and creating new ones. After all, you never know....

◐ ◐ ◐

"I never shave on days I'm gonna pitch. I try to look extra mean on those days. It helps me get batters out."

—Cleveland fireballer Sam McDowell, *The Suitors of Spring*

Big-League Blunders

What's that they say about life? Oh yeah, that it's not fair. Well, baseball legacies aren't always fair either. Consider Fred Merkle, Mickey Owen, and Bill Buckner, for example. All were above-average players, at times All-Star caliber performers, who were assets to pennant-contending teams. Sadly, this was not to be their legacy in the game. A bonehead play, a passed ball, a missed grounder. Big blunders in baseball are hard to forget.

Merkle's Boner

September 1908. With the pennant on the line in a crucial late-season game against the Chicago Cubs, Al Bridwell of the New York Giants swatted an apparent game-winning two-out RBI single in the bottom of the ninth. Rookie Fred Merkle was the runner at first. When Moose McCormick scooted home from third to score, all Merkle had to do was advance to second base and touch the bag in order for the run to officially count, according to major-league rules. When young Merkle failed to do so and instead ran toward the clubhouse in center field, Cubs second baseman Johnny Evers frantically called for the ball to force him out. The Giants' manager, Joe McGinnity, wrestled the ball away from him, even going so far as to throw it into the stands, but Evers retrieved it and touched second base.

Oddly, this wasn't the first time this had happened. It wasn't even the first time Evers had been involved in such a play. Just two weeks prior, umpire Hank O'Day had turned down a similar appeal by Evers, in part because O'Day had already left the field and hadn't seen the second baseman touch the bag. Furthermore, umpires of the day rarely enforced the rule that stipulates each runner must advance to the next base on a game-winning play with two outs. This time, O'Day came up with a different decision, though he did not announce it right away. Either on the field or later that night—it's not clear which—O'Day declared the game a tie. Amid a sea of confusion, and with countless fans scattered over the field, O'Day and his umpiring partner left the field. Well after thousands of fans had poured onto the field and most of the play-

ers had made their way back to the clubhouse, he called Merkle out, negating the run. Enraged by O'Day's decision, the Giants filed a protest but were turned down by National League president Harry Pulliam.

This tie game meant all the difference to the two teams, who finished the regular season in a flat-footed deadlock. It came down to a tie-breaking game on October 8 to decide the pennant. The Giants lost 4–2, and even though Merkle didn't even play in that deciding game, his name became forever linked with the infamous "Merkle's Boner"—no matter that he went on to become an excellent defensive first baseman and a respectable hitter.

Owen's Passed Ball

October 1941. Thirty-three years after Merkle's Boner, a normally sure-handed catcher let the Brooklyn Dodgers down at the worst possible moment. With Brooklyn trailing the Yankees two games to one in the World Series and clinging to a 4–3 lead in the ninth inning of Game 4, All-Star catcher Mickey Owen failed to catch what should have been a game-ending third strike to Tommy Henrich, who swung and missed. As the ball glanced off Owen's mitt and squirted away toward the Brooklyn dugout, Henrich raced to first, igniting a four-run rally for the Yankees that earned them a miraculous 7–4 victory. Now up three games to one and with momentum on their side, the Yankees beat Owen's Dodgers the next day to wrap up the World Series.

"It was all my fault," said Owen in a report filed the next day in *The New York Times.* "It wasn't a strike. It was a great breaking curve that I should have had. But I guess the ball hit the side of my glove."

Ironically, earlier in the season Owen had set the NL record for catchers with 476 consecutive errorless chances accepted; he also set a Dodger record with a .995 fielding percentage. Despite these achievements, and his election to the All-Star team in each of the next three years, he would never live down his blunder of 1941. That single play, rather than Owen's defensive excellence over time, would remain firmly embedded in the memories of Brooklyn fans and in the annals of baseball.

Between Buckner's Legs

October 1986. Call it "The Curse of the Bambino," if you will. With the Red Sox leading Game 6 of the World Series by two runs, the New York Mets found themselves with no one on base and two out in the bottom of the tenth, on the verge of elimination. As Red Sox fans jubilantly began to prepare for postgame parties, the Mets suddenly strung together three consecutive singles, bringing them within a run and putting the tying run on third base.

Mookie Wilson stepped up to the plate, and Sox reliever Bob Stanley threw a wild pitch that eluded catcher Rich Gedman, allowing Kevin Mitchell to score and Ray Knight to advance to second. With the game tied, Wilson then chopped a bouncer down the first base line. But as Boston fans watched helplessly and Mets fans looked on with mounting joy, the ball skipped between Bill Buckner's legs and slid down the right-field line. It's debatable whether Buckner would have had a play on the speedy Wilson, but the error left no doubt about the outcome, allowing the winning run to score from second base and handing the Red Sox yet another defeat in their quest for a world title.

After the game, Red Sox manager John McNamara faced a barrage of questions regarding his decision not to replace the aging and hobbled Buckner with utilityman Dave Stapleton as a defensive caddy. It was a maneuver McNamara had used throughout the season, but one he decided to forgo because he wanted Buckner on the field to celebrate the world championship. Alas, it was Buckner's error that ensured there would be no Red Sox celebration. The Mets took Game 7 as well, overcoming a three-run deficit to win the game and the Series. And Buckner, who otherwise would have been remembered as a gritty and skilled .289 lifetime hitter, would forever be linked in infamy with a World Series collapse.

Magical Moment

Move over, Babe—here comes Henry!

The Setting: Atlanta-Fulton County Stadium; April 8, 1974
The Magic: Hammerin' Hank passes Ruth with his 715th homer.

In spring training 1969, Hank Aaron felt old. He was seriously considering retirement. But Lee Allen, one of the first great baseball historians, took him aside and explained how close he was to setting some serious lifetime records. He was just one homer behind Mel Ott and two behind Ernie Banks for second place in NL history. The 3,000-hits milestone wasn't far away, and Aaron even had a chance to get the most at-bats of all time.

Aaron listened, and he heard the deeper truth behind Allen's comments. If he could set those records, people would have to take notice, and Aaron could use his increased visibility to see that changes were made within the game—against discriminatory hiring practices and segregation in spring training. Aaron accepted the challenge and went on to finish his career second in at-bats, third in games played and hits, and tenth in doubles.

But the big record was broken in Atlanta on a chilly April night, and not everyone was happy about it. Although many fans were cheering him on, Aaron also received racist hate mail and death threats from people around the country, including his hometown of Atlanta; police even provided him with a bodyguard. But Aaron maintained his cool, as he always had. And, just as he had done 714 times before, he stepped up to the plate and hit a round-tripper, depositing an Al Downing pitch into the Atlanta bullpen. Babe Ruth's home run record had been surpassed. But this moment wasn't just about Aaron's place in baseball history; it resonated throughout the country on many different levels.

◐ ◐ ◐

"How do I pitch him? I wish I could throw the ball under the plate."

—Opposing pitcher Don Newcombe on Aaron

"Freak" Pitches

Keep your eye on those spitballers and greasers.

Pitchers began seeking an advantage over hitters almost as soon as Jim Creighton developed the wrist snap in the 1850s. The rules were much simpler then, leaving more room for creative interpretation. So in 1868, when 16-year-old Bobby Matthews of the Lord Baltimores spat on the ball and fired it with the underhand stiff wrist the rules required, the ball danced, and the batters went crazy.

Doctoring the Ball

The spitball has had dozens of names, from "country sinker" to the "aqueous toss" and "humidity dispenser" or, more directly, "the wet one." But the spitball belongs in a larger class of pitches in which the ball is altered in one way or another to break or twist when it heads toward the batter. These pitches haven't always been fair, but they've usually done the trick.

In the 1890s, Clark Griffith, who amassed more than 200 wins in his pitching career, would bang the ball against his spikes, leaving it cut up and subject to off-balance aerodynamic forces. In later years, pitchers would cut a hole in their gloves through which they could scrape the ball on a doctored ring. Or they would have a teammate wear a belt with a sharp buckle and tear it against the ball as they warmed up between innings.

How the Spitball Got Its Name

In the early 1900s, Ed Walsh of the White Sox learned how to moisten a ball on the tips of his fingers so it would slide off and be harder to hit. Before long, the spitter was the pitch of choice for dozens of hurlers. Historians John Thorn and John Holway have said, "The dead-ball era could be called the doctored ball era."

Walsh's spitball was especially devastating because he could make it break four different ways: down and in, straight down, down and out, and up (which he threw underhand). Walsh put his hand to his face on every pitch so that the batters wouldn't know what to expect, but he threw the spitter only about half the time.

He and fellow spitball artist Jack Chesbro became the only two pitchers to win 40 games in one season in the 20th century.

Cleaning Up and Playing Dirty

After years of wild pitches (culminating in the 1920 death of Ray Chapman, who was hit in the temple by a pitched ball), baseball decided to clean up its act. Since the 1890s, it had been "illegal" for pitchers to damage a ball to alter pitches, but that rule was rarely enforced. The spitter was officially banned before the 1920 season (with stricter punishments for rule-breakers), although 17 pitchers were grandfathered in and allowed to throw it until their careers ended. The new rule outlawed spit, sandpaper, resin, talcum powder, and other "foreign substances" that produced trick pitches. So hurlers had to find better ways to cheat.

Some did and later admitted it; some have denied all wrongdoing. Hall of Famer Whitey Ford of the Yankees has been accused of using every trick he could muster, from gouging the ball with a ring, to covering one side of the ball with mud, to creating a special invisible gunk that he slathered on his fingers between innings. Lew Burdette of the Braves in the 1950s always said that having the hitters *think* he had a spitter was just as good as actually throwing one. He'd wipe his hands on his pants and in his hair and then spit between his teeth. But the all-time artist of loading the ball was Gaylord Perry, who used his wiles (and a lot of Vaseline) to win Cy Young Awards in both leagues. Perry's gyrations between each pitch were phenomenal. He'd grab here, scratch there, flick here, wipe there. No one could possibly know what was coming. In his 22 years of pitching, Perry was caught cheating just once.

◎ ◎ ◎

"I think the ball disintegrated on the way to the plate and the catcher put it back together again. I swear, when it went past the plate it was just the spit that went by."

—Sam Crawford on Ed Walsh's spitter

All-Time Great

Mickey Mantle

The slugger, speedster, and party animal overcame injury and charmed the fans.

Born: October 20, 1931; Spavinaw, OK
MLB Career: New York Yankees, 1951–68
Hall of Fame Resume: 536 home runs • 1,509 RBI • Named to 16 All-Star teams • Played in 12 World Series • Three MVP Awards • Led league in runs six times
Inside Pitch: Mickey was named after Hall of Famer Mickey Cochrane.

To those who saw him play, Mickey Charles Mantle was something special: a combination of power, speed, and presence possessing so much natural talent that some viewed him as an underachiever despite his titanic accomplishments. A switch-hitter from the time his father pitched to him in the family's Commerce, Oklahoma, backyard, he overcame the bone disease osteomyelitis in his left leg to make the Yankees as a 19-year-old outfielder in the spring of 1951.

Mantle was touted as the next Joe DiMaggio (who, for one year before retiring, played alongside Mantle in the outfield). He recovered from a tough start to have a fine rookie year dimmed only by an injury to his good leg in the Yanks' World Series win over the New York Giants. It was just the beginning of the health hazards that would plague Mantle's career, but as the starting center fielder on the most dominant team in baseball history, Mantle's star rose quickly. He batted .311 his second season, and he had already hit 121 homers by age 23, when he led the AL with 37 in 1955.

Superb defense, blistering power (the term "tape-measure home run" was coined after his 565-foot shot in Washington), and annual totals of 100-plus runs and 90 to 100 RBI were not enough for some fans awaiting the next DiMaggio. Only after putting together an MVP/Triple Crown season in '56 (pacing the league with a .353 average, 52 homers, 130 RBI, 132 runs, and a .705 slugging percentage) did Mantle win everyone over. He hit a career-high .365 with 34 home runs to cop a second straight MVP trophy in '57, and in 1961 he waged a season-long assault against Babe Ruth's single-season record of 60 homers. He wound up six short when he was sidelined in September by a hip infection, and teammate Roger Maris broke the record with his 61st blast.

Mick had become the fan favorite, and when he recovered to win a third MVP Award in 1962 (.321–30–89), it was still thought he might challenge Ruth's all-time record of 714 homers. But injuries (including surgeries on one shoulder and both legs) and years of hard drinking had worn down Mantle's body. After a strong year in '64 capped by three World Series home runs (his 18 homers in 12 Series broke Ruth's record), he and the Yankees began a rapid decline. Mantle was in constant leg pain and had been relegated to first-base duties when he retired in 1968 at age 37.

Mantle's 536 homers, 1,509 RBI, and leadership of seven World Series champions guaranteed him a Hall of Fame plaque, but his perseverance alone became legendary. When he died in 1995, baseball fans who came of age in the 1950s and '60s found themselves questioning their own mortality. If the great Mickey Mantle was vulnerable, they wondered, how safe are any of us?

◖◗ ◖◗ ◖◗

"Nobody is half as good as Mickey Mantle."

—Al Kaline, responding to a young boy who told him he wasn't half as good as Mickey Mantle

◖◗ ◖◗ ◖◗

"You say Mickey Mantle, I'll say Willie Mays; if you say Henry Aaron, I'll say Roberto Clemente. When you're competing at that level of ability, the margins of difference aren't that great."

—Tom Seaver, *The Greatest Team of All Time*

Learning the Lingo

To live in the world of baseball, one must speak the language.

Airmail: A throw, often from the outfield, that overshoots its intended target. **Origin:** Descriptive.

Banjo hitter: A hitter with little power. **Origin:** Refers to the banjo's twangy sound and/or describes the fragile musical instrument as if it were a bat.

Barber: A talkative player. **Origin:** Descriptive of the stereotypical chatty barber.

Battery: The pitcher and catcher, together. **Origin:** Telegraphy, referring to the transmitter (pitcher) and receiver (catcher).

Bees in the hands: The "stinging" sensation that occurs after swinging the bat, particularly when not wearing protective gloves and/or in cold weather. **Origin:** Descriptive of stings.

Bullpen: Where relievers warm up. **Origin:** "Bull Durham" tobacco advertisements often appeared on outfield walls near the area. May also refer to an area of the park where relief pitchers gather and "shoot the bull" for long stretches of the game.

Catbird seat: A favorable ball-strike situation for a pitcher or a hitter. **Origin:** Refers to the perch of the catbird. Popularized by broadcaster Red Barber.

Cleanup hitter: The fourth batter in the lineup. **Origin:** He clears, or cleans, the bases occupied by the first three hitters.

Deuce: Curveball. **Origin:** Usually signaled for with two fingers.

Fireman: A relief pitcher, usually the ace. **Origin:** Descriptive.

Get the thumb: To be ejected from the game. **Origin:** Descriptive of an umpire's hand signal.

The good face: A positive but unscientific assessment of a player's fitness, attitude, and "makeup." **Origin:** Scouting. A player possessing such qualities is said to have "the good face."

Hospital throw: A throw to a base that forces the fielder to take his eye off an approaching runner. **Origin:** Descriptive of the potential for injury.

Jack: A home run, or to hit a home run. **Origin:** Descriptive of jack, meaning "to lift."

Keystone: Second base, or the second baseman. **Origin:** Like the keystone of an arch, second base is considered a key supporting element (for scoring runs) and a key defensive position.

Matador: A timid fielder. **Origin:** Bullfighting. Refers to a player who fields a ball to his side, like the movement of a bullfighter, rather than get in front of it.

O-fer or Ohfer: Going hitless over a game or other period. **Origin:** Puns. O-fer is "zero-for," and "ohfer" includes the exclamation "oh" as in "oh-for-5."

Ribbies: Runs batted in. **Origin:** Phonetic, plural pronunciation of the acronym "RBI."

Southpaw: A left-handed pitcher. **Origin:** In most ballparks, home plate faces east so as to keep the sun from a batter's eyes, meaning south would be on the pitcher's left side.

Tablesetter: The first and second hitters in a lineup, or a player who reaches base early in an inning. **Origin:** Descriptive of preparation for the cleanup hitter.

Baseball by the Numbers

On some players, uniform numbers can make a statement.

From Babe Ruth's "3" in the 1930s to Albert Pujols's "5" today, baseball numbers on uniforms have given fans a chance to recognize, cheer on, and—in the case of countless Little Leaguers—imitate their favorite players. At times they have also served as a way for athletes to display their individuality.

Ruth's Yankees wore jerseys that corresponded to their spot in the vaunted New York lineup: Earle Combs "1," Mark Koenig "2," Ruth "3," Lou Gehrig "4," and so on down the line. Giants pitcher Bill Voiselle received special permission from the National League during the 1940s to wear "96"—a tribute to his beloved hometown of Ninety Six, South Carolina.

Just before 3′7″ Eddie Gaedel made his surprise pinch-hitting appearance for the hapless St. Louis Browns in 1951, the team's maverick owner, Bill Veeck, gave the crowd a hint of what was coming by printing Eddie's name and number in that day's scorecard: "Gaedel, ⅛." Veeck, in fact, was the man who became the first big-league boss to add player names atop their uniform numbers while running the White Sox a decade later. This gave TV viewers a better idea of who they were watching and enabled Chicago outfielder Carlos May to become the first and only major-leaguer to "wear" his birthday: "May 17."

Others making a statement with their backs more recently have included Al Oliver and Rey Ordonez, who presumably wore "0" so that their numbers would more closely match their names, and wacky left-hander Bill "Spaceman" Lee, who took "37" because, when turned upside down, it matched his name minus one "E." Minor-leaguer Johnny Neves, however, had them all topped. In 1951, he wore "7" backward on his Fargo-Moorhead jersey because, of course, his name spelled backward was "seveN." On the creativity scale, that's got to be #1.

Undercover Catcher

*When it comes to character assessments, you gotta listen to
Casey Stengel. And the Ol' Perfessor claimed Moe Berg was "the
strangest man ever to put on a baseball uniform." But Berg wasn't
just strange in a baseball uniform, he was strange and mysterious
in many ways—some of them deliberate.*

Moe Berg lived a life shrouded in mystery and marked by contradictions. He played alongside Babe Ruth, Lefty Grove, Jimmie
Foxx, and Ted Williams; he moved in the company of Norman
Rockefeller, Albert Einstein, and international diplomats; and yet
he was often described as a loner. He was well-liked by teammates
but preferred to travel by himself. He never married, and he made
few close friends.

"The Brainiest Guy in Baseball"

Moe was a bright kid from the beginning, with a special fondness
for baseball. As the starting shortstop for Princeton University,
where he majored in modern languages, Moe was a star. He was
fond of communicating with his second baseman in Latin, leaving
opposing baserunners scratching their heads.

He broke into the majors in 1923 as a shortstop with the
Brooklyn Robins (Dodgers). He converted to catcher and spent
time with the White Sox, Senators, Indians, and Red Sox throughout his career. A slow runner and a poor fielder, Berg nevertheless
eked out a 15-season big-league career. Pitchers loved him behind
the plate: They praised his intelligence and loved his strong, accurate arm. But while he once went 117 games without an error, he
rarely nudged his batting average much past .250. His weak bat
often kept him on the bench and led sportswriters to note, "Moe
Berg can speak 12 languages flawlessly and can hit in none." He
was, however, a favorite of sportswriters, many of whom considered him "the brainiest guy in baseball."

He earned his law degree from Columbia University, attending classes in the off-seasons and even during spring training and
partial seasons with the White Sox. When Berg was signed by the

Washington Senators in 1932, his life took a sudden change. In Washington, Berg became a society darling, delighting the glitterati with his knowledge and wit. Certainly it was during his Washington years that he made the contacts that would serve him in his post-baseball career.

Time in Tokyo and on TV

Berg first raised eyebrows in the intelligence community at the start of World War II, when he shared home movies of Tokyo's shipyards, factories, and military sites, which he had secretly filmed while on a baseball trip in 1934. While barnstorming through Japan along with Ruth, Lou Gehrig, and Foxx, Berg delighted Japanese audiences with his fluency in their language and familiarity with their culture. He even addressed the Japanese parliament. But one day he skipped the team's scheduled game and went to visit a Tokyo hospital, the highest building in the city. He sneaked up to the roof and took motion picture films of the Tokyo harbor. Some say those photos were used by the U.S. military as they planned their attack on Tokyo eight years later. Berg maintained that he had not been sent to Tokyo on a formal assignment, that he had acted on his own initiative to take the film and offer it to the U.S. government upon his return. Whether or not that was the case, Berg's undercover career had begun.

On February 21, 1939, Berg made the first of several appearances on the radio quiz show *Information, Please!* He was an immense hit, correctly answering nearly every question he was asked. Commissioner Kenesaw Mountain Landis was so proud of how intelligent and well-read the second-string catcher was that he told him, "Berg, in just 30 minutes you did more for baseball than I've done the entire time I've been commissioner." But Berg's baseball career was winding down; 1939 was his last season.

Secret Agent Man

Berg's intellect and elusive lifestyle were ideal for a post-baseball career as a spy. He was recruited by the Office of Strategic Services (predecessor to the CIA) in 1943, where he served in several capacities. He toured 20 countries in Latin America during the early days

of World War II, allegedly on a propaganda mission to bolster the morale of soldiers there. But what he was really doing was trying to determine how much the Latin American countries could help the U.S. war effort.

His most important mission for the OSS was to gather information about Germany's progress in developing an atomic bomb. He worked undercover in Italy and Switzerland and reported information to the States throughout 1944. One of his more daring assignments was a visit to Zurich, Switzerland, in December 1944, where he attended a lecture by German nuclear physicist Werner Heisenberg. If Heisenberg indicated the Germans were close to developing nukes, Berg had been directed to assassinate the scientist. Luckily for Heisenberg, Berg determined that German nuclear capability was not yet within the danger range.

Life After the War

On October 10, 1945, Berg was awarded the Medal of Freedom (now the Presidential Medal of Freedom) but turned it down without explanation. (After his death, his sister accepted it on his behalf.)

After the war he was recruited by the CIA. It is said that his is the only baseball card to be found in CIA headquarters. After his CIA career ended, Berg never worked again. He was often approached to write his memoirs. When he agreed, in 1960 or so, the publisher hired a writer to provide assistance. Berg quit the project in fury when the writer indicated that he thought Berg was Moe Howard of the Three Stooges. But his unusual career turns were later immortalized in the Nicholas Dawidoff book *The Catcher Was a Spy*. At age 70, Berg fell and injured himself. He died in the hospital. His last words were to ask a nurse, "What did the Mets do today?"

⚾ ⚾ ⚾

"There are two things I teach the boys that are all-American. One's the good old flag and one's baseball."

—Sportswriter Tim Murnane, 1908

Greatest Games of All Time

1951 NL Playoff, Game 3

Giants 5, Dodgers 4

The Setting: Polo Grounds, New York

The Drama: The Dodgers had held a 13½-game lead in the National League, but they found themselves in a playoff series with the crosstown Giants—in the third and final game.

No rivalry in any professional sport has ever surpassed the intensity and wackiness of the one between the New York Giants and Brooklyn Dodgers. And no game typified this brash, brilliant rivalry more than the third game of the 1951 playoff. It was the culmination of a sensational pennant race featuring the greatest come-from-behind charge to the top ever, which ended the season in a flat-footed tie. Yet the winner would not be crowned until another comeback in the final half of the final inning of the final playoff game, with the outcome ultimately sealed by the most dramatic home run in baseball history—the "Shot Heard 'Round the World."

The Dodgers, who had won the pennant in 1947 and '49 and narrowly missed in '50, were expected to win the National League once again. By the middle of May, they had established themselves in first; the Giants were second.

But then two important things happened. First, the Giants promoted Willie Mays from Minneapolis, where he was batting .477. Mays had a poor start for the Giants, but manager Leo Durocher made it clear to Willie that the kid would be in center field "as long as I'm the manager." Second, with Mays in center, a place had to be found for Bobby Thomson. He obligingly took over at third base, and the team began to click.

In early July, the Giants were in second place, but the Dodgers were still comfortably in front. On August 11, in fact, Brooklyn had a 13½-game lead, and Dodger manager Charlie Dressen offered this opinion to a writer: "The Giants is dead."

Durocher's boys didn't take kindly to that. They went on an incredible tear, winning 39 of 47 games, including the last seven of the regular season. It took a 14th-inning home run by Jackie Robinson on the final day of the season to keep the Dodgers from winding up in second. The two teams finished with identical 96–58 records, and the National League prepared for its second-ever playoff, a best-of-three confrontation.

Monte Irvin and Thomson homered off Ralph Branca to give the Giants a 3–1 victory in Game 1 in Brooklyn, but Clem Labine shut them out 10–0 at the Polo Grounds in Game 2. The amazing season was down to one game again.

For Game 3, the teams started their aces: Don Newcombe for Brooklyn, Sal Maglie (nicknamed "The Barber" for his willingness to throw close to batters) for New York. Maglie stumbled in the first, allowing two walks and a single to give the Dodgers a run. After that, he was untouchable for six innings. Newcombe was unscored on until the seventh, when the Giants tallied on a double, bunt, and sacrifice fly.

In the eighth, the Dodgers punched out four singles around a wild pitch and intentional walk for three runs and a lead that looked insurmountable. From his station in the third base coaching box, Durocher had been trying to rattle Newcombe, calling him every name he could think of. But Newk wasn't being affected. He put the Giants down in order in the last of the eighth.

But in the bottom of the ninth, Newcombe tired. Alvin Dark singled. Don Mueller pushed a single to right past Gil Hodges's outstretched glove. One out later, lefty hitter Whitey Lockman went with a Newcombe outside pitch and comfortably slapped it into the left-field corner. One run scored to make it 4–2, and runners were on second and third.

Dressen called for a new pitcher, and Branca headed into the game. When he unleashed the second pitch, a high inside fastball, Thomson turned on it, muscling it down the left-field line. When it cleared the fence 315 feet away, fans went berserk, and Giants broadcaster Russ Hodges screamed, "The Giants win the pennant!" into his microphone over and over again. The Giants had come back again. No one had ever seen anything like it.

Not Just America's Game

Baseball continues to grow in popularity across the globe.

Of the 16,000-plus players to have competed in the major leagues, nearly 1,000 have come from the Dominican Republic, Puerto Rico, Venezuela, and Japan (combined). Even Canada, not considered a baseball hotbed, has sent more than 200 players, including Hall of Famer Ferguson Jenkins, to the majors. Mexico has produced more than 100 big-leaguers, among them national icon Fernando Valenzuela. With most of these countries sitting so close to the United States, it seems logical that such a high-paying, high-profile job would attract neighbors. But what about countries far from the United States? Turns out the game is a hit with many of them, too.

One reason is the Little League World Series. The winner-take-all-the-glory tournament is immensely popular in many nations. While U.S. teams slug it out in Williamsport for a spot in the national bracket, the rest of the world competes in the other bracket. And the competition is fierce.

In 2006, the World Baseball Classic also brought the game to a world stage. Even as Americans groused about the timing of the WBC (during spring training) and its effect on pitchers' arms (a handful of participants suffered injuries), the passion for the tournament in other countries made it a success. Teams from the United States, Dominican Republic, Puerto Rico, and Korea—all considered favorites—were eliminated in early

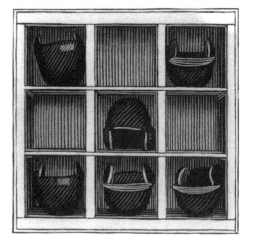

rounds. The Cubans, winners of three of the first four Olympic gold medals in baseball, reached the finals, where they went up against the Japanese. Using only two players from the American major leagues, Japan won the inaugural title. They could rightfully be called world champions. Other countries, too, hope to have a baseball title of their own someday.

Australia

American goldminers brought baseball to Australia in the 1850s. Joe Quinn, who moved to the United States as a teenager, was the first Australian to reach the major leagues, in 1884. It took another century for the second, Craig Shipley, to make it to the bigs. About 20 Aussies have followed, even as the game has declined in popularity at home. Despite the death of Australia's professional league, the country's silver medal in the 2004 Olympics provided baseball a boost in its battle with cricket.

Taiwan

Taiwan won 17 Little League World Series titles between 1969 and 1996; all other non-U.S. countries won just 13 championships *combined*. Yankee Chien-Ming Wang, Taiwan's first bona fide major-league star, has caused such a stir that thousands of his compatriots watch his games—broadcast live from New York—in the middle of the night local time on Taiwanese public television. Taiwan's own major league has had to deal with the aftershocks of a gambling scandal, but the renewed interest in baseball—plus Taiwan's history of Little League world dominance—should only nurture a game introduced to the island by the Japanese colonial government in the 1920s.

Korea

Like Taiwan, Korea has become a baseball power in recent decades. Introduced to the game by an American missionary in 1905, Korea started its first professional league in 1982. The Korean Baseball Organization's first alum to reach the major leagues was Chan Ho Park in 1994. More than a dozen Koreans (and counting) have followed.

China

China may have been the last country to host baseball on an Olympic stage. Both baseball and softball are marked for elimination after the 2008 Games in Beijing. The International Olympic Committee will consider bringing baseball back for the 2016 Games, but with the exception of Italy, few of the influential European IOC countries have ever really taken to baseball. Inroads have, however, been made in the People's Republic of China.

The game was first introduced there in the 1860s by Americans in Shanghai; its slow progress was halted a century later during the Cultural Revolution because the government considered baseball elitist. Yet the government has been instrumental in resuscitating the game in the Middle Kingdom. The Chinese Baseball League has been operating since 2002, and has given budding ballplayers a chance to hone their skills.

While few Chinese attend the games, despite no admission charge, that didn't stop the New York Yankees from visiting in January 2007. The Yanks met with government officials, promising to send coaches, scouts, and doctors to observe and interact with Chinese players. Their goodwill trip was the first real outreach by the major leagues to China. It may not bear fruit for another generation in terms of players, but from a country with 1.3 billion people, the Yankees are betting they might find a future superstar.

⚾ ⚾ ⚾

"Baseball is just the great American pastime. I think it's the joy of feeling part of [the game] more than other sports."

—President George H. W. Bush, *The Washington Post*,
March 31, 1989

⚾ ⚾ ⚾

"The game of baseball is a clean, straight game, and it summons to its presence everybody who enjoys clean, straight athletics. It furnishes amusement to the thousands and thousands."

—President William Howard Taft

It Ain't Nothing 'Til Bill Klem Calls It

There have been other fine umpires—Al Barlick, Doug Harvey,
Billy Evans. But there was only one Bill Klem.

Try to start a discussion that begins, "Who was the greatest [blank] of all time?" and you'll be in for some argument—unless the blank is "umpire." In that case, the answer is unquestionably Bill Klem. He was so good, and it was so obvious that he was so good, that for 16 of his record-setting 37 years as a National League arbiter, he umpired behind the plate only. That wasn't a reward for years of quality service—it started the first day he umped in the major leagues. He was uniquely skilled at calling balls and strikes.

Klem wasn't large, but he commanded respect because of his hard work and integrity. He took grief from some of the game's legendary grief-givers, but when the heat got to be too much, Klem would draw a line in the dirt with his toe, announce, "Don't cross the Rio Grande," and turn his back. Anyone who crossed that line was headed for the showers. He was often called "The Old Arbitrator," and that nickname (which Klem loved) is on his Hall of Fame plaque. But if you called him "Catfish" (because of his looks), you were tossed immediately.

Klem pioneered the inside chest protector, which allowed for a better view of the pitch than protectors that were worn outside the shirt. And he was one of the first to use hand signals for strikes and fouls. He umpired 104 World Series games in 18 Series—almost twice as many Series as any other ump—and he worked the first All-Star Game in 1933. When he retired in 1941 at age 67, he was the oldest ump in baseball history. (Bruce Froemming surpassed the mark in 2007.)

Klem did one very important thing that many umpires never do, although they should: *wait.* He would hesitate and let the facts clarify themselves in his mind before making a call. Once when Klem paused before signaling safe or out, the frustrated catcher shouted, "Well, what is he?" Klem answered, "He ain't nothing 'til I call it."

Casey Is a Hit

The famous poem always hits a home run with fans.

The outlook wasn't brilliant when, in 1888,
A man named Ernest Thayer penned a poem blessed by fate.
Its printed form drew little praise but when performed aloud,
"Casey at the Bat" brought forth great cheering from its crowd.

Then all around this favored land his words gained new steam,
They turned up in the papers and were learned by every team.
And somewhere Thayer's smiling now—you can be sure of that,
For decades later we're still cheering "Casey at the Bat."

"Casey at the Bat" is much more than a poem about a baseball team from Mudville whose star player strikes out with the game on the line. It has become part of the very fabric of American culture: a fun-to-read—or, better yet, fun-to-hear—story about not only baseball, but also hope.

Rhymes and Recitations

When former *Harvard Lampoon* editor William Randolph Hearst took over the *San Francisco Examiner* from his father, he brought three former *Lampoon* staffers on board with him. Ernest Lawrence Thayer was one of them. Thayer wrote "Casey at the Bat" under the pen name "Phin" on June 3, 1888. He was reportedly paid $5 for his efforts. It rhymed well and told a wonderful story under the heading, "Casey at the Bat, a Ballad of the Republic," but it did not hold great significance for many readers. Fortunately, it did make an impression on one of them.

Novelist Archibald Gunter kept a clipping of the poem from the *Examiner* as possible subject matter for a novel. Months later, when he learned that members of the New York Giants and Chicago White Stockings would be attending a comedy show in New York, he suggested to a comedian friend that he recite the poem for the players. DeWolf Hopper did just that, and the entire audience—not only the ballplayers—responded loudly.

Hopper later wrote in his memoir, *Once a Clown, Always a Clown,* "When I dropped my voice to B flat, below low C, at 'But one scornful look from Casey, and the audience was awed,' I remember seeing [Giants standout] Buck Ewing's gallant mustachios give a single nervous twitch."

Something for Everyone

The rest, one might say, is history—more than 120 years of it. The poem grew to such popularity that several people tried to take credit for writing it under the name "Phin." When Thayer came forward years later, he signed over the ballad's rights to Hopper, feeling it was not one of his greatest writings. Audiences felt differently, as Hopper went on to recite "Casey at the Bat" an estimated 10,000 times.

The poem has been performed by countless others in theaters, ballparks, classrooms, and stages everywhere. Comic magicians Penn and Teller have performed it. It has graced the airwaves of *Saturday Night Live* and entertained crowds waiting to see their heroes inducted into the Baseball Hall of Fame. It has been performed by Disney cartoon characters in a 1946 production, by legendary radio personality Garrison Keillor, by actor/comedian Jackie Gleason, by horror-film master Vincent Price, and by sportscaster Bob Costas, to name a few.

Magic in Mudville

Legend has it that Casey was modeled after a Stockton, California, player named John Cahill, whom Thayer had reportedly watched play. To honor that story, and presumably to drum up a little publicity, the Class-A Stockton Ports changed their name to the Mudville Nine during the 2000 and 2001 seasons. Others speculate that the name Mudville represents an area in Boston where Thayer grew up before going to Harvard.

This much is certain: In every true recital of one of the most recognized poems in American history, Flynn and Blake set the table for the Mighty Casey with two-out hits for Mudville. And with runners on second and third base and two outs, poor Casey always—as he did in 1888—strikes out.

"Casey at the Bat"
by Ernest L. Thayer

The outlook wasn't brilliant for the Mudville nine that day:
The score stood four to two, with but one inning more to play.
And then when Cooney died at first, and Barrows did the same,
A sickly silence fell upon the patrons of the game.

A straggling few got up to go in deep despair. The rest
Clung to that hope which springs eternal in the human breast.
They thought, "If only Casey could but get a whack at that.
We'd put up even money now, with Casey at the bat."

But Flynn preceded Casey, as did also Jimmy Blake,
And the former was a lulu, while the latter was a cake.
So upon that stricken multitude, grim melancholy sat;
For there seemed but little chance of Casey getting to the bat.

But Flynn let drive a single, to the wonderment of all.
And Blake, the much despised, tore the cover off the ball.
And when the dust had lifted, and men saw what had occurred,
There was Jimmy safe at second, and Flynn a-hugging third.

Then from 5,000 throats and more there rose a lusty yell;
It rumbled through the valley, it rattled in the dell;
It knocked upon the mountain and recoiled upon the flat,
For Casey, mighty Casey, was advancing to the bat.

There was ease in Casey's manner as he stepped into his place,
There was pride in Casey's bearing and a smile lit Casey's face.
And when, responding to the cheers, he lightly doffed his hat,
No stranger in the crowd could doubt 'twas Casey at the bat.

Ten thousand eyes were on him as he rubbed his hands with dirt;
Five thousand tongues applauded when he wiped them on his shirt.
Then, while the writhing pitcher ground the ball into his hip,
Defiance flashed in Casey's eye, a sneer curled Casey's lip.

And now the leather-covered sphere came hurtling through
    the air,
And Casey stood a-watching it in haughty grandeur there.
Close by the sturdy batsman the ball unheeded sped—
"That ain't my style," said Casey. "Strike one!" the umpire said.

From the benches, black with people, there went up a muffled roar,
Like the beating of the storm waves on a stern and distant shore.
"Kill him! Kill the umpire!" shouted someone on the stand;
And it's likely they'd a-killed him had not Casey raised his hand.

With a smile of Christian charity, great Casey's visage shone;
He stilled the rising tumult; he bade the game go on.
He signaled to the pitcher, and once more the spheroid flew;
But Casey still ignored it, and the umpire said, "Strike two!"

"Fraud!" cried the maddened thousands, and echo answered
    "Fraud!"
But one scornful look from Casey and the audience was awed.
They saw his face grow stern and cold, they saw his muscles strain,
And they knew that Casey wouldn't let that ball go by again.

The sneer has fled from Casey's lip, his teeth are clenched in hate;
He pounds, with cruel violence, his bat upon the plate.
And now the pitcher holds the ball, and now he lets it go,
And now the air is shattered by the force of Casey's blow.

Oh, somewhere in this favored land the sun is shining bright.
The band is playing somewhere, and somewhere hearts are light.
And somewhere men are laughing, and somewhere children shout,
But there is no joy in Mudville—mighty Casey has struck out.

The Brooklyn Giant

Roy Campanella's tragic car accident halted his ability to catch—but not to inspire.

Roy Campanella's brilliant catching career ended on a slick road on January 28, 1958, when his car slid into a telephone pole. Paralyzed below the shoulders, Campanella could no longer be a ballplayer, but he could still be an inspiration. He'd already inspired many during his baseball journey: starting in the Negro Leagues at age 16, taking a steep pay cut to sign with the Dodgers in 1946, integrating the American Association, helping Brooklyn win its only world championship, catching in five World Series, and becoming the only catcher to win three NL Most Valuable Player Awards. He hit 41 home runs in 1953—a record for catchers that stood until 1996—and had an NL-high 142 RBI that same year. He ended his career with a .276 batting average, 242 home runs, and 856 RBI.

On May 7, 1959, a major-league-record crowd of 93,103 came to the Los Angeles Memorial Coliseum for Roy Campanella Night, even though Campy had never played in that city. The Yankees traveled across the country for the benefit game against the Dodgers. The lights were turned down, and everyone in the crowd lit a match in tribute to Campanella. "This is something I will never forget," he said. "I thank God I'm here living to be able to see it. It's a wonderful thing."

The event raised an estimated $75,000 for Campy, who faced mounting debt in the days before lucrative autograph sessions and big-league pensions. The Dodgers hired Campanella to work in the community relations department, and the always upbeat Hall of Famer—he was elected to Cooperstown in 1969—served as a spring training instructor and a mentor to young catchers. Campy died in 1993 at the age of 71, years beyond the life expectancy of most quadriplegics. But then, Roy Campanella wasn't most men.

The All-American Girls Baseball League

Imagine a ballplayer who reaches base 215 times, attempts 203 stolen bases (caught only twice)—and happens to be a woman.

There was such a ballplayer, and her name was Sophie Kurys. She was a star in the All-American Girls Baseball League (AAGBL) of the 1940s and '50s. Kurys's mark of 201 steals in 1946, a year in which the basepaths were actually lengthened, was six times greater than Brooklyn Dodger Pete Reiser's major-league high of 34 that year—and Pistol Pete didn't have to slide with bare legs. Sliding was excruciating in the short skirts of the All-American Girls Baseball League, especially in Fort Wayne, Indiana, where the grounds crew burned the infield with gasoline to dry it on rainy days. But the players all slid, and never headfirst. It was a running league, and the constant sliding caused deep cuts—known to ballplayers as strawberries—that would painfully stick to clothes after games. "I had strawberries on strawberries," Kurys recalled.

Kurys stole 1,114 bases in just eight seasons—most of them as a Racine Belle—and her 140-steal annual average was higher than major-league career record holder Rickey Henderson's best season. Kurys's most memorable moment, though, was beating the throw home for the only run of a 14-inning game to win the 1946 league championship. Max Carey, then the all-time National League stolen-base leader (with 738) and president of the AAGBL, called it "even in the majors, the best game I've ever seen."

The league was started in 1943. Many able-bodied men were enlisted in the armed services, and the major leagues—not to mention the minors—were forced to use many players who would have been laughed out of the ballpark before World War II started. The AAGBL wasn't just a wartime phenomenon, though. The league lasted until 1954 and made several attempts to branch out. A 1949 tour of Central America featured exhibition games in four different countries. There were also junior teams, most notably the Junior Belles in Racine, where teenage girls learned fundamentals, participated in a short-season schedule, and occasionally played before the start of AAGBL contests.

The AAGBL had some outstanding players. Two-time batting leader Dorothy Kamenshek (.292 lifetime) was sought by a men's minor-league team in Fort Lauderdale, but she turned them down. Joanne Weaver, at 14, followed her sister Betty into the league and later became the only .400 hitter in AAGBL history. Bonnie Baker, a Saskatchewan-born catcher and former model, was the only player ever hired as a manager in the league. Pitcher Jean Faut, whose husband would eventually be her manager, had a baby in March 1948, then went out and won 16 games on the season while also playing third base; she later pitched two perfect games and led South Bend to consecutive championships. Rose Gacioch once had 31 outfield assists in a season and converted to pitcher, helping the Rockford Peaches win four titles. Dottie Schroeder was the only woman to play every season—and nearly every game—of the league's existence, winning her only title in 12 seasons by driving in the winning run for the Kalamazoo Lassies in the last game in league history.

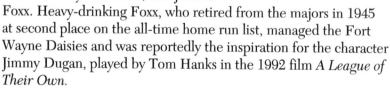

The managers were better known: ex-Cub Woody English, former Pirate Carson Bigbee, Bill Wambsganss (who was noted for turning an unassisted triple play in the 1920 World Series), and future Hall of Famers Max Carey, Dave "Beauty" Bancroft, and Jimmie Foxx. Heavy-drinking Foxx, who retired from the majors in 1945 at second place on the all-time home run list, managed the Fort Wayne Daisies and was reportedly the inspiration for the character Jimmy Dugan, played by Tom Hanks in the 1992 film *A League of Their Own*.

Hollywood likes to stretch the truth, but *A League of Their Own* wasn't too far off base. If anything, the movie condensed the 12 seasons the league existed into one year and pieced many real-

life stories together to create characters with fictional names. The most memorable aspects of the film are mostly true: the Midwestern locale, the mass tryout in Chicago, the compulsory charm school, the chaperones, the bus trips, the camaraderie, a player's child in uniform on the bench, and the candy magnate who started the whole thing (fictional Walter Harvey—a thinly disguised version of Chicago Cubs owner Philip Wrigley). A 1993 television series with the same name as the film could have shed more light on other facets of the league, but its six-episode run was shorter than some homestands.

Contrary to what was depicted in the movie, though, the league began with a 12-inch softball thrown underhand from 40 feet away. The ball got smaller, the mound was moved back, and the distance between the bases grew as the league wore on. By 1954, the ball was 9¼ inches, approximately the same size as a regulation major-league ball; the mound was 60 feet from home plate; and the bases were 85 feet apart—just shy of the dimensions of a major-league diamond (60 feet, 6 inches; 90 feet). But all these changes weren't enough to keep the league from folding.

Mismanagement by independent owners, too much expansion, and dwindling attendance eventually killed off the AAGBL. In the last year, the players drove their own cars to games when teams could no longer afford a bus, and they even played without pay at the end. The ride had been a good one, though. The $45–$75 average weekly salary was far more than most women would have earned in occupations that they enjoyed far less. What's more, the 600 women who made the grade earned the right to play baseball professionally. That's something only a handful of women have been able to claim in the half-century since then.

⚾ ⚾ ⚾

"We had to look like ladies and play baseball like men."

—Pepper Paire

Signs of the Times

*Communication between coaches and players is like
a well-choreographed game of charades.*

Anyone who has watched a base coach flash crazy-looking signs
to a hitter knows that baseball has a hidden language. Sometimes,
however, that language isn't really so hidden. Take the case of a
Dodgers player who gave third base coach Preston Gomez a quiz-
zical look while being given a squeeze-bunt sign and yelled out,
"This pitch?" The squeeze was taken off.

Nonverbal Communication

Coaches convey signs to hitters in a variety of ways—touching
a hand to their ear, to their cap, to their chest. The order of the
signs can mean completely different things from different coaches.
There is no "how-to" book for signaling. Where the coach is standing, how many times he claps his hands, where in a progression of
hand signals a shoulder-touch falls—these can all indicate that a
batter should hit away, take a pitch, or bunt. "It's one of the biggest parts of baseball," former Mets manager Davey Johnson once
said of this nonverbal communication. "And it always has been."

Baseball historian Paul Dickson estimates that more than
1,000 nonverbal instructions are given in the course of a nine-
inning major-league baseball game. This includes a variety of signs
from catchers to pitchers for every hitter, but it also includes a
number of subtle and not-so-subtle signals from coaches to batters and baserunners—signals that might be completely lost on
the average fan. A player must watch carefully and be prepared to
hit and run, steal a base, throw to second, or do whatever else the
coach is directing him to do.

Vital Signs

Coaches and managers consider their instructions vital to the
outcome of a game. Former Yankees skipper Billy Martin once
relayed signs via phone from a hospital bed. Legend has it that
Jack McKeon, after being ejected from a game, returned in the

team mascot's uniform and continued calling plays. (McKeon, for the record, denies that story.) After having been ejected from a minor-league game in the Florida State League, Don Zimmer once climbed a light pole and flashed signs from outside the park.

Signs and signals have been around in baseball for more than a century, perhaps for as long as the game has been played. And while the gestures have gone from simple hand waves and numbers-of-fingers to elaborate brushes of the chest, doffs of the cap, and swipes of the sleeve, the most effective signs are still those that are easiest to remember and see from the batter's box or from the basepaths. Each coach comes up with his own set of signals for the team, so it's his responsibility to make sure the players understand the messages he's sending.

Stealing Signs

Still, signs that are *too* simplistic can lead to easy sign-stealing from the opposing team. The Cleveland Indians of the 1940s were said to have used an elaborate sign-stealing system that included an arm wave from a man in the outfield scoreboard each time a curveball was coming. Other teams have been accused of using everything from old-fashioned telescopes to modern video equipment to swipe opponents' signs, whether they are from coaches to players or catchers to pitchers.

To combat such tactics, coaches and catchers frequently flash decoy signs that have nothing to do with the called-for pitch or plays. However, these decoys and extra gyrations of the body can fool one's own players, too. And if not executed correctly, they might not even serve their purpose in fooling the opposition.

"If you rush through the decoy signs and go slow when you're giving the real signs, they'll know something is going on," explains former Yankees coach and player Luis Sojo. Players have to pay close attention for an "indicator" sign that lets them know the next sign is not a decoy.

Baseball teams can be orchestras of sorts, with managers, coaches, and catchers serving as the conductors. They're trying to create a harmony that only their team can understand. Because in baseball, some of the most compelling strategy is best left unsaid.

One Is the Loneliest Number

The music world has one-hit wonders. Baseball has something similar: players who have one season of greatness.

Every baseball player dreams of leaving a legacy of sustained greatness—quality play year after year. Most have their ups and downs, but there are some who leave their typical stats behind for one brilliant season. In some cases, their outstanding season was sparked by a change in ballpark or team; in other cases, a hotshot rookie simply caught the league by surprise. Then there were those players who benefited from a league-wide shift, a change in the equipment, or adjustments to their conditioning and approach. If only these players could have bottled their single season of glory and carried it through the rest of their career, they would all be residing in Cooperstown today.

Earl Webb

Webb entered the majors in 1925 at age 27, playing sporadically for the New York Giants and Chicago Cubs. He showed flashes of hitting potential but had little extra-base power. He was a below-average outfielder and couldn't run very fast. It seemed as though Webb would be a quick blip in the baseball annals, but things changed when he joined the Boston Red Sox in 1930. Playing half of his games at Fenway Park, Webb batted .323 (up from .250 in 1928), clubbed 16 home runs, and even improved his defensive play.

In 1931, Webb raised his level of play even higher. He had a career-high .333 batting average, 14 home runs, and 103 RBI. But his most amazing feat was banging out 67 doubles—more than doubling his career-best output for one year and setting a single-season major-league record that stands to this day.

Not to take anything away from his improved play, but some sportswriters believed that Webb developed a habit of intentionally stopping at second base when he could have advanced to third. This was not exactly a team-first concept, which might partially explain why Webb's major-league career came to an end two years later.

Walt "Moose" Dropo

With some one-year wonders, the first impression is the best. That was certainly the case with the 6'5", 220-pound Dropo, who had one of the best rookie seasons in major-league history. In 1950, Dropo hit .322, pounded out 34 home runs, and tied for the league lead with 144 RBI while playing first base for the Boston Red Sox. Dropo's performance earned him American League Rookie of the Year honors, a nice topping to a season in which he also won a spot as the starting first baseman in the All-Star Game.

But Dropo's sophomore effort was a letdown for Red Sox fans who thought they had found the perfect right-handed complement to Ted Williams: Dropo batted a disappointing .239 as opposing pitchers found some holes in his swing. One year later, the Red Sox sent him packing as part of a nine-player trade with the Detroit Tigers. Dropo hit well for the Tigers over the balance of the 1952 season, but he would never come close to his first-year numbers. Over the last nine seasons of his career, Dropo hit no more than 19 home runs in a single season and posted batting averages that never topped .281. All in all, he had a decent career, but it wasn't the stuff of legends, which many had expected after his incredible rookie season.

Jim Hickman

A right-handed hitter with power and patience, Hickman experienced some moments of brilliance at the start of his major-league career. He became the first player in Mets history to hit three home runs in a single game. He also became the first Met to hit for the cycle. Yet the Mets felt that Hickman could do more. They fretted over his lack of aggressiveness at the plate and grew frustrated with his batting choices. All in all, Hickman provided the Mets with some power but didn't become the star they had hoped he would be. After the 1966 season, the Mets traded Hickman to the Los Angeles Dodgers, who passed him on to the Chicago Cubs.

Things finally clicked in 1970. Hickman hit 32 home runs for the Cubs, eclipsing his previous high of 21. He also reached career highs in doubles (33) and RBI (115). Hickman's breakthrough season earned him a trip to the All-Star Game, where he drove in the game-winning run for the National League.

So what happened to make Hickman a star in 1970? Well, there may have been something going around the National League that summer. Hickman, like a number of other NL players—including Bob Bailey, Donn Clendenon, Dick Dietz, Clarence Gaston, Billy Grabarkewitz, and Wes Parker—all enjoyed breakout seasons. While it's impossible to prove, it's conceivable that something may have been done to juice up the baseball in the NL that season. If that's the case, no one benefited more than Hickman, who experienced the biggest breakthrough of any player—and who would never put up such impressive numbers again.

Brady Anderson

For much of his career, Anderson was a fine defensive center fielder who stole bases with regularity and hit 15 to 20 home runs a season. In 1992, his first-half performance with the Baltimore Orioles earned him a place on the American League All-Star team.

Yet it all paled in comparison to his accomplishments in 1996. That year, Anderson muscled up and by June had already exceeded his best single-season home run total, hitting 27 round-trippers in the first three months of the season. By season's end, he had hit a stunning 50 homers, more than doubling his career best. Anderson also set a record (since broken) by hitting 12 lead-off home runs. He was aided by a serious commitment to weight lifting and a batting approach that emphasized swinging harder. Not even an attack of appendicitis could prevent Anderson from putting up one of the best offensive seasons ever enjoyed by a major-league center fielder.

Unfortunately, Anderson was never able to duplicate those numbers—he never hit more than 24 dingers in a season again. In fact, many speculate that his 1996 accomplishments were fueled by the use of steroids. After the 2001 season, he was released by the Orioles and signed by the Cleveland Indians. He left baseball altogether in 2003.

Heard on the Mound

"You're only as smart as your ERA."

—Jim Bouton, *I'm Glad You Didn't Take It Personally*

"When Steve and I die, we're going to be buried 60 feet, six inches apart."

—Tim McCarver, Steve Carlton's "personal" catcher
for much of his career, *The Pitcher*

"Against that guy, we should all get four strikes."

—Anonymous batter on facing Sandy Koufax

"Maybe a pitcher's first strikeout is like your first kiss—they say you never forget it."

—Bob Feller, *Now Pitching, Bob Feller*

"You can learn little from victory. You can learn everything from defeat."

—Christy Mathewson

"Age is a question of mind over matter. If you don't mind, it doesn't matter."

—Satchel Paige

"The saddest words to a pitcher are three: Take him out."

—Christy Mathewson

"Throw strikes. The plate don't move."

—Satchel Paige

Merkle's Boner

In the last week of a red-hot pennant race in 1908,
this game between the top contenders had one
of the strangest endings ever.

The 1908 National League season was the culmination of a thrilling start to the 20th century. The Pirates (who had won the pennant in 1901, '02, and '03) were tangled in a bristling pennant race with the Giants (who had won in 1904 and '05) and the Cubs (winners in '06 and '07). The entire season turned on one bizarre play in one game—a play that unfortunately labeled a smart ballplayer, Fred Merkle, a "bonehead" for the rest of his life.

On September 22, the Cubs had tightened the race by beating the Giants in both games of a doubleheader. The next day, legendary pitcher Christy Mathewson started for New York; Jack "The Giant Killer" Pfiester was Chicago's starter. Mathewson allowed only five hits for the contest. The Giants scored their lone tally in the sixth on a single, an error, a sacrifice, and a single. The sky was darkening when the Giants came to bat in the last of the ninth. The score was 1–1.

With one out, Giants third sacker Art Devlin singled off Pfiester. Next up, Moose McCormick figured if he pulled the ball to the right side, Devlin could advance to second. He was able to hit it where he wanted, but second baseman Johnny Evers flagged down the hard grounder and forced Devlin.

Batting next was Fred Merkle, who was playing because regular first baseman Fred Tenney was out with a sore back. It was the only game that entire season in which Tenney failed to start at first for John McGraw's men. Nineteen-year-old Merkle rose to the occasion, rifling a single over first baseman Frank Chance's head down the right-field line. McCormick hustled into third. When Giants shortstop Al Bridwell followed with a liner into right-center, McCormick trotted across the plate, and the sellout mob at the Polo Grounds surged jubilantly onto the field. Some even carried Mathewson on their shoulders as they celebrated on the field.

The problem was, Merkle (apparently) never touched second. A couple weeks earlier, the Cubs had been involved in a similar situation in Pittsburgh. A Pirate single drove in the apparent winning run in the last of the tenth, and the Pirate runner on first failed to step on second. Keen-eyed Johnny Evers appeared with the ball, stepped on the base, and announced the third out, which meant the run couldn't count. Umpire Hank O'Day muttered something to the effect that no one ever bothered to enforce that rule, which was true, even though the books stated it clearly. The Cubs protested his decision, to no avail.

When the same thing happened in New York, O'Day was the umpire again. Even though the fans were pouring onto the field and the place was bedlam, O'Day headed toward second to see if Merkle touched the sack as he rounded the bases. After a scrap to get the ball away from at least one Giant and several fans (some maintain to this day that the real ball never reached second), Evers once again appeared on second with a ball and announced the runner was out.

This time O'Day was on the spot, and he ruled in favor of Evers, although not until after he left the field—wisely avoiding a riot. After meeting with National League president Harry Pulliam that night, he stated that the runner was out, and because of the thousands of fans on the field and impending darkness, the game was to be declared a 1–1 tie.

The papers of the day were full of charges and countercharges. Mathewson assured everyone that he had grabbed Merkle by the arm and made certain the youngster had touched second. But the league upheld O'Day's tardy decision, and the game entered the record books as a tie. And ever since then, the rule that you must touch the next base has been dutifully enforced.

Because of that tie, the Cubs and Giants finished the pennant race in a dead heat. The game was replayed after all the other games had been played, and the Giants and Mathewson lost to the Cubs and Pfiester 4–2, sending Chicago on to the postseason.

All-Time Great

Cy Young

No other pitcher was so consistently good for so long.

Born: March 29, 1867; Gilmore, OH
MLB Career: Cleveland Spiders, 1890–98; St. Louis Cardinals, 1899–1900; Boston Pilgrims, 1901–08, 1911; Cleveland Naps, 1909–11; Boston Braves, 1911
Hall of Fame Resume: Most wins by a pitcher (511) • Most complete games (749) • Five 30-win seasons • Ten other 20-win seasons • Led league in shutouts seven times • Started 40 games a season 11 times • Six seasons with an ERA below 2.00
Inside Pitch: The last seven batters Young faced in his career hit a triple, three doubles, and three singles.

At one point, Babe Ruth's mark of 714 homers was the career baseball record most people predicted would never be broken. Once Henry Aaron topped it, Lou Gehrig's streak of 2,130 consecutive games became the popular choice. Now that Cal Ripken, Jr., has put that thought to rest, the question arises anew: 511 wins? Twenty-five a year for more than 20 years? Don't worry, Mr. Young; your mark appears safe.

Walter Johnson, Lefty Grove, and others have each been lauded as the greatest pitcher of all time, but Denton True Young's record of 511 victories remains the benchmark for all hurlers—and far ahead of runner-up Johnson's 417. Pitching in an era when arms often burned out after a handful of 350-inning seasons, Young exceeded that total 11 times over a 14-year span and was a 20-game winner on a record 15 occasions. His 7,354 innings pitched are more than 1,300 ahead of runner-up Pud Galvin, and even his record 316 losses looks secure for the moment.

Growing up just after the Civil War in Gilmore, Ohio, Young picked up his nickname (shortened from "Cyclone") from a minor-league catcher who was impressed by his speed. The hardy 6'2" farm boy reached the majors with the National League's Cleveland Spiders in 1890, and after a 9–7 debut, won 20 or more games each of the next nine seasons. Those early years were spent hurling from a pitcher's "box" some 50 feet from home plate, and when the distance was increased to 60′6″ and a mound was added in 1893, the right-hander didn't seem to miss a beat.

The hard-throwing Young led the NL only twice in wins, and he routinely gave up more hits than innings pitched (although that was the norm in the 1890s). Far from dominant in many of his first 11 seasons, he improved his records instead through consistency and durability. His best NL years came in 1892 (36–12 with a league-leading nine shutouts and a 1.93 ERA) and 1895 (35–10), but it was after joining the Boston Pilgrims of the new American League in 1901 that Young had his most dominating campaigns. Leading the AL in victories his first three years with Boston (going 33–10, 32–11, and 28–9), he had a 1.95 ERA and walked just 127 in 1,098 innings over the span—topping it off in 1903 with two wins as Boston beat Pittsburgh in the first modern World Series.

Author of three no-hitters (including a 1904 perfect game), Young went 21–11 with a 1.26 ERA at age 41. After his career ended in 1911, he lived well over 40 more years, attending old-timer's functions and tossing out the first ball at the 1953 World Series. Others may have been flashier, but when the two major leagues honor their best pitchers each season, they do so with a plaque named for the game's winningest hurler—Cy Young.

◯ ◯ ◯

"I pitched 874 major-league games in 22 years, and I never had a sore arm until the day I quit. My arm went bad in 1912 when I was in spring training, and I guess it was about time."

—Cy Young, *Baseball Digest,* October 1943

◯ ◯ ◯

"Son, I won more games than you'll ever see."

—Cy Young, responding to a youthful reporter

Power Hitters

Baseball's strongest sluggers: They didn't just hit the ball, they hurt it.

Baseball is not a game of brute strength. But it doesn't hurt to have a bit of muscle, especially when combined with terrific eyes, sensational reflexes, and superior hand-eye coordination. Having the brains to adapt to different pitchers' styles is helpful, too.

Jimmie Foxx

Foxx's nickname was "The Beast" for good reason. His rippling muscles terrified American League pitchers for years. When he slugged 58 homers in 1932, he became only the third player to top 50. Foxx was second in lifetime homers until Willie Mays surpassed him in 1966. Jimmie's pokes were often the longest balls ever hit in (or out of) the park.

Josh Gibson

Called the "black Babe Ruth," power-hitting Gibson slammed a number of homers that exceeded 500 feet. The color line kept him from the majors, but stories of Gibson's slugging feats have become legendary. In his Negro League career (1930–46), he was the home run king nine times.

Ryan Howard

In his first five seasons, through 2008, Howard belted 177 home runs for the Philadelphia Phillies. At the age of 26, he won the Home Run Derby at the 2006 All-Star Game and finished the

season with 58 homers. It's said he once hit a 430-foot homer—when he was only 12 years old.

Harmon Killebrew
When Killebrew slugged long home runs, they didn't just go far—they sometimes caused damage. A long ball he hit in 1967 in Minneapolis's Metropolitan Stadium went more than 530 feet and shattered two seats in the process. He hit more than 40 home runs eight times on his way to a lifetime total of 573, ninth best all time.

Dave Kingman
"King Kong" was not a good hitter, was a poor fielder, and wasn't even considered a nice person. But boy, could he slug the ball. At 6′6″, he wound up and sent balls high into the stratosphere. In 1976, while playing for the Mets, he hit one out of Wrigley Field, over Waveland Avenue, and off a house on Kenmore Avenue.

Mickey Mantle
No one ever walloped home runs from both sides of the plate like Mantle. He often played in pain, with injuries ranging from childhood osteomyelitis to a knee torn apart in the 1951 World Series. Mantle is given credit for the longest ball ever hit in Yankee Stadium, and a famous photo shows him smiling at the tattered ball he belted out of Washington's Griffith Stadium on April 17, 1953.

Willie McCovey
McCovey didn't have rippling muscles like Jimmie Foxx or Harmon Killebrew, but when he connected, the ball could almost be heard to whimper in pain. Only five men have ever hit more homers in the National League than his 521. Though not a home run hitter when his career began, he hit full stride from 1963 through 1970, when he hit (in order) 44, 18, 39, 36, 31, 36, 45, and 39.

Mark McGwire
He was called one of the "Bash Brothers" when he played with Jose Canseco for the Oakland A's, but McGwire didn't rewrite the record books until he was traded to St. Louis, where he broke

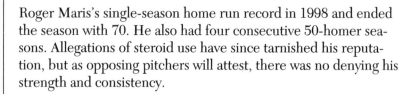

Roger Maris's single-season home run record in 1998 and ended the season with 70. He also had four consecutive 50-homer seasons. Allegations of steroid use have since tarnished his reputation, but as opposing pitchers will attest, there was no denying his strength and consistency.

Babe Ruth

Ruth's prowess as a hitter for distance so far surpassed anyone ever before seen that they had to invent a new word for it: "Ruthian." In his first spring training game in the minor leagues in 1914, Babe cracked the longest ball fans in Fayetteville, North Carolina, had ever seen. His last homer in the majors was the longest ball ever hit out of Forbes Field; it cleared the double-deck right-field grandstands. In between, he hit hundreds more.

Willie Stargell

It was a frightening image for the opposition: Willie Stargell, poised at the plate, absolutely motionless except for his bat as he wristed it in fat circles. The way he flipped it around, it seemed to weigh less than an ounce. That strength and that bat came together to hit homers completely out of Dodger Stadium; he's the only person to do it twice, in 1969 and '73. Stargell also smashed more balls out of Pittsburgh's Forbes Field and Three Rivers Stadium than anybody else.

"People ask me how I'd like to be remembered. I tell them I'd like to be remembered as the guy who hit the line drive over Bobby Richardson's head."

> —Willie McCovey, who ended the seventh game of the 1962 World Series with a vicious liner caught by Yankee second baseman Richardson with runners at second and third in a 1–0 New York win, *Baseball Anecdotes*

Magical Moment

Ripken achieves the "unachievable."

The Setting: Oriole Park at Camden Yards; September 6, 1995
The Magic: Cal Ripken, Jr., breaks Lou Gehrig's "unbreakable" consecutive-game streak.

We don't just want our baseball heroes to be good; we want them to be good for a long time. Lou Gehrig's incredible record of 2,130 consecutive games played had been a testament to his greatness. It seemed to be a feat that no one else could achieve . . . until Cal Ripken came along, playing inning after inning, game after game, year after year. Ripken's appearance in every game for more than 13 seasons is especially monumental when you realize that during his streak more than 3,700 players spent time on the disabled list.

That September night in Baltimore, as Ripken prepared to beat Gehrig's streak, President Bill Clinton and Vice President Al Gore were in the stands, as were Joe DiMaggio and Frank Robinson. The crowd of more than 46,000 cheered for Cal when he took the field, when he batted in the second, and when he homered in the fourth. But when the last out was made in the top of the fifth with the Orioles leading (thus making it an official game), the ovation was deafening. Ripken left the dugout three times to acknowledge the cheers. Finally his teammates Bobby Bonilla and Rafael Palmeiro convinced Cal to take a lap around the field. "If you don't, we'll never get this game going again," they said. Cal obligingly circled the field, waving to fans, shaking hands and slapping palms. The outpouring of affection lasted 22 minutes. But then it was time to get back to work, and the Orioles went on to beat the Angels 4–2. And Ripken just kept going, playing another 501 games before ending his streak at 2,632 in 1998. In a game sometimes known for its overblown paychecks and egos, Ripken proved to be a class act year after year after year.

Baseball's Best Ballparks

Great ballyards have as much appeal and personality as the athletes who play in them. Here are some all-time top venues.

Fenway Park, Boston
Year Built: 1912
Who Plays There: Boston Red Sox
Cost to Build: $650,000 ($12.8 million today)
Capacity: 36,108
Outfield Dimensions: L 310, C 389, R 302
Notable Fact: The runs and hits numbers for the scoreboard are 16 inches by 16 inches large and weigh three pounds each.

There's no other place on Earth where the purity of the game and the fan's experience of it is as powerful as in Boston's Fenway Park. It's not just a place where people go to watch baseball; it *is* baseball. It's the oldest ballpark in the bigs, dating back more than 95 years. Maybe it doesn't smell like a new rose, and maybe it isn't sparkly clean, but here you can feel the history of the game emanating from every square inch. It hosted the utterly bizarre and wonderful 1912 World Series, it's where Babe Ruth played his first big-league game, and it stood witness to the immortal feats of Ted Williams. Boston's deeply knowledgeable fans will tell you all about it between bites of a Fenway Frank, but only *between* pitches; if you're a Red Sox fan, you stay focused on the game. Fenway's famed "Green Monster," a 37-foot-high wall, stands like a national monument in left field. And now there are seats on top of it.

PETCO Park, San Diego
Year Built: 2004
Who Plays There: San Diego Padres
Cost to Build: $450 million
Capacity: 42,445
Outfield Dimensions: L 334, C 396, R 322
Notable Fact: The left-field foul pole is attached to the southeast corner of a former iron and steel foundry that was built in 1909.

Stucco-walled PETCO Park opened to glowing reviews in 2004. Upon entering the ballpark, Padres fans pass a palm court, jacaranda trees, and waterfalls. Once inside, they're treated to views of the city skyline, as well as other attractions beyond the outfield fence, including a beach and a park for fans to enjoy. The four-story Western Metal Supply building in the left-field corner now includes the Padres Team Store, a standing-room area, luxury suites, a restaurant, and rooftop seating for 800 fans. Need to check some stats from your laptop during the game? No problem: PETCO is wired.

AT&T Park, San Francisco

Year Built: 2000
Who Plays There: San Francisco Giants
Cost to Build: $357 million
Capacity: 41,503
Outfield Dimensions: L 339, C 399, R 309
Notable Fact: A giant baseball glove decorates the left-center seats, 501 feet from home plate.

The first privately financed major-league ballpark since Dodger Stadium (built in 1962), AT&T Park has an authentic San Francisco feel: charming and intriguing, yet not too brash or boisterous. Just beyond the right-field fence (once a Barry Bonds home run away) is San Francisco Bay—or McCovey's Cove, as it has come to be called in honor of Hall of Famer Willie McCovey. You can watch the sailboats pass by between innings, or you can marvel at the nine-foot statue of Giants superstar Willie Mays. An architectural marvel, AT&T Park features a terrific play area with a gigantic Coke bottle that kids can slide down, and the scoreboard has a dozen categories of stats for every hitter and pitcher. The park is always immaculate, and there's a greater variety of first-class food (don't miss the garlic fries!) than you'll find in most other parks.

Ebbets Field, Brooklyn

Year Built: 1913
Who Played There: Brooklyn Dodgers and Brooklyn Eagles (Negro National League)
Cost to Build: $750,000 ($14.3 million today)

Capacity: 31,903
Outfield Dimensions: L 348, C 393, R 297
Notable Fact: Braves batter Bama Rowell rapped a ball off the Bulova clock in the right-field scoreboard in 1946, shattering the glass and providing inspiration for a scene in the 1984 movie *The Natural.*

Built on the site of a former garbage dump, the intimate, unusual, and altogether enjoyable Ebbets Field is what today's retro ballparks are paying homage to. Ebbets hosted the often zany, often brilliant Brooklyn Dodgers and their outrageous fans, including the "Dodger Sym-Phony" and Hilda Chester, who always brought along a pair of cowbells that she used to clank out noisy encouragement to her team. The outfield fences jutted every which way, providing enough angles to tax the talents of any geometrician (or outfielder), while the upper deck hung out over the field. Batters hoped to hit clothier Abe Stark's ad in right field, with its elegantly simple offer: "Hit Sign, Win Suit." The last game played at Ebbets was on September 24, 1957, and the park was demolished in 1960.

Oriole Park at Camden Yards, Baltimore
Year Built: 1992
Who Plays There: Baltimore Orioles
Cost to Build: $110 million
Capacity: 48,876
Outfield Dimensions: L 333, C 400, R 318
Notable Fact: A red seat in left field (Section 86, Row FF, Seat 10) marks the spot where Cal Ripken hit his 278th home run in 1993, breaking Ernie Banks's record for the most home runs hit by a shortstop. Ripken hit the same seat in 1995 during consecutive game number 2,130—the game that tied Lou Gehrig's record.

This is the park that changed everything. It tolled the death knell for the cookie-cutter oval stadiums that had dominated the sports scene for decades. Camden Yards was the first of the magnificent retro ballparks that have now become the standard. Bleacher seats, a picnic area behind part of the center-field fence, and ivy growing on the hitters' backdrop contribute to the park's nostalgic feel. Perhaps most important, Camden Yards is integrated into the urban landscape, not slapped down into the middle of an ocean of parking lots. The park is buffered by the 100-year-old eight-story B&O Warehouse beyond the right-field fence. Inside, Camden Yards boasts comfortable seats, a dual-level bullpen, and fresh flowers along the walkways. The outstanding concessions include freshly squeezed lemonade and ex-Oriole Boog Powell's succulent barbeque.

Wrigley Field, Chicago
Year Built: 1914
Who Plays (Played) There: Federal League Chicago Whales, 1914–1915; Chicago Cubs, 1916–present
Cost to Build: $250,000 ($4.7 million today)
Capacity: 41,160
Outfield Dimensions: L 355, C 400, R 353
Notable Fact: The scoreboard, erected in 1937, is still manually operated and has never been hit by a batted ball.

Nestled into a charming North Side neighborhood, Wrigley Field lives up to its nickname, "The Friendly Confines." Fans—including the infamous Bleacher Bums—are treated to magnificent views of Chicago, ivy-covered walls, and home runs galore, especially when the Windy City gales are blowing out. Best of all, the Wrigley experience connects everyone to what is wonderfully timeless about this sport. Since most of Wrigley's games are played during the day (Wrigley was the last park to add lights, in 1988—40 years after the next-to-last), the idea of ducking out of work early to catch a game is still sinfully, deliciously alive in Chicago. The ballpark seats just 41,160, so some fans watch the action live from the rooftops of buildings behind the outfield fences.

Yankee Stadium, New York
Year Built: 1923 (renovated 1974–75; reopened 1976)
Who Played There: New York Yankees
Cost to Build: $2.5 million ($27.6 million today); $48 million for 1974–75 renovation
Capacity: 57,478
Outfield Dimensions: L 318, C 408, R 314

Notable Fact: The outfield fences were moved in five times to up home run totals.

Until the Babe showed up, the Yanks comfortably shared the Polo Grounds with the Giants. When the Yanks moved into their new stadium in 1920, Ruth christened the place with a home run on Opening Day. "The House That Ruth Built" was the first ballpark to be classified a "stadium" because of its size. The park hosted 37 World Series, with the Bronx Bombers prevailing in 26 of them. The stadium's signature features included a short porch in right, "Death Valley" in left center, and monuments to pinstriped legends—including Ruth, Lou Gehrig, Joe DiMaggio, Mickey Mantle, and manager Miller Huggins—beyond the outfield fence. On September 21, 2008, the Yankees played their last game there before moving across the street to their new $1.3 billion, 51,000-seat stadium.

PNC Park, Pittsburgh
Year Built: 2001
Who Plays There: Pittsburgh Pirates
Cost to Build: $237 million
Capacity: 38,496
Outfield Dimensions: L 325, C 399, R 320
Notable Fact: The Outback in the Outfield restaurant, overlooking left field, allows fans to watch the game while they dine.

With the emergence of many great new ballparks, discussion rages as to which is the best. Both ESPN and the Web site Ballparks of Baseball named Pittsburgh's PNC Park tops. With only two decks of seats, PNC Park is baseball's second-smallest venue (after Fenway Park). The Roberto Clemente Bridge, which is closed to vehicles on game days, leads pedestrian fans from downtown Pittsburgh to an intimate setting with a panoramic view of the city's skyline. Paying homage to the team's past greats are gigantic statues of Clemente, Willie Stargell, and the team's first superstar, Honus Wagner. The out-of-town scoreboard shows not just the score, but the inning, outs, and men on base for every game being played. PNC's food includes the legendary Primanti's all-on-one sandwich and ex-Pirate Manny Sanguillen's barbeque.

The Roy Chapman Tragedy

*The pitch that cut Ray Chapman's life short
haunted Carl Mays all his life.*

"Nobody remembers anything about me except one thing—that I threw a pitch that caused a man to die," wrote Carl Mays in an article in *The Sporting News* in 1963.

Forty-three years after the Yankees sidearmer let loose a fastball that fatally struck the Indians' Ray Chapman, the incident still haunted Mays. He went to his grave in 1971 at the age of 79, professing that the beaning was an accident and that the memory of it denied him enshrinement in the Hall of Fame.

On August 16, 1920, in a showdown between pennant contenders at the Polo Grounds in New York, Mays's first pitch of the fifth inning struck Chapman squarely in the side of the head. Chapman attempted to walk to the clubhouse, but he collapsed and was rushed to a nearby hospital, where he was diagnosed with a massive skull fracture. Doctors performed emergency surgery, but the Cleveland shortstop wouldn't live through the night. It was the first and, thus far, only fatal accident involving a play on a major-league diamond.

Although Mays had a magnificent record, he had a reputation as an ornery loner. He defended his right to pitch inside, suggesting that a worn-out ball was to blame for the accident. Others pointed to Mays's otherwise extraordinary control and his long history of hit batsmen and doctored pitches, casting him as a villain.

The tragedy prompted officials to rigorously discard used or scuffed balls and added urgency to a recent ban on spitballs, shine balls, and other doctored pitches. These changes hastened an end to the "dead-ball era" and ushered in a new age of offense. One innovation that might have saved Chapman's life, the batting helmet, wouldn't come into popular use until the 1950s.

Heartbroken, but inspired by the memory of their popular teammate, the Indians would hold off the Yankees and the White Sox to win the 1920 American League pennant and defeat the Brooklyn Dodgers in the World Series.

Ty's Temper

Ty Cobb had to be the best at whatever he did, whether it was hitting a baseball or hitting someone who got in his way. The Georgia Peach did plenty of both.

Legend has it that at a function in the late 1950s, a catcher confessed to Ty Cobb that some 40 years earlier he had used a trick (tagging a runner at home with two outs and then tossing off his mitt to indicate the third out, even when the runner was safe) that led to Cobb being called out at home when he had really been safe. It probably happened seven or eight times, the old catcher chuckled. Cobb reached out and started strangling the old-timer. "You cost me eight runs!" Cobb seethed as his hands grew tighter on the man's neck. The game was never over for Ty Cobb.

He had a burning desire to win, no matter who got hurt or what the personal cost. Cobb was like this at age 18, and he was this way until a combination of alcoholism, diabetes, and cancer ended his life in 1961 at age 74. He made millions through shrewd investments and endowed a hospital and an educational fund in his hometown in Georgia, yet he lived a miser's life. Cobb never mellowed, never relented.

Tyrus Raymond Cobb was raised by a disciplinarian father in Royston, Georgia, among relatives who had served as Confederate officers in the Civil War. His mother shot and killed his father accidentally, mistaking him for a prowler. Cobb, then 18, was playing minor-league ball at the time, and the tragedy made the focused young ballplayer bitter and angry at the world. He debuted with the Tigers just three weeks after his father was killed. Sam Crawford was there when Cobb arrived in Detroit in 1905.

"Every rookie gets a little hazing," Crawford recalled, "but most of them just take it and laugh. Cobb took it the wrong way. He came up with an antagonistic attitude, which in his mind turned anything into a life-or-death struggle. He always figured everyone was ganging up against him."

God help anyone who was. In 1912, a heckler in New York loudly questioned the bigoted Cobb's racial ancestry, and the Tiger tore into the man, punching him mercilessly. Cobb was suspended from the team indefinitely. His teammates stood up for their meal ticket by refusing to play the next game. In 1921, Cobb pulverized Hall of Fame umpire Billy Evans under the stands following a game in which two calls went against him.

Off the field, accolades were hard to come by. Cobb carried a revolver and was as mean to people on the street as he was to the players in the other dugout. He attacked elevator operators, butchers, and groundskeepers over perceived slights. Three men who tried to steal his Chalmers automobile—the one he'd won in an epic batting race with Cleveland's Nap Lajoie in 1910—were beaten senseless by their would-be victim.

Davy Jones, who played alongside Cobb and Crawford in Detroit's outfield, admitted that he was Cobb's only friend on the team. "He was one of the greatest players who ever lived, but he had very few friends. I always felt sorry for him."

Jones, like Crawford, disclosed his teammate's shortcomings to Lawrence S. Ritter in *The Glory of Their Times,* which was published a few years after Cobb's death. Few dared go on the record maligning or pitying Cobb while he was still alive and kicking.

⚾ ⚾ ⚾

"I recall when [Ty] Cobb played a series with each leg a mass of raw flesh. He had a temperature of 103 and the doctors ordered him to bed for several days, but he got three hits, stole three bases, and won the game. Afterward he collapsed on the bench."

—Grantland Rice, *Cooperstown: Where the Legends Live Forever*

⚾ ⚾ ⚾

"Every great batter works on the theory that the pitcher is more afraid of him than he is of the pitcher."

—Ty Cobb, *The Tiger Wore Spikes*

Baseball's Origins

*One thing's for sure: The Abner Doubleday Fan Club
isn't going to like this.*

It was long believed that Abner Doubleday invented baseball in
1839. While we now know this is not true, we still don't know
exactly how baseball came to be. Games involving sticks and balls
go back thousands of years. They've been traced to the Maya in
the Western Hemisphere and to Egypt at the time of the Pha-
raohs. There are historical references to Greeks, Chinese, and
Vikings "playing ball." And a woodcut from 14th-century France
shows what seem to be a batter, pitcher, and fielders.

Starting with Stoolball

By the 18th century, references to "baseball" were appearing in
British publications. A book printed in France in 1810 laid out the
rules for a bat/base/running game called "poison ball," in which
there were two teams of eight to ten players, four bases (one called
"home"), a pitcher, a batter, and flyball outs. Different variations
of the game went by different names: "Tip-cat" and "trap ball"
were notable for how important the bat had become. It was no
longer used merely to avoid hurting one's hand; it had become a
real cudgel, to swat the ball a long way.

In an 1801 book entitled *The Sports and Pastimes of the
People of England,* Joseph Strutt claimed that baseball-like games
could be traced back to the 14th century and that baseball was
a descendant of a British game called "stoolball." The earliest
known reference to stoolball is in a 1330 poem by William Pagula,
who recommended to priests that the game be forbidden within
churchyards.

In stoolball (a game that is still played in England today,
mostly by women), a batter stands in front of a target, perhaps an
upturned stool, while another player pitches a ball to the batter.
If the batter hits the ball (with a bat or his/her hand) and it is
caught by a fielder, the batter is out. Ditto if the pitched ball hits
a stool leg.

The Game Evolves

It seems that stoolball eventually split into two different styles. One became English "base-ball," which turned into "rounders" in England but evolved into "town ball" when it reached the United States. The other side of stoolball turned into cricket. From town ball came the two styles that dominated baseball's development: the Massachusetts Game and the New York Game. The former had no foul or fair territory; runners were put out by being hit with a thrown ball when off the base ("soaking"), and as soon as one out was made, the offense and defense switched sides. The latter established the concept of foul lines, and each team was given three "outs" to an inning. Perhaps more significantly, soaking was eliminated in favor of the more gentlemanly tag. The two versions coexisted in the first three decades of the 19th century, but when the Manhattanites codified their rules in 1845, it became easier for more and more groups to play the New York style.

The Knickerbocker Club

In the early 1840s, Alexander Cartwright, a New York City engineer, was one of a group of men who met regularly to play baseball, and he may have been the mastermind behind organizing, formalizing, and writing down the rules of the game. The group called itself The Knickerbocker Club, and their constitution, which was enacted on September 23, 1845, paved the way for the game we know today.

The Myth Begins

Even though the origins of baseball are murky, there's one thing we know for sure: Abner Doubleday had nothing to do with it. Albert Spalding organized the Mills Commission in 1905 to search for a definitive American source for baseball. They "found" it in an ambiguous letter spun by a Cooperstown resident. But Doubleday wasn't even in Cooperstown when the author of the letter said he had invented the game. Also, *The Boy's Own Book* presented the rules for a baseball-like game ten years before Doubleday's alleged "invention." (See pages 220–21 for more information about the Doubleday myth.) Chances are, we'll never know for sure how baseball came to be the game it is today.

All-Time Great

Hank Aaron

Simply put, Hammerin' Hank was one of the greatest hitters ever to pick up a bat.

Born: February 5, 1934; Mobile, AL
MLB Career: Milwaukee/Atlanta Braves, 1954–74; Milwaukee Brewers, 1975–76
Hall of Fame Resume: 755 home runs (second) • 2,297 RBI (first) • 2,174 runs (tied for fourth) • 3,771 hits (third) • 21 All-Star selections
Inside Pitch: Unlike many superstars who shriveled and faltered in the postseason, Aaron batted .362 and slugged .710 in 17 postseason games.

He never hit 60 home runs in a season—or even 50. Henry Aaron held the career home run record for more than 30 years, accumulating his considerable cache of records not by pumping out statistics that jumped off the paper, but rather with a career of steady, consistent play. Each time a current player hits 30 homers a few years in a row, comparisons to great sluggers of lore are made, but consider this: For *20 seasons,* from 1955 through '74, Hank Aaron averaged 36 home runs a year.

How could production like this go unnoticed? The former Negro Leaguer had a fine rookie season with the Milwaukee Braves in 1954 (.280 with 13 homers), yet even as he blossomed into one of the National League's top hitters, the slim, shy man from Alabama with the quick and powerful wrists was overshadowed by sluggers such as Willie Mays, Mickey Mantle, and Duke Snider, all of whom played in New York.

A batting title in '56 (.328) and a World Series win and MVP Award the following year (.322–44–132) garnered Aaron some notoriety, but when talk turned to someone breaking Babe Ruth's season homer mark (60) or career home run record (714), Hank's name was rarely mentioned. The heir to Babe's throne would have to be a muscle-bound masher like Mays or Mantle, not a skinny line-drive hitter—even if those drives happened to find the outfield fence with regularity. Over the next several years, Aaron garnered a second batting title (.355 in 1959) and three Gold Gloves for his outfield play, but he remained in the shadows of teammates Warren Spahn and Eddie Mathews.

But in the mid-1960s, Willie and Mickey began slowing down, and after the Braves moved their franchise to the homer-friendly climate of Atlanta in 1966, Aaron began heating up. He led the National League with 44 and 39 home runs, respectively, in his first two Southern summers, and in 1968 he clubbed his 500th homer. He slugged 44 more in 1969, became the ninth major-leaguer to reach 3,000 hits (1970), and slammed home run No. 600 off Gaylord Perry of the Giants in '71 en route to a career-high 47 home runs at age 37.

When "Hammerin' Hank" passed Mays with his 649th dinger in June 1972, the race to catch Ruth began—a race against age, time, and bigotry. Aaron received 930,000 pieces of mail in 1973, containing racial slurs, death threats, and plots to kidnap his children. He survived that pressure and rallied to hit 40 homers in just 392 at-bats, finishing the '73 season just one home run short of Ruth.

On the first day of the 1974 season (April 4), Aaron tied it up when he popped his 714th homer. He entered the game on April 8 needing just one more to pass the Babe's hallowed career record. At 9:07 P.M. in Atlanta, Aaron lined a 1–0 slider from L.A.'s Al Downing over the left-center-field fence. The scoreboard blazed: "Move over, Babe, here comes Henry!" The new home run king was mobbed by teammates when he reached home plate, where his mother gave him the biggest hug of all.

Hank finished up two years later with 755 homers, 2,297 RBI, 3,771 hits, and 2,174 runs (the same number of runs accumulated by Babe Ruth). Although Barry Bonds has since surpassed Aaron's home run record, that doesn't diminish the legacy of a man whose years of consistency made him one of the greatest hitters of all time.

World Series Perfection

Don Larsen summoned greatness once,
when it mattered the most.

The Setting: Yankee Stadium; October 8, 1956
The Magic: Don Larsen's perfect World Series game is one for the ages.

In 1954, Don Larsen, then a member of the Baltimore Orioles, had a record of three wins and 21 defeats. He was one of seven Orioles swapped for ten Yankees that off-season, and he obviously took to his new surroundings, posting a 9–2 record in a partial '55 season and an 11–5 record as a swingman in '56. That year he started 20 games and relieved in 18 others.

But on one October afternoon, the solid but, until then, unremarkable Larsen gave one of the greatest pitching performances of all time, retiring all 27 Brooklyn Dodgers he faced. There were three turning points in his perfecto (the first perfect game in the majors in 34 years). One was a heads-up piece of defensive work on a second-inning Jackie Robinson grounder, which third baseman Andy Carey deflected to shortstop Gil McDougald, who threw to first in time to nail Robinson by an eyelash. Second was Mickey Mantle's fourth-inning home run (the first hit allowed by Sal Maglie that day). And third was Mantle's nifty running grab of a Gil Hodges line drive the next inning. Beyond that, Larsen was utterly dominant: He threw only 97 pitches, and only one batter ever saw a three-ball count. Larsen lasted ten more years in the bigs, mostly as a reliever and without much success, but his one perfect day of World Series glory is an achievement that remains unmatched.

◖◖ ◖◖ ◖◖

Two of the worst records posted by pitchers in the 20th century were Baltimore Oriole Don Larsen's 1954 campaign, in which he went 3–21 for a .125 winning percentage, and New York Met Roger Craig's 1962 slog, during which he went 10–24 (.294).

World War II

Shortages, from food to baseballs, didn't deter Americans from playing their favorite game at home or abroad.

Americans learned to do without many things during the Second World War—meat, coffee, gasoline, and loved ones who were thousands of miles away—but one thing they did not forgo was baseball.

"I honestly feel it would be best for the country to keep baseball going," President Franklin D. Roosevelt wrote in his famous "green light letter" to Commissioner Kenesaw Mountain Landis on January 15, 1942.

The Changing Face of Baseball

Cleveland Indians owner Alva Bradley, perhaps following the lead of the NFL's Cleveland Rams, who sat out the 1943 season, advocated shuttering baseball near the war's end. But the War Department identified baseball as the favorite sport of 75 percent of American servicemen; football placed a distant second. So there would be baseball, but it would be different.

More games were played at night to accommodate factory workers, travel and supplies were restricted, and fans were as likely to buy a war bond as a hot dog. Because many of the game's

biggest stars eventually served in the armed forces, teams had to get creative with their lineup cards. Rosters were filled with players deemed unfit for military service, teenagers too young for the draft, or players too old to serve. Scouts began recruiting Latin American players, and fans took great interest in new professional women's teams, which started up in 1943.

Pitcher Joe Nuxhall remains the youngest player in major-league history, appearing at age 15 for the

Reds in 1944. Hal Newhouser, who was rejected four times from the Army Air Corps because of a heart problem, won the American League MVP Award two years in a row for the Tigers.

Have Ball, Won't Travel

The Yankees lost all their starters to the service over a two-year period. With so many strong ballplayers from other teams serving in the war, in 1944 the St. Louis Browns won their only pennant. They played—and lost to—the St. Louis Cardinals in the World Series (no travel required). In '45 the Browns defended their pennant with the one-armed Pete Gray in the outfield. His 51 hits and 11 strikeouts in 234 at-bats were commendable, but the time it took him to transfer the ball from his glove to his hand allowed opponents to run wild.

The 1945 All-Star Game was canceled due to travel restrictions, and the standard home/away/home setup was changed for that year's World Series between the Tigers and Cubs. The first three games were played at Detroit's Briggs Stadium, and the last four were played at Chicago's Wrigley Field. (Detroit won the Series, 4–3.)

Soldiers Stay in the Game

Soldiers serving overseas didn't want to give up their favorite sport. Baseball equipment was supplied to servicemen through the Bat and Ball Fund, which was established by Washington Senators owner Clark Griffith and National League president Ford Frick. Major-league clubs also passed along used equipment, including foul balls returned by fans. During America's first year in the war, the fund provided close to 100,000 baseballs to the Mediterranean theater alone.

Friend and foe alike took notice. The Japanese, who had their own infatuation with baseball, shouted at American soldiers: "To hell with Babe Ruth." (He, apparently, returned the sentiment.) The Germans often targeted baseball diamonds when they bombed the American military in Europe, in order to undermine the morale of servicemen who used the fields as a major source of recreation. Yet the 1945 finals of the Eastern Theater of Opera-

tions baseball championship took place at the same Nuremberg stadium where numerous Adolph Hitler rallies had been held.

Baseball also made a big impression in Italy. American servicemen stationed in the town of Nettuno, for example, stirred up interest in baseball among the locals; to this day, many young boys there still receive bats and gloves as gifts for their First Communion.

The Pastime Post-War

By the end of 1945 the war was over, and fans were flocking to ballparks in record numbers. The world had changed greatly over the past four years, and baseball had changed, too. Some ballplayers came back as war heroes, while others were forever lost. Women gradually receded from playing pro ball, but their involvement in the workforce at large continued to grow. And through all the changes, during the war and since, Americans have clung to their love for a pastime that still connects us all.

⚾ ⚾ ⚾

"[Ted Williams] was great enough to become a Hall of Fame player. He was caring enough to be the first Hall of Famer to call for the inclusion of Negro Leagues stars in Cooperstown. He was brave enough to serve our country as a Marine in not one but two global conflicts. Ted Williams is a hero for all generations."

—Dale Petroskey, President of the Baseball Hall of Fame

⚾ ⚾ ⚾

"Baseball in the Navy was always much more fun than it had been in the major leagues."

—Bob Feller

Counting Cards

*After more than a century, card collecting remains
a simple pleasure.*

Long before ESPN and MLB.com provided the opportunity to
keep up-to-the-inning tabs on ballplayers, baseball cards allowed
generations of fans to feel connected with their heroes. And while
big-league salaries may have reached outrageous levels, for many
devotees of the game, cardboard is still as good as gold.

Trade Cards, Tobacco, and the T-206

Today's cards are aimed primarily at the Little League crowd,
but the first commercial cards in the 1870s (then called "trade
cards")—which featured pictures of top teams on one side and
advertisements on the other—were marketed to adults. By the
1880s, the game's rising popularity prompted several tobacco companies to insert cards into packs of their products, and stars such as
King Kelly and Cap Anson began appearing on their own cards.

The cards considered by many collectors to be the most beauti-
ful ever produced appeared during the 1900–1915 era and featured
color drawings of players who were posed or in action. Usually
smaller than today's standard 2½″×3½″ cards, they picked up a
younger audience when candy companies also began producing
them. The "Mona Lisa of baseball cards"—the T-206 White Borders Honus Wagner—was introduced during this time. Only about
50 of these cards were made before a dispute between the tobacco
firm and the Pirates shortstop halted their production. In 2007, one
of the cards reportedly sold to a private collector for $2.35 million.

Kids Get On Board

Back then, of course, nobody was worried about a card's monetary
value. By the 1930s, when Goudey and other gum companies
began producing hundreds of individual player cards each year,
kids began trading the cards—either to complete numbered sets
or to pick up a favorite player. Many kids stuck cards into the
spokes of their bikes to get just the right machine-gun sound.

Baseball's post–World War II boom extended to baseball cards, which reached new heights in popularity during the 1950s. The king then was the Topps Company, which had a virtual monopoly on card production from 1952 through 1980 and offered as many as 800 new cards each year. Almost every major-leaguer signed an annual deal with Topps; each plastic-wrapped pack that was available at the corner drugstore contained several cards with players' vital statistics and complete playing records on the back, along with a rectangle of rock-hard pink bubblegum. Cards featured everything from league leaders and All-Stars to fathers and sons, boyhood photos, and even (briefly) umpires.

The Card Collecting Explosion

The Topps monopoly ended in 1981, when two other companies—Fleer and Donruss—won the legal right to produce their own sets. Card collecting as a hobby exploded. Kids, faced with numerous choices, bought more cards than ever, and adults who had grown up with Topps paid $10, $20, even $100 to replace the ones they had purchased for nickels as youngsters—and that their parents had long since thrown out. In addition to baseball card conventions, fans at one point had some 10,000 card shops in which to seek out treasures. Young collectors now put their top cards in protective cases rather than in their bike spokes, and gum (which damaged cards, as well as teeth) faded from the scene.

The sheer glut of cards produced in the late 1980s and early '90s eventually led to a rapid decline in their monetary value, and this, plus fallout from the 1994 players' strike, forced many shops to close their doors. Recently, however, there has been another revival: Topps and numerous rivals now produce a seemingly endless array of specialty cards, including "relic" versions, with shavings from actual game-used bats attached, and "heritage" versions that are designed to look like cards from the 1950s. Gum has even made a comeback, and the Internet—and especially eBay—has made it easier than ever to find an elusive card. The cards of such Golden Age players as Willie Mays and Mickey Mantle—at least those that have survived in decent condition—are valued in the thousands of dollars. And don't forget that T-206 Wagner!

Greatest Games of All Time

1986 World Series, Game 6

Mets 6, Red Sox 5

The Setting: Shea Stadium, New York

The Drama: It looked like "The Curse of the Bambino" had finally been put to rest—but then the Mets kicked it up a notch and the Sox imploded.

For a game ending that moves past improbability into the realm of science fiction, Game 6 of the 1986 World Series is unsurpassed. Both the Mets and the Red Sox had been through debilitating League Championship Series. Both had fought back from near-certain defeat with near-miraculous effort. What nobody could have predicted was how much fight was still left in these two teams. The Sox won the first two games; the Mets the next two. The 4–0 lead the Red Sox held after five innings of Game 5 was whittled in half before the Mets came up short in the ninth inning.

Leading three games to two, the Red Sox had their chance to avenge both "The Curse of the Bambino" and ugly comments about their character and guts. They needed a good pitching performance, and they had their best hurler, Roger Clemens, starting. Clemens had a 24–4 record that season and the lowest ERA in the American League. The Mets countered with Bob Ojeda, who had pitched an effective seven innings in their Game 3 win.

The Sox scored in the first, on a single by batting champ Wade Boggs and a Dwight Evans double. They scored again in the second, on singles by Spike Owen, Boggs, and Marty Barrett. Clemens set down six of the first nine Mets he faced on strikes. Darryl Strawberry walked to open the fifth, however, and after a stolen base, a single, and an error, the Mets were able to plate the tying run when Danny Heep grounded into a double play.

Boston reclaimed the lead in the top of the seventh. Barrett walked to lead off and moved to second on Bill Buckner's ground-out. Ray Knight gloved a smash by Jim Rice but threw poorly to first. Rice was safe; Barrett went to third. Then the Mets botched an Evans double-play grounder, which allowed Barrett to score. Rich Gedman singled to left, but Mookie Wilson made a huge throw, nailing Rice as he tried to score. The Sox held on to a 3–2 lead.

The Mets tied things up in the eighth. Lee Mazzilli hit a pinch single, and Lenny Dykstra was safe when Sox hurler Calvin Schiraldi (who had replaced blister-fingered Clemens) tried to turn his bunt into a force at second but made a bad throw. Next hitter Wally Backman bunted, too, and this time Schiraldi made the wise play. Both runners advanced. After an intentional walk, Gary Carter's fly to left was deep enough for Mazzilli to tag and score.

The first two Mets reached in the last of the ninth, but Schiraldi hung tough, and the game headed into extra innings. The tenth inning was almost too much to believe. Dave Henderson yanked a Rick Aguilera pitch over the left-field wall. The Sox were in business. Two outs later, the Boggs/Barrett tandem struck again: Boggs hit a double and Barrett drove him in with a single, and Boston had a two-run lead heading into the bottom of the tenth.

Schiraldi got both Backman and Keith Hernandez to fly out, and some of the Mets faithful began to leave the ballpark. Red Sox fans prepared to celebrate after 68 years of waiting. But the game wasn't over yet. Carter lofted a soft single to left field. Kevin Mitchell rapped a pinch single up the middle. Knight's bloop to center barely fell in for a single, scoring Carter and moving Mitchell to third. It was now 5–4 Boston.

Schiraldi was replaced by Bob Stanley to pitch to Wilson. The result was one of the greatest at-bats in Series history. With the count 2–2, Mookie fouled off consecutive pitches. The next was wild inside; Wilson bent himself in half to avoid the pitch. Mitchell roared home and Knight headed to second. The game was tied.

After two more foul balls, Wilson tapped the tenth pitch down the first base line. There stood Bill Buckner, long a solid defensive first sacker. The ball rolled under his glove, between his legs, and into short right. The Mets had pushed home three runs to stave off World Series defeat in spectacular—and bizarre—fashion. The Mets took the title two days later, winning the final game 8–5.

Baseball's Great Ambassador

When we think of baseball legends, we usually place them into one category: player, manager, or pioneer. But there are some icons who defy typecasting, and Buck O'Neil—one of baseball's greatest ambassadors—was one of them.

Buck O'Neil was a solid player in the Negro Leagues, with a career batting average of .288. The first baseman was a strong clutch hitter and had a league-leading .353 average in 1946; the next year he hit .358. He went on barnstorming tours with teammate Satchel Paige, played in the 1942 Negro League World Series, and was named to the Negro Leagues' celebrated East-West All-Star Game in 1942, '43, and '49.

Yet there was so much more to Buck O'Neil than what he accomplished as a player. In 1948, he became manager of the Negro American League's Kansas City Monarchs, where he won four pennants, led his clubs to two Negro American League championships, and guided his teams to a perfect record of 4–0 in the East-West Game.

The Negro Leagues began to dissolve in the late 1940s, and O'Neil segued into a career with the major leagues. After joining the Chicago Cubs as a scout, O'Neil played crucial roles in signing Hall of Famers Lou Brock and Ernie Banks and quality major-leaguers such as Joe Carter and Oscar Gamble. O'Neil also became the first African American coach in major-league history, joining the Cubs' "College of Coaches" (which unsuccessfully employed a group of managers rather than just one) in the early 1960s, though he was never its head coach.

O'Neil's contributions to baseball reached far off the field. After leaving scouting and coaching, O'Neil probably did more than anyone else to promote the legacy of the Negro Leagues. Whether charming audiences on Ken Burns's *Baseball* documentary or appearing on David Letterman's talk show, or through his work as a voting member of the Hall of Fame's Veterans Committee, O'Neil always did his best to praise the abilities and personalities of other Negro League stars. While modest about himself, he said that

Oscar Charleston was the equal of Ty Cobb and praised Satchel Paige for bringing out the best in everyone—even the opposition.

O'Neil's storytelling greatly enhanced the public's knowledge of and familiarity with the Negro Leagues, which had been largely overlooked until the 1990s. In 2000, O'Neil visited the Hall of Fame and discussed the ability that black players showed when they barnstormed against white teams featuring major-leaguers. "They [the major-leaguers] were just out there for a payday, but we wanted to prove a point that they weren't superior," O'Neil told the Cooperstown audience. "So we would stretch that single into a double, that double into a triple, that triple into a home run. This was Negro Leagues baseball, this was the baseball Jackie Robinson brought to the major leagues." O'Neil emerged as an unofficial ambassador for the Negro Leagues, exposing younger generations to the rich culture of black baseball.

Even in Buck's final summer, he persisted in advancing the awareness of Negro League baseball. He continued his work as the chair of the Negro Leagues Museum in Kansas City, Missouri, which he had started through tireless promotional and fundraising efforts. At the 2006 Hall of Fame induction ceremony, O'Neil stole the show with a humorous, lively, and uplifting speech. Unfortunately, the one thing O'Neil was not able to accomplish during his life was his own election to Cooperstown. In 2006, he fell one vote short, which shocked his fans and supporters and certainly caused O'Neil a deeper disappointment than he ever admitted. He passed away on October 6, 2006, at the age of 94.

In considering someone's candidacy for the Hall, most people feel it is not enough merely to focus on what one did as a player. Rather, the accomplishments of an entire *career* must be taken into consideration. In the case of O'Neil, his efforts as a manager, scout, coach, and ambassador raise his status, making him one of the most diversely skilled and respected figures in baseball history. And it's the entirety of those accomplishments that posthumously earned Buck O'Neil what he so richly deserved, when in 2008 a statue was erected in his likeness just beyond the National Baseball Hall of Fame and Museum's entrance and he became the first recipient of the Hall's Buck O'Neil Lifetime Achievement Award.

Eccentric Owners

Some baseball owners make a lot of noise and stir up controversy.
Some are lovable, some despicable, and most a measure of both.

Chris Von der Ahe, the heavily accented and profit-driven German immigrant, took notice of the increase in sales at his St. Louis saloon on game days in the late 1870s. Before long, he owned the American Association's St. Louis Browns and became a sensational (and wealthy) promoter, à la Bill Veeck, and a noisy meddler, à la George Steinbrenner, even though he never really understood the game. In 1895, he modified Sportsman's Park to include nightly horse races and shoot-the-chute rides. Four years later, he had to double its seating capacity. After every game, Von der Ahe would roll a wheelbarrow full of that day's gate to the bank, sometimes stopping at the saloon to buy the fans a few rounds. But in 1898, part of the ballpark was destroyed in a fire, and Von der Ahe, whose fortunes had dwindled, lost his team.

Born into a prosperous banking family in 1890, **Larry MacPhail** became a lawyer and then used his legal wits to maneuver himself into baseball. He was an innovator for the Reds and then the Dodgers, and was responsible for the proliferation of night baseball, radio broadcasting of games, airplane travel for teams, and the use of batting helmets. MacPhail's hot-tempered battles with manager Leo Durocher were both legendary and frequent. He fired Leo dozens of times, only to hire him right back. MacPhail left the Reds after the 1937 season and went on to work for the Dodgers and Yankees before hanging up his cap for good in 1947.

Self-made millionaire **Charlie Finley** bought the Kansas City A's in 1960. His slew of wacky promotions—such as using orange baseballs or having a mechanical rabbit hand balls to the umpire behind home plate—didn't help attendance (the team still stunk). So he moved them to Oakland. He hired good scouts because they were cheaper than good players and built a strong team—perhaps made even stronger because of the players' total unity in their hatred for him. Finley was well known—and infamously disliked—

for micromanaging the team and the management. He often demanded that players change their playing style, and he fired any manager who publicly disagreed with him. He paid bonuses to players who would grow mustaches; pitcher Rollie Fingers' handlebar mustache was the most famous result of this. He tried to institute a "designated runner," and he dressed his players in garish green and gold uniforms. But it was his poor business decisions that ultimately did him in, and he stepped away from baseball in 1980.

Marge Schott inherited her husband's Cincinnati business empire when he died in 1968. Under her guidance, the businesses flourished, and she used a portion of her earnings to become partial owner of the Cincinnati Reds, eventually taking control in 1985. Not only was she a woman in a man's world; her abrasive personality and controversial statements made her even more of an outsider. Fined and suspended for her racial and ethnic slurs, Schott didn't seem upset at all. But she was essentially forced out of the game in 1999 and sold her controlling interest in the Reds that year. She died in 2004 at the age of 75.

George Steinbrenner is the only major-league owner to be a character on a hit TV comedy show (though he was portrayed by an actor on *Seinfeld*). His personality is almost a cliché—the boisterous, bullying, infuriating meddler, as capricious as he is strong. His most famous quote came the day he, as leader of a limited partnership that was buying the Yankees, said, "I won't be active in day-to-day club operations at all." In fact, he did little else—berating his players, firing his managers (including Billy Martin on five occasions), and "apologizing" to the fans when his team lost the 1981 World Series. After Steinbrenner paid a small-time gambler $40,000 for "dirt" on Yankees outfielder Dave Winfield in 1990, baseball commissioner Fay Vincent banned him from baseball for life. Word of his exile began to spread during a game that was being played at Yankee Stadium, and the crowd erupted into applause and a standing ovation. Steinbrenner was reinstated three years later and helped lead the Yankees to the American League East championship in 1994 and World Series wins in 1998, '99, and 2000.

Major League Mascots

Mascot alert! The unforgettable and the regrettable.

Baseball teams have employed mascots as good luck charms and used illustrated characters to promote themselves for as long as the game has been played. But the furry and feathery variety that can be found dancing atop dugout roofs today can trace its heritage to a San Diego radio station promotion in 1974. It was then that KGB radio convinced a college student, Ted Giannoulas, to dress up as a chicken and distribute eggs to children at the San Diego Zoo. Encouraged by the success of the stunt, Giannoulas began appearing in costume at Padres games that year and in short stead became the biggest baseball star hatched in San Diego since Ted Williams. By the end of the 1970s, the Chicken's success had prompted other teams—including the Pittsburgh Pirates (the Pirate Parrot), Philadelphia Phillies (the Phillie Phanatic), Montreal Expos (Youppi), and St. Louis Cardinals (Fredbird)—to introduce their own characters. In the 1990s, a second wave of mascots arrived as part of an effort to market the game to children. In 2008, every team except the Dodgers, Angels, Cubs, and Yankees employed at least one mascot. (Though the Angels have an unofficial mascot in their beloved Rally Monkey.)

The San Diego Chicken: Despite never having been an "official" Padres character—the Swinging Friar has filled that role since the team's founding in 1969—the Chicken has become a traveling attraction. It is famed for physical comedy routines that include presenting an eye chart to umpires in a mock challenge to calls that don't go in the Padres favor and, with the help of a participating catcher, re-creating the Pete Rose–Ray Fosse All-Star Game collision, complete with slow-motion replay.

The Phillie Phanatic: Against the better judgment of team owner Bill Giles, the Phillies introduced this wide-bodied, long-snouted creature in 1978. It won cheers in a city that is otherwise famous for its hair-trigger boo reflex. Originally portrayed by Phillies mail-

room clerk Dave Raymond, the Phanatic was at his best when making a straight man of whichever Phillie opponent *least* wanted to be part of the act. Dodgers manager Tommy Lasorda, with his low tolerance for on-field antics, was a favorite foil.

Mr. Met: The original live-action costumed mascot, the baseball-domed Mr. Met first appeared on the cover of a 1963 yearbook and debuted live at the opening of Shea Stadium in 1964. His cheery gait and smiling eyes delight children but hide a mischievous nature, perhaps suggesting that the disappearance of his one-time companion, Lady Met, is a mystery best left unsolved. Though entering his late 40s, Mr. Met is still one of the most visible and active Mets. His schedule of party and event appearances, merchandise tie-ins, and TV commercial spots rivals that of the team's most marketable stars.

Youppi: The fluffy orange giant, whose name means "Hooray" in French and whose uniform number was !, became the first two-sport anthropomorphized character. He served the Montreal Expos from 1979 until they carelessly left him behind when they moved to Washington, D.C., and became the Nationals in 2005. Their loss was the Montreal Canadiens' gain: Youppi bolted to the NHL, signing a reported six-figure deal with the Canadiens.

The Pirate Parrot: Kevin Koch, the actor behind the green mask of the Pittsburgh Pirates' mascot for its first six years, was undercover in more ways than one: He made a drug deal while wearing a hidden transmitter to help the FBI secure evidence in its investigation of drug use among ballplayers. The dealer, whom Koch

reportedly introduced to some Pirates players, later pleaded guilty to 20 counts of selling cocaine during the 1985 Pittsburgh drug trials.

Dandy: A pinstriped bird with a mustache resembling

that of relief pitcher Sparky Lyle, Dandy was the official mascot of the Yankees from 1982 to 1985—a fact the team's own stuffed shirts, including owner George Steinbrenner, profess not to recall. Ultimately, the cuddly mascot had difficulty finding a home within the Yankees' stodgy corporate image. Dandy rarely made an appearance beyond the upper reaches of Yankee Stadium.

Crazy Crab: Intentionally hideous, Crazy Crab was unveiled as a subversive "anti-mascot" in 1984 by the San Francisco Giants, who encouraged fans to boo the bug-eyed, belligerent crustacean and whose scoreboard admonitions—PLEASE DO NOT THROW THINGS AT THE CRAZY CRAB—practically begged fans to do just that. After a season of fan abuse, both physical (bottles and garbage hurled from the stands) and verbal (booing, hissing, and epithets), the Crazy Crab was retired. In 2006, sparked in part by a fan petition, Crazy Crab appeared during an '80s throwback promotion. The Crab, true to his sullen nature, attacked Stomper, the mascot of the visiting Oakland A's. It made a brief appearance again in July 2008, when 20,000 Crazy Crab bobbleheads were given away as a promotion.

Mettle: Ignoring the fact that they had a perfectly acceptable mascot in Mr. Met, in 1979 the New York Mets unveiled a live mule as their new mascot. Mettle, like the team that year, often left a mess on the field, and he was quietly sent out to pasture after a single season, the worst at the gate in Mets history.

Baseball team names often change, sometimes because the club moves to a new location, and sometimes just because. A few National League teams with creative names prior to 1900 were the Indianapolis Blues, the Buffalo Bisons, the Troy Trojans, the Worcester Ruby Legs, the Detroit Wolverines, the Kansas City Cowboys, and the Cleveland Spiders.

Hall of Fame Talk

"One of the secrets of the Babe's greatness was that he never lost any of his enthusiasm for playing ball, and especially for hitting home runs. To him a homer was a homer, whether he hit it in a regular game, a World Series game, or an exhibition game."

— Sportswriter Frank Graham on Babe Ruth, *The New York Yankees*

"Guessing what the pitcher is going to throw is 80 percent of being a successful hitter. The other 20 percent is just execution."

—Hank Aaron, *Hank Aaron...714 and Beyond*

"Nobody taught me about hitting. I learned."

—Ted Williams, *Voices from Cooperstown*

"After the game, it took me 20 minutes to walk to where he had hit the ball in a split second."

—Yankee ace Lefty Gomez on a homer he allowed to Jimmie Foxx

"Above anything else, I hate to lose."

—Jackie Robinson, *The Boys of Summer*

"We Who Are About to Cry Salute You."

— Sign hanging from the left-field stands at Shea Stadium the night Willie Mays said good-bye to baseball and his fans, September 1973

"I believe the joy of getting paid as a man to play a boy's game kept me going longer than many other players."

—Stan Musial

Playing the Field

Baseball is the national pastime, but it's not the only sport around.
Here are several athletes who did double duty.

Danny Ainge
Baseball:
2 HRs, 37 RBI, .220 BA in 3 seasons
Basketball:
11.5 points per game, 1,002 3-pointers, 2 NBA championships in 14 seasons
Verdict:
Swish.
Danny Ainge was an infielder by summer and a shooting guard by winter who ultimately was better served shooting the three than turning two. But it wasn't an easy transition. Ainge was drafted by the Blue Jays out of high school in 1977 and toiled for five years in baseball while attending Brigham Young University on a basketball scholarship. He was midway through a three-year baseball contract when the Celtics drafted him in 1981, sparking an intersport legal battle that was ultimately resolved when Toronto released Ainge from his contract in exchange for a reported half-million-dollar payment from Boston. It was money well spent: Ainge made his NBA debut in December 1981, 79 days after playing his last MLB game, and went on to a 14-year career and two NBA championships. He went on to serve as a Celtics executive, where he was instrumental in assembling Boston's 2007–2008 NBA championship team.

Chuck Connors
Baseball:
2 HRs, 18 RBI, .238 BA in 2 seasons
Basketball:
4.5 points per game in 2 seasons
Verdict:
Action!
Chuck Connors played pro basketball and pro baseball but didn't become a star until he played "The Rifleman" in the TV show of

the same name. Connors originally served as a reserve forward on the 1947 and '48 Celtics, but he gave that up to be a first baseman with the Dodgers (1949) and the Cubs (1951). Farmed out to the Cubs' minor-league team in Los Angeles in 1952, Connors caught the eye of a casting director and before long was a television star.

Dave DeBusschere
Baseball:
3–4, 2.90 ERA in 2 seasons
Basketball:
8 All-Star Games and 6 All-Defense mentions in 12 seasons, NBA Hall of Fame
Verdict:
Slam dunk.
A 6'6" right-hander with a lively fastball, Dave DeBusschere played four years of pro baseball, including parts of two seasons with the White Sox, compiling a big-league record of 3–4 with a respectable 2.90 ERA. But he did his best work preventing scoring on the basketball court as one of the NBA's best-ever defenders.

George Halas
Baseball:
.091 BA in 1 season
Football:
Rose Bowl MVP, six-time NFL coach of the year, NFL Hall of Fame
Verdict:
Gridiron.
The year before Babe Ruth joined the New York Yankees, George Halas was a young outfielder for the team. Halas eventually became a legend in his own right as a pioneering player, coach, and owner in the National Football League. For the man known as "Papa Bear," baseball was only a passing fancy. His 12-game stint with the Yankees was preceded by a stellar college football career at the

University of Illinois and followed by a founding ownership of an NFL franchise, the Decatur Staleys, in 1920. That team eventually relocated to Chicago, where Halas chose the nickname Bears as a tribute to the city's North Side baseball residents, the Cubs.

Cal Hubbard

Baseball:
16-year umpiring career, Hall of Fame
Football:
Star offensive lineman, 4 NFL championships in 9 seasons, Hall of Fame
Verdict:
Football—in a close call.
The only man enshrined in both the Pro Football Hall of Fame and the National Baseball Hall of Fame, Cal Hubbard was a legendary Packers offensive lineman of the 1920s and '30s who spent his off-seasons as a minor-league baseball umpire. He reached the majors as an American League umpire in 1936, his final year as a football player, and dispensed baseball justice for the next 15 years, working four World Series and three All-Star Games. His experience running football plays helped him design various patterns of positioning for umpires that are still used today.

Bo Jackson

Baseball:
141 HRs, 415 RBI, 1 All-Star Game in 8 seasons
Football:
Heisman Trophy winner, 1 Pro Bowl invitation, 2,782 yards rushing, 18 TDs (16 rushing, 2 receiving) in 4 seasons
Verdict:
Let's play two!
Simultaneous and frequently spectacular success on the diamond and gridiron made Bo Jackson a cultural phenomenon of the 1980s. A slugging outfielder for the Royals, White Sox, and Angels and a bruising running back with the Oakland Raiders, Jackson is the only man to be named a starting All-Star in both sports. He claimed football was his "hobby" and didn't return to that game

following a hip injury suffered in 1990. Aftereffects of the injury eventually ended his baseball career by age 31.

Brian Jordan

Baseball:
184 HRs, 821 RBI, .282 BA in 15 seasons
Football:
1 Pro Bowl in 3 seasons
Verdict:
Can o' corn.
Drafted as an outfielder by the Cardinals (1st round) and as a defensive back by the Buffalo Bills (7th round), Brian Jordan spent minor-league off-seasons playing safety for the Atlanta Falcons, where he was named a Pro Bowl alternate in 1992. Though Jordan would say football was his first love, he gave up the game to sign a baseball-only contract with the St. Louis Cardinals and began a 15-year major-league career that included an All-Star campaign in 1999 and five trips to the postseason.

Michael Jordan

Baseball:
.202 in 1 season in Class AA
Basketball:
14-time All-Star, all-time NBA career points-per-game leader
Verdict:
Are you kidding?
Michael Jordan was already considered among the greatest basketball players of all time when, on October 6, 1993, he shocked the world by announcing his intention to retire from basketball and give pro baseball a try. He signed a contract with the White Sox, where he managed to hit just .202 in one season

as a Class-AA outfielder. Humbled, Jordan was back in a Chicago Bulls uniform a year later.

Ron Reed
Baseball:
146–140, 3.46 ERA, 103 saves in 19 seasons
Basketball:
8 points per game in 2 seasons
Verdict:
Out of the park.
A star basketball player at Notre Dame, the 6′6″ Reed was drafted by the Detroit Pistons in the first round of the 1965 draft. He played two seasons as a reserve forward in the NBA while toiling in the minor leagues for the Milwaukee Braves' system. But Reed gave up hoops for good after emerging as an All-Star pitcher in his rookie baseball season of 1968. A control artist, Reed was an anchor of the 1969 Braves' rotation and later had a long run as a set-up man with the Phillies in the 1970s, pitching into his 40s.

Deion Sanders
Baseball:
.263 BA, 186 SBs in 9 seasons
Football:
8 Pro Bowls in 14 seasons; excelled as a defensive back, kick returner, and wide receiver
Verdict:
Touchdown!
On October 11, 1992, Deion Sanders played an afternoon football game for the Atlanta Falcons in Miami, then flew to Pittsburgh in time for the Atlanta Braves' NLCS game against the Pirates. Though Sanders didn't get into the latter game, he would end his dual-sport career as the only man to appear in both a Super Bowl and a World Series. Though far more accomplished as a rare two-way player in football, Sanders was a fine basestealer and outfielder in baseball, and, had he chosen neither sport, he might even have made it as a track star.

Jim Thorpe
Baseball:
7 HRs, 82 RBI, .252 BA in 6 seasons
Football:
52 pre-NFL games in 6 seasons, 6 TDs, Hall of Fame
Olympics:
Gold medals in the decathlon and pentathlon, 1912 Olympics
Verdict:
What season is it?

Considered among the greatest American athletes of all time, Jim Thorpe achieved worldwide prominence by blowing away the field in the pentathlon and decathlon events at the 1912 Games in Stockholm, Sweden. When it was revealed that Thorpe had played semipro baseball for pay prior to the Olympics, his medals were stripped. But the scandal called attention to Thorpe's baseball skills, and he was subsequently signed to a contract by the New York Giants. Thorpe played outfield for three teams over six seasons, ending in 1919. At the same time, Thorpe was a magnificent fullback for pre-NFL teams and the first president—and superstar—of what would become the NFL, playing for six different teams until 1928.

⚾ ⚾ ⚾

The ten states that produced the most major-leaguers in the 20th century were: California with 1,828 players; Pennsylvania with 1,324; New York with 1,107; Illinois with 985; Ohio with 956; Massachusetts with 635; Missouri with 552; Michigan with 405; New Jersey with 377; and North Carolina with 368.

⚾ ⚾ ⚾

"Baseball is pitching, fundamentals, and three-run homers."

—Earl Weaver, *How Life Imitates the World Series*

All-Time Great

Babe Ruth

*Not just the greatest ballplayer (hitter and pitcher) of all time,
but a unique American icon.*

Born: February 6, 1895; Baltimore, MD
MLB Career: Boston Red Sox, 1914–19; New York Yankees,
1920–34; Boston Braves, 1935
Hall of Fame Resume: 714 homers (third) • In the top three
lifetime in runs, home runs, home run percentage, RBI, on-base
percentage, walks, and walk percentage
Inside Pitch: When Babe Ruth died, he owned 56 major-league
records plus ten more AL marks—including the best winning percentage for a pitcher, lifetime, *against* the New York Yankees.

No one in baseball history has matched the achievements of
the most well-rounded player of all time: George Herman "Babe"
Ruth, pitcher and slugger extraordinaire.

A kid of the streets who learned to play ball while he attended
St. Mary's Industrial School for Boys, George made the majors in
1914 at age 19 with the Boston Red Sox. From 1915 to '18, he went
78–40 with an ERA under 2.30, helping the club to three World
Series titles. The left-hander posted a Series-record 29 consecutive
scoreless innings in 1918, yet he was such a successful hitter that
manager Ed Barrow began giving him outfield assignments on non-
pitching days. The 6'2" hulk liked the arrangement, and when he
was allowed to roam the outfield almost exclusively in 1919, he hit a
major-league-record 29 home runs.

Theatrical producer and Red Sox owner Harry Frazee was not
impressed. Needing money for his latest show and believing the
uninhibited Ruth and his exorbitant $10,000 salary were to blame
for a sixth-place slide in 1919, Frazee sold Babe to the New York
Yankees in January 1920 for $125,000—plus a $300,000 loan on
Fenway Park. Babe put his stamp of approval on the stupidest

move in baseball history with a record-shattering 54 homers in 1920—more homers than 14 of the 16 major-league *teams* compiled—and the spark was lit. Fans wanted excitement after the hard realities of World War I and the Black Sox scandal, and Ruth supplied it—he showed that one swing could accomplish what had previously taken a series of bunts, steals, and slides.

He was the quintessential hero of the Roaring '20s, a ham for the cameras who enjoyed having every move followed and could back up his bravado. Dominating as no player before or since, he averaged 47 home runs and 133 RBI during a decade in which just four other players hit as many as 40 homers even once. Over his career, Ruth would lead the Yankees to seven pennants and four World Series championships (hitting 15 homers in Series play), despite regular indulgences in women, booze, and food. He drew suspensions from his managers and screams of delight from kids—and it was the kids who seemed to matter to him most.

Even when his 94–46 pitching mark is not factored in, Ruth's records are remarkable. He slugged .849 in 1920 and averaged .690 slugging and .474 on-base percentages over his career. When the .342 lifetime hitter retired, his mark of 714 home runs was almost double that of his nearest competitor. That career total and Babe's season high of 60 homers in 1927 have both since been topped, but his impact on the game remains undisputed. He was baseball's most beloved performer—and its finest.

⚾ ⚾ ⚾

"Ruth made a grave mistake when he gave up pitching. Working once a week, he might have lasted a long time and become a great star."

—Tris Speaker on Babe Ruth's switch to the outfield, 1919

⚾ ⚾ ⚾

"I stopped telling people stories about how great he was because I realized no one believed me."

—Ruth teammate and fellow Hall of Famer Waite Hoyt

Jackie Breaks Through

Big talent, in a new kind of package.

Setting: Ebbets Field, Brooklyn; April 15, 1947
The Magic: Baseball's color line is finally shattered as Jackie Robinson makes his big-league debut in front of 26,623 fans.

Of all the historic events in baseball, this is the one that most transcended sports history and became American history. When Jackie Robinson stepped onto the field, the game was forever changed. Yet Robinson's groundbreaking appearance as the first 20th-century African American in the previously all-white professional leagues received little fanfare the day it happened. The crowd, though predominantly black, didn't roar, and most major newspapers did not carry this story on their front page. It seems that many in the baseball world treated this as they would any other Opening Day—even though it was anything but.

Jackie's wife, Rachel, was both nervous and excited as she watched from the stands, cradling five-month-old Jackie Jr. While Robinson had the support of some teammates, most notably Pee Wee Reese, others had actively campaigned against him. But Dodgers general manager Branch Rickey, baseball commissioner Happy Chandler, and Dodgers manager Leo Durocher had all worked to ensure that this milestone event would take place.

Robinson went 0–3 that day; he hit into a rally-killing double play, but he also scored the winning run later when his speed forced an error. (The Dodgers won 5–3.) It wasn't pressure or nerves that kept him hitless, he said—it was the talent of pitcher Johnny Sain.

Robinson went on to hit .297, steal 29 bases, and score 125 runs that season, and he was named Rookie of the Year. His team won the pennant and returned to the World Series for only the second time in 27 years.

On that spring day in 1947, Jackie Robinson opened the door, but of course many more had to follow for the "experiment" to truly be a success. It didn't take long for Robinson to make his mark and for baseball to throw off the stigma of segregation, helping it to truly become "America's game."

Life in the Little Leagues

Little League baseball has produced a parade of stars, but it's the everyday heroes that make it a success.

For Nolan Ryan, Little League was the first stop on his way to the Hall of Fame and an important one on his journey through fatherhood. The latter, its founders might say, is precisely what Little League baseball was engineered to be about.

Youth baseball leagues were formed in the United States as early as the 1880s. In 1938, Carl E. Stotz started a league for children in Williamsport, Pennsylvania, and devised rules and field dimensions for what would become Little League baseball. The next year, the first three teams—Lycoming Dairy, Lundy Lumber, and Jumbo Pretzel—took the field, and the parents who organized the teams formed the first Little League board of directors.

By 1946 there were 12 similar leagues, all in Pennsylvania. Three years later, there were more than 300 such leagues throughout the United States, and in 1951 Little League took hold in Canada. The league has now spread worldwide. Little League baseball is the world's largest organized youth sports program, with nearly 200,000 teams in more than 100 countries.Williamsport, though, has remained a central location. The Little League World Series (LLWS)—a truly international event—is played there each year, and its finale hit the national television airwaves in 1963.

Of the hundreds of thousands of teams, only 16 compete for the title of Little League World Series champion. To make it to the finals in Williamsport, teams of 11- and 12-year-olds must advance through the International Tournament—a process that requires more games worldwide than six full major-league seasons!

Eight teams from the United States battle for the U.S. championship as eight teams from other countries fight for the international crown in a ten-day tournament that culminates with the top international team and the winning U.S. squad battling for the LLWS title. Fans from all over the world pack hotels throughout central Pennsylvania each summer for the event. In 2008, the 32-game World Series drew 323,444 fans.

The format of the event has been tweaked through the years, and as the young players have gotten better, the dimensions of the park have grown. From 1947 through '58, the finals were played at Original Field, where the outfield fences were all less than 200 feet from home plate. Beginning in '96, a 205-foot blast was required to clear the fences in all fields; as of 2008, those fences stand at 225 feet.

Through all its growth, some things have remained pleasantly constant. For example, the World Series champions get invited to the White House. And Little League's founding goal remains this: to teach children the fundamental principles of sportsmanship, fair play, and teamwork, just as Stotz envisioned nearly 70 years ago.

That these principles can help talented young players advance their baseball careers is a bonus Stotz may or may not have foreseen. Nolan Ryan's first organized sports experience was in Little League. "The first field in Alvin [Texas] was cleared and built by my dad and the other fathers of the kids in the program. I played Little League from the time I was nine years old until I was 13. Some of my fondest memories of baseball come from those years."

Little League remains a big deal in towns all over America. Ryan knows: Not only did he pitch a Little League no-hitter long before he threw seven of them in the majors, but he also helped coach his own sons' Little League teams. Less famous mothers and fathers do the same for their sons and daughters on diamonds around the world.

Ryan, of course, graduated from Little League ball to the Hall of Fame, as did George Brett, Steve Carlton, Rollie Fingers, Catfish Hunter, Jim Palmer, Mike Schmidt, Tom Seaver, Don Sutton, Carl Yastrzemski, and Robin Yount. None of those greats ever played in the Little League World Series, but all were boosted by their organized baseball experience as youngsters, as were countless other major-league stars.

Only a small fraction of Little League players go on to the ranks of professional baseball, of course. But where would one be without dreams? And Little League baseball is about so much more than reaching the majors.

Little League/Major League Notables

Boog Powell
Little League: Powered Lakeland, Florida, to the 1954 World Series.
Major Leagues: Won the 1970 American League MVP Award and led Baltimore to four World Series trips in six years.

Lloyd McClendon
Little League: Socked home runs in five consecutive at-bats for Gary, Indiana, in the 1971 World Series.
Major Leagues: Served as a valuable utility man for the Reds, Cubs, and Pirates from 1987 to '94 before graduating to a managerial career with Pittsburgh.

Dwight Gooden
Little League: Served as the ace of a powerhouse Belmont Heights team from Tampa, Florida, that reached the 1979 World Series.
Major Leagues: Named NL Rookie of the Year in 1984, won Cy Young Award in 1985, and pitched the Mets to a 1986 World Series title. Considered one of the most dominant pitchers of his day.

Derek Bell
Little League: Took the same Belmont Heights team with whom Gooden starred to back-to-back World Series in 1980 and '81, reaching the finals both years.
Major Leagues: The first big-leaguer to play in two Little League World Series won a title with Toronto in '92 and hit .276 over 11 seasons.

Gary Sheffield
Little League: Teamed with Bell in 1980 as stars of the United States team that fell to Taiwan in the World Series championship game.
Major Leagues: Has slugged nearly 500 career home runs, has twice batted .330, and helped the Marlins claim the 1997 World Series championship.

Learning the Lingo

To live in the world of baseball, one must speak the language.

Ace: Top pitcher on a staff. **Origin:** In playing cards, ace is high.

Around the horn: The path of a baseball being thrown around the infield, either following a strikeout, as part of a warmup, or in a double or triple play. **Origin:** Nautical term referring to sailing ships that would pass Cape Horn in southern Chile.

Band box: A small ballpark. **Origin:** From small bandstands that are frequently found in parks and town squares.

Barnstorming: A tour, often of exhibition games. **Origin:** An old vaudeville term that implied the performers were so eager to strut their stuff they'd even play in a barn during a storm.

Bermuda Triangle: Any area between three or more fielders in which a ball drops safely for a hit. **Origin:** Refers to the triangular area in the Atlantic Ocean where, legend has it, numerous boats have mysteriously disappeared.

Billyball: An aggressive style of play. **Origin:** The style favored by former manager Billy Martin.

Bleeder: A safe hit that just eludes the grasp of a fielder. **Origin:** Like blood, it often trickles.

Climbing the ladder: When a pitcher tries to retire a batter by using a series of ascending pitches. **Origin:** Descriptive.

Five o'clock hitter: A player who does his best work in batting practice. **Origin:** Refers to the hour at which batting practice usually takes place.

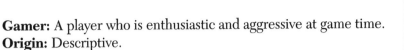

Gamer: A player who is enthusiastic and aggressive at game time. **Origin:** Descriptive.

Goat: A player who is held responsible for a loss or poor play. **Origin:** Variation of scapegoat, meaning the one held responsible for a loss, but not necessarily the culprit.

Hot corner: Third base. **Origin:** Scene of hard, pulled hits by right-handed batters.

In his wheelhouse: A pitch that is placed precisely where the batter likes to hit it. **Origin:** Nautical term referring to the room where the boat is controlled.

Jake: To beg out of the lineup with a dubious injury, or to fake an injury. **Origin:** Probably refers to Garland "Jake" Stahl, the early 20th-century ballplayer and manager who reportedly begged out of a game citing a sore foot.

Murphy money: Per-diem stipend provided to players for meals and spring-training expenses. **Origin:** Named for Robert Murphy, an attorney who led an unsuccessful attempt to unionize the Pirates in 1946. He did succeed in getting owners to provide the stipend as a preventative measure against future uprisings.

Rubber arm: A pitcher who is, or can be, used frequently. **Origin:** Descriptive of the flexibility and durability of rubber.

Station-to-station: An offense that tends to move baserunners one base at a time, either due to a relative lack of speed or a need to play conservatively. **Origin:** Descriptive of commuter trains.

Walk-off hit: A hit that ends a game, often a home run. **Origin:** Recent term, descriptive of the losing team walking off the field dejectedly. Similar to a sayonara home run.

Big Numbers for Big Sluggers

While a few of the numbers are a bit exaggerated, there have been some incredible long-distance shots worth noting.

Big sluggers have had big numbers attached to their names throughout history. Dan Brouthers hit a 500-plus-foot homer on May 4, 1884, at Union Park in Baltimore. And Honus Wagner is said to have tagged one 450 feet at Brooklyn's Washington Park in 1903—and then another at the Polo Grounds.

Ruth's Rockets
The story of the breathtaking home run really starts where the home run came to life—with Babe Ruth. As a rookie, the Babe cracked a Ruthian shot at St. Louis's Sportsman's Park that was measured at 470 feet. In 1921 alone, he hit at least one 500-foot home run in all eight American League cities.

Killebrew Can-Do
On June 3, 1967, Harmon Killebrew smashed a pitch six rows into the upper deck at Metropolitan Stadium in Minneapolis. What was impressive wasn't just the distance (about 530 feet), but the force. The blast shattered two seats. The next day, he hit another one almost as far. He is also one of the only players (along with Jimmie Foxx, Frank Howard, Cecil Fielder, and Mark McGwire) to clear the left-field roof at Tiger Stadium.

It's Outta Here—Really Outta Here!
Reggie Jackson's 1971 Tiger Stadium All-Star Game blast, which bounced off the light tower, came in an exhibition game but can still draw gasps on the highlight reel. Willie Stargell hit the ball out of Dodger Stadium twice—once in 1969 and again in 1973. But Stargell's greatest slugging feats probably came at his first home park, Forbes Field. Only ten men ever cleared the right-field roof there. Babe Ruth was the first; Stargell did it seven times.

McGwire Makes His Mark

From 1982 through 1995, there was only one genuine 500-plus-foot home run hit in the major leagues. Cecil Fielder did it in Milwaukee in September 1991, hitting the ball clear out of Milwaukee County Stadium.

During "the era of the homer," from roughly 1996 through 2003, single-season home run totals seemed to explode, and the career homer record began to be threatened. The Cardinals' Mark McGwire was at the center of that explosion, in terms of both distance and frequency. In 1998, the year he tagged 70 homers to outdo Roger Maris's 61, four of his long balls reached 500 feet. (The longest one, hit 545 feet to center field at Busch Stadium, was commemorated with a bandage on the spot on the wall where it hit.) Fourteen others topped 450 feet.

Even Mickey Wasn't That Good

Unfortunately, some long-ball memories are just myth—or, at least, exaggerated truth. The story goes that Mickey Mantle once hit a ball 734 feet, which is nearly impossible given the laws of physics. By his own testimony, the hardest ball Mantle ever hit was on May 22, 1963, at Yankee Stadium. The ball struck the facade on the right-field roof approximately 370 feet from home plate and 115 feet above field level. An optical illusion led observers to believe that the ball was still rising when it hit the facade and "would have gone 620 feet."

A claim that Mantle reached 600 feet in 1960 is questionable, as are those of other "legendary" shots, such as Dave Nicholson clearing the Comiskey Park roof on May 6, 1964, and Dave Kingman's homer out of Wrigley Field a dozen years later. *The New York Times* said Kingman's blast went 630 feet; it probably was more like 530. Josh Gibson's famous homer out of Yankee Stadium in 1930 never happened. Gibson's own recollection of his longest home run was measured at "only" 512 feet.

Magical Moment

Could a Rose by any other name hit as sweet?

The Setting: Riverfront Stadium, Cincinnati; September 11, 1985
The Magic: Pete Rose becomes the new all-time hit leader.

His longtime Reds manager, Sparky Anderson, once said of Pete Rose, "He is Cincinnati. He's the Reds." And even though Rose played for two other teams in his career (and helped one of them to a World Series title), there was only one place for him to be when his career began to wind down—back home in Cincinnati. It was there that he chased the seemingly unconquerable record of Ty Cobb's lifetime total of 4,189 hits.

Rose was both playing for and managing the Reds in 1985 when he faced San Diego pitcher Eric Show at 8:01 P.M. this September night. (Actually, Rose had broken Cobb's record several days earlier, but Major League Baseball had redefined the record as 4,191 hits, so that's the one Pete was after.) The count was two balls and one strike when Pete shot a line drive into left field for his 4,192nd hit, and Cincinnati celebrated as though it had just won the World Series as its favorite son marched (or hustled, if you will) himself atop the leader board for all-time hits. With fireworks blazing above them, the crowd cheered for a full seven minutes.

Rose racked up an amazing lifetime total of 4,256 hits—nearly 500 more than Hank Aaron; 800 more than Carl Yastrzemski, Cap Anson, and Honus Wagner; and 1,000 more than Nap Lajoie, Cal Ripken, Jr., and George Brett. Pete's later actions have taken some of the bloom off the Rose, but for that one night, Cincinnati's hustling hometown hero deserved all the adulation he got.

Old Hoss's Endurance

When the Providence Grays lost one of their two pitchers to a rival franchise in 1884, Charley "Old Hoss" Radbourn literally took matters into his own hands.

Charley "Old Hoss" Radbourn had a rubber arm and an iron will. When his team, the Providence Grays, found themselves without one of their pitchers in 1884, the gritty right-hander made a deal with team owners: He would pitch the rest of the season, he said, but if the Grays won the National League pennant, he'd get a bonus and the right to free agency.

So began one of baseball's most remarkable tales of endurance: When it was all over, the Grays were pennant winners and Radbourn had logged 73 starts—including a stretch of 19 consecutive starts and wins—and 678⅔ innings, just four outs short of Will White's all-time record of 680 innings in a season, set in 1879. Radbourn's 59 victories that year are an all-time record and six more than his closest challenger. Radbourn then pitched the Grays to three straight victories over American Association champion New York, sweeping the Metropolitans in what some consider the first World Series. He collected a $2,000 bonus (more than $40,000 by today's standards) and then re-signed with Providence in 1885.

Radbourn's stamina was outstanding even in his day—an era in which teams carried two pitchers, 30-win seasons weren't uncommon, and the concept of relief pitching was barely developed. Radbourn tried to conserve his achy arm by using a variety of deliveries, but the strenuous workload took its toll nonetheless; the dependable Old Hoss reportedly had difficulty combing his hair before and after games.

The record feats of rubber-armed 19th-century hurlers such as Radbourn and White get safer every year. Bill Hutchison, who threw 622 innings in 1892, was the last pitcher to surpass 600— and 500—innings in a season. Ed Walsh in 1908 was the last 400-inning pitcher. And it's been more than a quarter-century since Steve Carlton in 1980 was the last player to throw more than 300 innings in one year.

Striking It Rich

"For it's one, two, three strikes you're out ... "—and sometimes those strikes come one right after the other, after the other.

A strikeout will put a bully in his place or get a pitcher out of a jam. It's baseball's ultimate act of defense, often displaying the dominance of the hurler, the incompetence of his bat-waggling opponent, or both. The following are some examples of baseball's foremost—and freakiest—feats of fanning.

19 Ks

In 1884, the birth of the overhand pitching motion resulted in several dominant one-game pitching performances. Charles Sweeney of the Providence Grays and Hugh "One Arm" Daily of the Chicago Unions both recorded 19-K outings. Dupee Shaw of the Boston Unions and Henry Porter of the Milwaukee Brewers each recorded an 18-strikeout game.

Steve Carlton of St. Louis struck out 19 Mets on September 15, 1969, but the celebration was muted: He lost the game 4–3 after surrendering a pair of two-run homers to Ron Swoboda.

In 1970, Tom Seaver of the Mets also reached the 19-strikeout mark, and he did it in spectacular fashion by blowing away the last ten Padres he faced. Seaver's mark is still the all-time record for consecutive batters struck out.

On June 24, 1997, Seattle's Randy Johnson struck out 19 Oakland A's—but allowed 11 hits, including two home runs, in a 4–1 loss. The Big Unit, however, won a 19-K game later that year, beating the White Sox 5–0. Johnson is the only man to strike out at least 19 men twice in the same season. He also holds the single-season record for strikeouts per nine innings pitched (13.4 in 2001). As of the end of 2008, Johnson holds the career standard of 10.67 K/9 and is the all-time strikeout leader among left-handers.

Nolan Ryan had four 19-K games (three in extra-inning affairs) and holds the modern-era single-season strikeout record, ringing up 383 victims in 1973, which is one more than Sandy Koufax had in 1965. Ryan broke Koufax's mark by striking out 16 Minnesota Twins

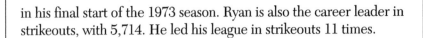

in his final start of the 1973 season. Ryan is also the career leader in strikeouts, with 5,714. He led his league in strikeouts 11 times.

20 Ks

Roger Clemens is the only pitcher to fan 20 men in a game twice, completing the tricks a decade apart for the Red Sox—in 1986 at Fenway Park against Seattle and in 1996 at Detroit. His record-setting 1986 outing received an unlikely assist from his first baseman, Don Baylor. With Gorman Thomas batting for Seattle in the fourth inning, Baylor dropped a foul pop behind first and was charged an error for prolonging the at-bat; Thomas proceeded to be called out on strikes. Clemens had a chance to retire 21 by strikeout in that game, but Ken Phelps grounded to shortstop for the final out. It should be noted that in neither of Clemens's two 20-strikeout games did he walk a single batter.

When rookie Kerry Wood of the Cubs struck out 20 Houston Astros in only his fifth career start, he tied Clemens's all-time nine-inning game mark and caused a sensation. Not only was the game a one-hitter, but it also marked only the second time in history that a pitcher had matched his age in years with strikeouts in a game. (Rookie Bob Feller whiffed 17 Philadelphia Athletics in 1936.)

21 Ks

Washington Senator Tom Cheney, a journeyman who would fashion a 19–29 career record, whiffed 21 Baltimore Orioles on September 12, 1962. Thirteen of those Ks came in the first nine innings, and he racked up the rest in the final seven innings of the 16-inning, 2–1 victory. Cheney's mark remains the highest total for any single baseball game.

Single-Season Ks

The single-season strikeout king of all time is Matthew Kilroy, who fanned 513 batters in 583 innings for the American Association's Baltimore Orioles in 1886. Kilroy, a 20-year-old left-handed rookie, ended up posting a disappointing 29–34 record that year, due in large part to the fact that in addition to his Ks, he walked 182 batters.

Unusual Ks

Because rules allow batters to try to advance to first base (if unoccupied) on a wild pitch or passed ball on strike three, there have been 51 occasions since 1900 when a pitcher has struck out four men in an inning. Remarkably, one pitcher, Chuck Finley, accomplished the feat on three separate occasions, including twice in one year (1999). No other pitcher has struck out four men in an inning twice. Finley is also among the 17 pitchers to record four strikeouts in one inning in consecutive order. Orval Overall of the Cubs is the only player to whiff four men in an inning of a World Series game. He did it in Chicago's decisive Game 5 victory in 1908.

A dropped third strike led to one of baseball's most unusual plays. On April 25, 1970, Earl Wilson appeared to have ended the Tigers' inning by striking out, but the ball was actually trapped by Twins catcher Paul Ratliff, who failed to tag or force Wilson and instead rolled the ball back to the pitcher's mound. The Twins trotted off the field as Wilson raced around the bases, rounding third before the Twins took notice. Left fielder Brant Alyea picked up the ball at the mound and threw to shortstop Leo Cardenas near home plate. Wilson retreated to third, but Alyea hustled there to receive a throw from Cardenas and tag him out.

Mark Whiten is among a handful of players in baseball history to hit four home runs in a game, but the outfielder is in even more select company as a pitcher. Called in by the Indians in 1998 for mop-up duty in a game they were losing by nine runs, Whiten struck out the side, becoming the only position player ever to do this in his only inning of work as a pitcher.

On May 29, 1982, Roy Smalley of the Yankees struck out into a triple play. With Bobby Murcer and Graig Nettles on the move from second and first, respectively, Smalley swung and missed at strike three. Twins catcher Sal Butera fired to third base to catch Murcer, who retreated to second only to find Nettles approaching from the other direction. Nettles then turned back to first base but was tagged out there by Kent Hrbek. In the meantime, Murcer broke once again for third but was nailed at the base when Hrbek fired to pitcher Terry Felton covering. Murcer later remarked, "We need a second base coach."

Presidential Pratter

"A couple of years ago, they told me I was too young to be President and you were too old to be playing baseball. But we fooled them."

—45-year-old John F. Kennedy to 41-year-old Stan Musial at the 1962 All-Star Game

"We cheer for the Senators, we pray for the Senators, and we hope that the Supreme Court does not declare that unconstitutional."

—Lyndon B. Johnson, July 10, 1962

"I don't know a lot about politics, but I know a lot about baseball."

—Richard Nixon, 1981

"A big enough boy to enjoy the national game—and a man big enough to guide our country through its greatest crisis."

—Words accompanying a picture of President Woodrow Wilson throwing out the first ball of the season on the cover of 1917 World Series program

"I know, but I had a better year than Hoover."

—Babe Ruth's response when a reporter pointed out that his 1930 salary demand of $80,000 topped the President's $75,000 salary

"Last year, more Americans went to symphonies than went to baseball games. This may be viewed as an alarming statistic, but I think that both baseball and the country will endure."

—John F. Kennedy

"Baseball is our national game."

—Calvin Coolidge

The Judge

Baseball's dictatorial but effectual commissioner Kenesaw Mountain Landis presided over the game from 1920 through '44. Having served as a judge, Landis had no problem laying down the law.

Judge Kenesaw Mountain Landis operated out of a Chicago office with one word written on the door: BASEBALL. Stubborn and conscientious, the Judge had the final say.

Supreme Power

Serving as Major League Baseball's first commissioner, from 1920 until his death in 1944 at age 78, Landis fought ferociously to protect what he called the "national institution" of baseball. He took office while the game's integrity was under fire (the baseball world was reeling from the Black Sox scandal); he died with its good name restored. And he didn't particularly care whose feelings or finances might be hurt along the way.

When baseball's owners named him commissioner in 1920, Landis demanded "supreme power" over the game. The Judge rapidly established that he wasn't kidding about supreme power. He immediately crossed AL president Ban Johnson by ignoring the idea that he was supposed to serve as head of a three-person "commission." The rule of baseball was his and his alone.

Laying Down the Law

At the time of the 1921 World Series, Landis hadn't even been on the job a year. But he had made his presence felt, with suspensions and expulsions of "dirty" players and the consolidation of his power. And the biggest confrontation yet was brewing.

It happened during the final days of the 1921 World Series—the first Series in which Babe Ruth's Yankees appeared. In those days players looked to extend their season and their income by playing postseason games in less-than-major-league locales. They called it "barnstorming," from an old vaudeville term that implied the performers were so eager to strut their stuff they'd even play in a barn during a storm.

The World Series was Landis's special interest. What happened within the leagues was the purview of the league presidents, but the Series was Landis's own. He understood that having an exhibition "Series" after the actual Series diminished the value of the original. There were rules in place that forbade such behavior, but no one was enforcing them. Landis decided to set things straight by telling Babe Ruth himself that he was not allowed to go on a barnstorming tour.

"It seems," Landis said, "I'll have to show somebody who's running this game."

Landis vs. Ruth

The Judge tried to reach Ruth to let him know he was laying down the law. Ruth, ever the big kid, didn't return the Judge's phone calls until after the final game of the Series. ("What has that long-haired old goat got to do with me?" Ruth wanted to know.) Ruth told the Judge he had a contract to play in a barnstorming series, which he couldn't (or wouldn't) break, and he was about to catch a midnight train to Buffalo to start the tour. Landis snarled, "If you do, it will be the sorriest thing you ever do in baseball."

It was the biggest power play in baseball history. The game's superstar versus the game's center of power. Babe had to feel he held the cards; who could stand up to *him*? When asked about Landis's wrath, Ruth replied, "Ah, let the old guy go jump in the lake." But when he ignored Landis's edict and went on the barnstorming trip anyway, the Judge suspended Ruth for six weeks and withheld his share of World Series money. When Babe appealed to the Yankee owners, they backed the commissioner. The Judge had laid down the law, and even the great Babe Ruth had to toe the line. The Judge had indeed proven who was running this game.

◖ ◖ ◖

When Kenesaw Mountain Landis was named commissioner of baseball, comedian Will Rogers concurred. "Might as well give it to the old fella," he opined. "He's at the game every day anyway."

All-Time Great

Rogers Hornsby

He was a nasty, rude person but possibly the greatest right-handed batter of all time. And he had power, too.

Born: April 27, 1896; Winters, TX

MLB Career: St. Louis Cardinals, 1915–26; New York Giants, 1927; Boston Braves, 1928; Chicago Cubs, 1929–32; St. Louis Cardinals, 1933; St. Louis Browns, 1933–37

Hall of Fame Resume: Won seven batting titles, six consecutively • Led the league in hits four times; had more than 200 hits three other times • His .424 batting average in 1924 was the highest in the 20th century • Led the league in homers and triples twice, in doubles four times

Inside Pitch: Hornsby refused to read or go to the movies for fear of damaging his eyesight.

It's been almost 70 years since Ted Williams last cracked it, but there was once an era in which a .400 batting average was not an unheard-of feat. Six men achieved the magic mark a total of 11 times from 1910 to 1930, but Rogers Hornsby's performance from 1921 to '25 should still be considered the greatest hitting stretch in major-league history. Through 696 games, 2,679 at-bats, and countless doubleheaders in the St. Louis sun, the Cardinals second baseman averaged a .402 batting mark.

Hornsby's achievement becomes even more remarkable upon viewing his early career. A 140-pound shortstop with a .232 average in the low minors during 1914, the righty-hitting Texan eventually put on 20 pounds and hit .313 in his rookie year with the Cards in 1916 before upping his mark to .327 (second in the National League) a year later. Hornsby was moved to second base in 1920 and paced the NL in batting (.370), slugging (.559), RBI (94), hits (218), and doubles (44) despite cranking just nine homers. It was, at the time, the best

offensive season by an NL second baseman in the 20th century, but it was only the beginning.

In 1921, the man called "Rajah" (for his regal, hazel-eyed appearance) upped his average to .397 with 44 doubles, 18 triples, 126 RBI, 131 runs, and 21 homers—leading the league in each department except the last while maintaining a hold on the NL batting, slugging (.639), and on-base-percentage (.458) leads that would last four more years. His first .400 season (.401) followed in 1922, with Hornsby completing his full maturation as a slugger by belting 42 homers (then a record for second basemen), driving in 152 runs, and winning the 1922 Triple Crown.

An aloof free-thinker who was nearly as despised as the only man to compile a higher lifetime average—Ty Cobb—Hornsby outdid even the Georgia Peach during his infamous 1921–25 run. Though limited by injury to 107 games in '23, he still averaged 216 hits, 123 runs, 41 doubles, 13 triples, 29 homers, and 120 RBI over the span—highlighted by the highest NL average of the 20th century (.424) in '24 and his second Triple Crown in 1925 (.403–39–143). After being named player/manager of the underachieving Cards that same year, he led St. Louis to its first pennant and a stunning seven-game World Series upset of the Yankees in 1926 while batting .317.

As with Cobb, however, success couldn't calm Hornsby's bitter disposition. He routinely clashed with Cardinals owner Sam Breadon over money matters and, before

the 1927 season, was traded to the Giants for Frankie Frisch and Jimmy Ring. After more quarrels with New York ownership during his lone season there (in which he hit .361), he passed through Boston (a seventh and final batting title at .387 with the '28 Braves) and Chicago (.380–39–149 totals in '29) before his production slipped. He eventually ended up back in St. Louis for part-time duty with the Cardinals and Browns, and his final .358 average, 301 homers, 1,584 RBI, and .577 slugging percentage earned him a Hall of Fame plaque—even if his attitude was anything but golden.

Latin American Players

Una pasión para el béisbol

When Major League Baseball summoned a group of prominent Latino players and ex-players to New York in 2005 to commemorate the contributions made to the game by players of Latin American heritage, it showed them a video of such past superstars as Luis Aparicio, Roberto Clemente, and Orlando Cepeda. Watching it had a visible effect on many of those in attendance.

"Watching that video gave me goose bumps," said Yankees relief pitcher Mariano Rivera, a native of Panama. "It was tremendous, watching some of the guys who made the path for us. I'm honored just to be mentioned with them."

A Way of Life

Meriting mention among those greats is indeed a high honor, given the number of All-Star players to hail from Cuba, the Dominican Republic, Venezuela, Puerto Rico, Nicaragua, Mexico, and other Latin American and Caribbean countries.

Though many of these players grew up in some of the poorest nations in the Western hemisphere, using cut-out milk cartons as gloves and swinging sticks at rolled-up cloth "baseballs," they are part of a parade of talent to the majors that seems to grow richer each year. Latino players will tell you that it's largely because of a collective love for the game that permeates their homelands—not unlike the deep connection Europeans and South Americans generally feel to soccer.

As former Dominican winter-league general manager Winston Llenas once said, "It's more than a game. It's our passion. It's almost our way of life."

Added St. Louis Cardinals manager Tony La Russa, "The Latin American player understands the game of baseball better than other players. They've been talking about it and playing it their whole lives; they're not confused and distracted by other sports."

Battling Prejudice

Although some Latinos played in the major leagues long before blacks were allowed to do so, others were denied the chance because of their darker skin. Cuban-born Negro Leagues Hall of Famer Martin Dihigo, for example, never got to show his considerable skills in the big leagues despite being considered one of the greatest, most versatile players of all time.

Like black players, the Latino players of the 1940s, '50s, and '60s endured segregation, ridicule, and hostility. Unlike their African American counterparts, most of them had a language barrier to overcome as well.

Today, nearly 30 percent of all major-league players are Latino. Every big-league team scouts Latin America for talent. The top Latino prospects earn invitations to academies set up by some of the American clubs. Some people call them "baseball factories" because they produce and train major-league talent at minimum wages.

Desire and Determination

The Dominican Republic has led the way among Latino countries to produce an abundance of major-league talent. Among its heroes: Joaquin Andujar, George Bell, Robinson Cano, Rico Carty, Luis Castillo, Mariano Duncan, Tony Fernandez, Pedro Guerrero, Guillermo Mota, Jose Offerman, Juan Samuel, Alfonso Soriano, Sammy Sosa, and Fernando Tatis.

Of youngsters in the Dominican Republic, sports anthropologist Alan Klein said in the documentary *Stealing Home,* "Every morning you would drive to the Academy, you would see 15, 20 kids out there—not one of them had a uniform; they all had pieces of one uniform or another, poor equipment, they would be right at the gate waiting for the security people to open up the gates, and they would go in for their tryout. If they got signed, they were happy. If they didn't get signed, it didn't even deter them for a minute; they would be on the road hitchhiking to the next location."

That desire has helped boost the number of Latinos playing American professional baseball exponentially over the last few decades.

Fueling the Fire

Beginning in the 1940s, an international amateur baseball tournament named Mundial fueled competitive fires between Latin American nations; interest in the game at all levels soared as a result. Caribbean basin nations won every one of these tournaments from 1940 to '72, with Cuba taking 11 titles in 18 years.

The creation of national agencies to foster amateur baseball development in Cuba and the Dominican Republic, among other countries, contributed to the passion in those nations. And the fact that pro baseball was banned by Cuba's communist regime after the 1961 season certainly helped push some of that island's talented players onto U.S. soil.

Glory and Greatness

The success of players such as Aparicio, Cepeda, and Clemente paved the way for others. And those others have followed in huge numbers. While about 28 percent of big-leaguers on 2008 Opening Day rosters were born outside the United States, that percentage was 47 in the minors, according to Major League Baseball. The vast majority of those non-American-born players were Latino.

Venezuelan Johan Santana has been one of the best major-league pitchers in recent seasons. Dominican-born David Ortiz stands near the top of the list of American League hitters, and his compatriot Albert Pujols has dominated the National League in a similar fashion. They are just a few of the big-name Latino stars who now set the standard for greatness.

Commissioner Bud Selig summed it up: "Over the years, major-league baseball has been blessed with a wealth of players of Latin American heritage who have contributed to some of the most memorable moments and accomplished some of the most storied feats in the history of the game."

Latino Legends

In 2005, Major League Baseball asked fans to vote for the Latino Legends team by choosing 12 players from a ballot of 60. The honored players:

Catcher: Ivan Rodriguez, Puerto Rico
First baseman: Albert Pujols, Dominican Republic
Second baseman: Rod Carew, Panama
Shortstop: Alex Rodriguez, Dominican Republic
Third baseman: Edgar Martinez, Puerto Rico
Outfielders: Roberto Clemente, Puerto Rico; Manny Ramirez, Dominican Republic; Vladimir Guerrero, Dominican Republic
Starting pitchers: Pedro Martinez, Dominican Republic; Juan Marichal, Dominican Republic; Fernando Valenzuela, Mexico
Relief pitcher: Mariano Rivera, Panama

⚾ ⚾ ⚾

The 2008 season opened with 28 percent of major-league players having been born outside the United States. The largest numbers came from the Dominican Republic, Venezuela, and Puerto Rico. Following is a breakdown of all the foreign countries in which 2008 Opening Day major-leaguers were born:

Dominican Republic (88)
Venezuela (52)
Puerto Rico (29)
Japan (16)
Canada (14)
Mexico (11)
Cuba (8)
Panama (5)
Australia (4)
Taiwan (3)
Colombia (2)
Korea (2)
Curaçao (1)
Netherlands (1)
Nicaragua (1)
U.S. Virgin Islands (1)

Dubious Honors
(The League's Worst Teams)

The teams that are found underneath the bottom of the barrel.

Many arguments have raged about the best baseball team ever. But the worst? Many qualify for the dubious honor of worst team for a single season. Each was terrible in its own way in its own time. Only teams that completed a season schedule are considered here (eliminating several fly-by-night clubs from the 19th century).

1899 Cleveland Spiders
How Bad Were They? 20–134 (84 games out)
Managers: Lave Cross (8–30); Joe Quinn (12–104)
Nightmare Season: Just three years earlier, the Cleveland Spiders had played in consecutive Temple Cups (the championship series of the day) and boasted Cy Young in his prime, as well as a cast of top hitters. With no rules prohibiting multiple team ownership, the best players from Cleveland were shifted to St. Louis—which was owned by the same group—in 1899. The result for Cleveland was the most losses in big-league history. The Spiders finished the year going 1–40. They were such a bad draw (fewer than 150 fans per home game!) that ownership forced them to play 112 road games.

1916 Philadelphia Athletics
How Bad Were They? 36–117 (54½ games out)
Manager: Connie Mack
Nightmare Season: Two years removed from consecutive pennants, Connie Mack's Athletics compiled the worst winning percentage (.235) of the 20th century. Competition from the Federal League, anger at being swept in the 1914 World Series, and dwindling finances led Mack to sell off his best players, leading to 109 losses in 1915 and seven straight last-place finishes from 1916 to '22. And Mack let his pitchers take the punishment: Despite being the only team in the American League with an ERA above 3.00 in 1916, the A's led the league with 94 complete games.

1935 Boston Braves

How Bad Were They? 38–115 (61½ games out)

Manager: Bill McKechnie

Nightmare Season: The Red Sox and Braves staged a heated contest for the dubious honor of worst team in Boston throughout the 1920s and '30s. With each racking up five 100-loss seasons, neither team was any good. But the Braves earned the prize with their doozy of a showing in 1935. After three consecutive .500 or better seasons, the Braves dropped off a cliff. Opponents batted .303, and Boston's 4.93 ERA was the highest in the NL since the offensive explosion of 1930. Aged Babe Ruth was on this team; he retired in May.

1941 Philadelphia Phillies

How Bad Were They? 43–111 (57 games out)

Manager: Doc Prothro

Nightmare Season: The Phillies lost 100 games six times in a seven-season span from 1936 to '42, with 1941 being the lowest point. Unlike in 1930, when the pitching staff racked up an unfathomable 6.71 ERA at the tiny Baker Bowl in a year in which the team batted .315, the '41 Phillies at Shibe Park couldn't hit, either. They were last in runs scored as well as runs allowed, hit for the lowest batting average yet had the highest batting average against, needed more relief appearances than any other team, and, not surprisingly, had the NL's lowest attendance. The Phils hired a new manager (Hans Lobert) and promptly lost 109 times in '42.

1952 Pittsburgh Pirates

How Bad Were They? 42–112 (54½ games out)

Manager: Billy Meyer

Nightmare Season: The Pirates have the distinction of being the worst team to play between America's entry into World War II and baseball's expansion era years. And what a bad team it was. The Bucs allowed more walks, hits, and home runs than any other NL team in 1952 and gave up 134 more runs than anyone else, as well. However, thanks to a shortened fence in left field, future Hall of Famer Ralph Kiner tied for the home run crown—his seventh straight year of winning or sharing it. When Kiner asked for a salary increase, owner Branch Rickey famously replied, "We finished last with you, we can finish last without you." After trading him to the Cubs, that's just what the Pirates did...for the next three seasons.

1962 New York Mets

How Bad Were They? 40–120 (60½ games out)
Manager: Casey Stengel
Nightmare Season: The 1962 Mets are the stars of this dreadful, gloomy list. Oh, they were bad. No one had piled up more losses since 1899. They were outscored by 331 runs. This expansion team lost the first nine games they played and had three losing streaks in double digits. But with players like "Marvelous Marv" Throneberry, the Mets lost with panache. New York was so starved for National League baseball that fans ate it up at the Polo Grounds and gleefully followed the team to Shea Stadium in 1964. More than 40 years later, books are still published about Casey Stengel's fun, flea-bitten crew.

1962 Chicago Cubs

How Bad Were They? 59–103 (42½ games out)
Managers: College of Coaches: El Tappe (4–16); Lou Klein (12–18); Charlie Metro (43–69)
Nightmare Season: It's hard to believe that two teams from the same league in the same year could have made it onto this list, but the 1962 Cubs are worthy thanks to the College of Coaches. Owner P. K. Wrigley's bright idea put the sputtering franchise in the hands of the overmatched coaching staff who managed the team on a rotating basis. Playing their tenth decade as a franchise, the Cubs lost 100 games for the first time, finished seven games behind expansion Houston, and were the only team with a .500 record against the moribund Mets. During the last week of the season, the Cubs drew crowds of less than 1,000 to Wrigley Field three times.

1969 San Diego Padres

How Bad Were They? 52–110 (41 games out)
Manager: Preston Gomez

Nightmare Season: You think the Mets are the only epically bad expansion team? The Padres suffered on the field and at the gate. Just 512,970 fans showed up for their first year of existence. (The Expos, playing at a tiny, frigid facility, drew twice that number the same year with the same record.) San Diego pitchers struck out the fewest batters in the bigs, while the .225-hitting offense fanned the most times in the NL. The Padres beat out the Expos and the 1977 Blue Jays as the worst first-year team not named the Mets, and they finished last in each of their first six seasons, averaging 101 losses.

1988 Baltimore Orioles
How Bad Were They? 54–107 (34½ games out)
Managers: Cal Ripken, Sr. (0–6); Frank Robinson (54–101)
Nightmare Season: While there were many terrible seasons between 1970 and 2002, the staggering start and finish of the 1988 Orioles helps them to edge out the likes of the 1979 A's, the 1991 Indians, and the 1998 Marlins. The O's began the season with three Ripkens and a record 21 consecutive losses. Cal Sr. was fired six games in. (Cal Jr. and Billy stayed on as players.) The team managed a 51–69 mark for Frank Robinson between May and mid-September before a dismal 3–17 finish.

2003 Detroit Tigers
How Bad Were They? 43–119 (47 games out)
Manager: Alan Trammell
Nightmare Season: The Tigers would have made the list anyway for their brutal 53–109 season in 1996, but let's not get greedy. The 2003 Tigers were terrible on an epic scale. Detroit had the most losses in American League history, the third-most ever in the major leagues, and the lowest AL batting average since the 1988 Orioles. Three years later, though, the Tigers took control of the AL Central, making it all the way to the World Series. Revenge is certainly sweet.

Who in the Hall?

There are some things about the game's star players that even the most seasoned baseball expert doesn't know. See if you can guess which Hall of Fame players are described here.

1) He began his career playing for a semipro team called the Amarillo Colts.

2) He once received a grand total of $20 for playing a night game in Lincoln, Nebraska.

3) When he was a child, his father would pay him a nickel in order to get him to play catch.

4) He operated a car dealership while playing in the major leagues.

5) An anonymous phone caller once made a death threat against him during spring training.

6) He never played in a World Series.

A: Ernie Banks

1) He flied out in his first major-league at-bat and made an error in his first game.

2) He suffered from osteomyelitis, an unrelenting bone disease, which caused doctors to remove two inches of bone from his left foot when he was eight years old.

3) He seemed to have little fear of injury, which, combined with his bone disease, may have led to his many broken bones. These included a broken collarbone and a broken hand—an injury that caused him to miss a month of the 1967 season and possibly cost his team the pennant.

4) In 1973, he hit a career-low .255 while playing only 91 games.

5) He finished his career playing primarily as a designated hitter.

A: Al Kaline

1) As a teenager, he temporarily suffered from a heart murmur.

2) He gave up a home run to the first major-league batter he faced.

3) He was partly responsible for Major League Baseball's decision to lower the pitcher's mound by five inches.

4) During one of his team's pennant-winning seasons, he missed two months with a broken leg.

5) He once lost the seventh game of the World Series.

6) He delayed his start in the major leagues to play basketball for the Harlem Globetrotters.

A: Bob Gibson

1) He was first signed by a scout for $1 and an autographed ball.

2) He missed three full seasons and part of a fourth in the middle of his career after he volunteered for service in World War II.

3) He once lost a World Series game in which he pitched a two-hitter.

4) His manager chose not to pitch him in his final World Series.

5) His mother was hit in the face by a foul ball hit off one of his pitches, leaving her in the hospital for two weeks with cuts, bruises, and two black eyes.

6) He openly feuded with Pete Rose and has been vocal in his opposition to Rose being considered for induction into the Hall of Fame.

A: Bob Feller

1) He began his career playing for Sandersville of the Georgia State League.

2) He went 4-for-4 against Hall of Fame pitcher Robin Roberts in his first major-league game.

3) He was platooned for several seasons at the beginning of his career.

4) His line drive, the final out of the World Series his team lost, was referenced in the *Peanuts* comic strip.

5) In 1977, he was forced to attend spring training as a nonroster player.

A: Willie McCovey

1) After struggling in Class D at Williamson, West Virginia, an official with his parent major-league team recommended that he be released.

2) On the verge of being released, he was switched from pitching to playing the outfield due to a shoulder injury.

3) He batted only .222 in his first World Series and also batted .222 in his last World Series.

4) He memorized the speed of the fastball, curve, and slider of every pitcher in the league. He said that he knew how the ball would move by the time it crossed the plate, because he could pick up its speed within its first 30 feet of flight.

5) He missed the entire 1945 season because of military service during World War II.

6) He is an accomplished harmonica player.

A: Stan Musial

1) He played for nine teams over 22 years, including one world champion.

2) Relying on an intimidating fastball and demeanor, he recorded at least 20 saves in 10 different seasons.

3) He was only the second pitcher to reach 300 saves.

4) Unlike many of today's closers, he often pitched three innings to earn a save.

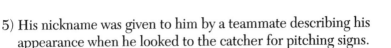

5) His nickname was given to him by a teammate describing his appearance when he looked to the catcher for pitching signs.

A: Rich "Goose" Gossage

1) He was put up for adoption immediately after he was born. Two days later, he was adopted.

2) He played his first professional season for a team in South Dakota in the Northern League.

3) He missed all of the 1968 season with a sore arm.

4) Late in his major-league career, he was an underwear model and donated all the proceeds from the sale of his advertising poster to the Cystic Fibrosis Foundation.

5) After pitching a no-hitter while allowing six walks, he called the game the "ugliest no-hitter ever."

6) He made an unsuccessful comeback seven years after his retirement.

A: Jim Palmer

1) As a minor-league player, he was threatened by a shotgun-toting fan who vowed to kill him if he picked up a hit that night.

2) As a rookie in the major leagues, he hit only .243.

3) During his second LCS, he went 0-for-14 at the plate.

4) Once, while trying to steal second base, he realized that he would be out easily and tried to call a time-out.

5) While attempting to break up a fight on the field, he suffered a pinched nerve in his elbow that brought his season to an early end.

6) Known for his monstrous home runs, he hit two of only four long balls ever hit completely out of Dodger Stadium and seven of the 18 ever hit out of Forbes Field.

A: Willie Stargell

One-of-a-Kind Ballparks

Ballparks' strange quirks keep fans—and fielders—on their toes.

A ballpark's beauty is in the eye of the ticket holder. Modern stadiums cater to the appetites of the modern fan, offering unobstructed views, ample seats, special club sections, and scoreboards that display images and play music. Ballparks of the past had far fewer—if any—frills and were contoured to their surroundings, creating unique, sometimes quirky features and distinctive environments in which to watch baseball.

Baker Bowl, Philadelphia
Home of the Philadelphia Phillies, 1894–1938

Erected as a wooden park in 1887, it was replaced with concrete and steel after seven years, following a fire. Sections of the stands collapsed in 1903 and 1927, but each time the Phillies moved back in within a few weeks. The stadium was built near a train yard, and the indentation of a tunnel in right field led to the park's nickname: "the Hump." The club tried to compensate for the short fence in right (280 feet) with a 40-foot tin wall, and a 15-foot in-play net was added in 1929. No matter—it was still the best hitter's park in the game: The National League batted .352 there in 1930.

Fate: Demolished in 1950.

Griffith Stadium, Washington, D.C.
Home of the Washington Senators, 1911–1960; expansion Washington Senators, 1961

The stadium, which was built in just one month after National Park burned down in March 1911, was one of the most cavernous parks in history. Its left-field wall, which was 407 feet away from home plate, was deeper than dead-center in 16 parks that were in use in 2007. Even stranger was the way the structure jutted in to accommodate neighboring houses. In 1924, the year of their only world championship, the Senators hit one home run there all season.

Fate: Demolished in 1965.

Polo Grounds, New York

Home of the New York Giants, 1911–1957; New York Yankees, 1913–1922; New York Mets, 1962–1963

This fifth incarnation of the Polo Grounds was erected in concrete and steel after a fire destroyed the previous one in April 1911. The horseshoe-shape ballpark allowed for very short home runs to left and right—279 and 257 feet, respectively—but extended 483 feet to the raised clubhouse in center. Only three major-leaguers ever reached the bleachers in center: Joe Adcock, Lou Brock, and Hank Aaron. Managers could only see the top half of their outfielders since the outfield was sunken for drainage, but the park was good enough for groundskeeper Matty Schwab, who was lured to the job because owner Horace Stoneham built him an apartment under the left-field stands in the 1950s.

Fate: Demolished in 1964.

Tiger Stadium, Detroit (formerly Navin Field and Briggs Stadium)

Home of the Detroit Tigers, 1912–1999

Detroit's landmark underwent many changes over the years, but fans were always close to the action (and perhaps a girder). The "Cash Register," a second-deck overhang in right field, caught many balls that outfielders had a bead on, while many other balls cleared the roof altogether. The 125-foot flagpole in center field was the tallest in-play obstacle ever at a major-league park. The same corner had previously housed Bennett Park, which opened in 1896 and closed in 1911. The Tigers moved out in 1999.

Fate: Most of the old stadium was dismantled in 2008, although a preservation group is trying to save a portion for youth leagues and a museum.

Ebbets Field, Brooklyn

Home of the Brooklyn Dodgers, 1913–1957

A half-century after the final game was played there, Ebbets Field remains the granddaddy of them all when it comes to ballpark nostalgia. Dodgers owner Charlie Ebbets bought up dozens of small parcels in what was known as "Pigtown" and wedged his elegant ballpark into a space near the Gowanus Canal. The wall/scoreboard in right, which was 318 feet from the plate, had a reported 289 different angles. The scoreboard featured an ad for Schaefer Beer, and the letters "h" (for a hit) or "e" (for an error) lit up in the sign to reflect the action on the field.

Fate: Demolished in 1960 after the Dodgers moved to L.A.

Braves Field, Boston

Home of the Boston Braves, 1915–1952

The first superstadium was built in response to Boston's "Miracle Braves" of 1914. A massive single deck held 40,000 spectators, and its vast dimensions—402 feet down the line in left and 542 to the right-center corner—held everything in. There were no home runs hit over the outer wall for the first decade of the park's existence. The Braves won their only world championship in Boston at Fenway Park in 1914; the Red Sox won the World Series at Braves Field in 1915 and 1916.

Fate: Sold to Boston University in 1952. The core remains today and serves as a football, soccer, and field hockey stadium named Nickerson Field.

Jarry Park, Montreal

Home of the Montreal Expos, 1969–1976

The first major-league foray into Canada stretched a recreational facility from a capacity of 3,000 to 28,000. Construction was still ongoing during the opening month of the inaugural Expos season. A swimming pool remained in right field, with long drives to right often getting wet. Montreal still managed to surpass one million fans in each of its first six seasons. The Expos moved into Olympic Stadium the year after the 1976 Montreal Games.

Fate: Part of Jarry's seating remains in Stade Uniprix, an indoor facility that's used for professional tennis events.

Exhibition Stadium, Toronto

Home of the Toronto Blue Jays, 1977–1989

It was a football stadium—a Canadian Football League stadium, at that—so fans in the center-field bleachers sat a mile (or rather a kilometer) from home plate. At least the bleachers were covered; the grandstand was not. Astroturf and cozy dimensions kept hitters happy (330 feet down the lines, 400 to center). But the frigid Toronto weather—snow covered the field for the first game in 1977, and high winds caused a game to be canceled in 1984—and an abundance of birds made Blue Jays fans happy to leave Exhibition for SkyDome in 1989.

Fate: Demolished in 1999.

Metrodome, Minneapolis

Home of the Minnesota Twins, 1982–present

It might be the shortest dome in history (186 feet high), and it is certainly one of the ugliest. The 23-foot-high wall in right covers seats that are used for football and is called "the Baggy" because of its resemblance to a trash bag. Past manipulation of the air conditioning ducts—and, therefore, ball flight—helped the team's offense, but a bigger advantage is the way the place traps noise and disrupts opponents. The dome, which is held in place by air pressure, has twice deflated temporarily.

Fate: Currently hosts the Twins and the NFL's Vikings, though the Twins have plans to move to a new park in 2010.

Minute Maid Park, Houston (formerly Enron Field)

Home of the Houston Astros, 2000–present

Houston has one of the quirkiest parks in the game. While the "Crawford Boxes"—so dubbed because that's the street on which they're located—make left field ridiculously short, a drive to more distant left-center must pass over a hard-to-see line that determines a home run. "Tal's Hill," named after team president Tal Smith, is downright dangerous, as it requires center fielders to race up a 30-degree hill to catch 430-foot pokes. Smith modeled this hill after a slope in old-time Crosley Field in Cincinnati, but while Crosley's slope was there of necessity (to bring the field level closer to street level), Tal's Hill was built merely as a quirk. While navigating the hill, outfielders also have to avoid running into the flagpole that is planted in center field.

Fate: Currently hosts the Astros.

"Stengelese"

Casey Stengel spent 55 years as a player and manager with a style, a sense of humor, and a language uniquely his own. As he might have put it: "There comes a time in everyone's life, and I've had plenty of them."

Charles Dillon Stengel was born in Kansas City, Missouri, in 1890 and made his major-league debut with the Brooklyn Trolley Dodgers in 1912. A fair hitter and outfielder, Stengel played 14 seasons, mostly with the Dodgers/Robins and New York Giants, where he worked under legendary managers Wilbert Robinson and John McGraw. He gained a reputation as a clown, which was cemented in 1918 when, as a member of the Pittsburgh Pirates, he gave booing fans at Ebbets Field the bird, literally—he removed his cap and out flew a sparrow. "The higher-ups complained that I wasn't showing a serious attitude by hiding a sparrow in my cap," he later said, "but I said any day I get three hits, I am showing a more serious attitude than a lot of players with no sparrows in their hats."

"The Ol' Perfessor" skippered some of the best and worst teams of his time, amassing a 1,905–1,842 record over 25 seasons. After managing the talent-poor Dodgers (1934–36) and Boston Braves (1938–43), his break came when he was unexpectedly

---

Classic Stengelese

Stengel called rookies "green peas." A good fielder was a "plumber," and a tough ballplayer was someone who could "squeeze your earbrows off."

"Good pitching will always stop good hitting and vice versa."

"I don't know if he throws a spitball, but he sure spits on the ball."

"Being with a woman all night never hurt no professional baseball player. It's staying up all night looking for a woman that does him in."

named manager of the New York Yankees in 1949. His appointment was unpopular with fans and the press, who couldn't believe the stodgy franchise would hire such a joker, but Casey had the last laugh: His Yankees would win ten pennants and seven World Series titles over the next 12 years.

As a manager, Stengel proved to have a keen eye for talent, often using positional platoons and his bullpen brilliantly. ("The secret of managing is to keep the guys who hate you away from the guys who are undecided," he said.) His unique patois—stream-of-consciousness ramblings peppered with large amounts of humor and nuggets of truth and practicality—was known as "Stengelese." He was a master of the malaprop and the mixed metaphor, and with his humor and ability to turn a phrase, he engaged writers, deflected attention from his players, and sparked interest in his clubs. These qualities were useful throughout his career, especially when managing the dismal expansion New York Mets, whom he led from their founding in 1962 until a hip injury midway through the 1965 season ended his professional career at age 75. He was inducted into the Hall of Fame a year later.

◖◖ ◖◖ ◖◖

"Can't anybody here play this game?"

—Manager Casey Stengel on his 1962 Mets team,
which went 40–120

◖◖ ◖◖ ◖◖

"Ruth, Gehrig, Huggins, somebody get that ball back to the infield!"

—Casey Stengel, reacting to a Yankee outfielder fumbling for a ball among the center-field monuments at Yankee Stadium

Learning the Lingo

To live in the world of baseball, one must speak the language.

Alibi Ike: An excuse-maker. **Origin:** A fictitious nickname often used by famed baseball writer Ring Lardner.

Antkiller: A hard-hit ball on the ground. Also known as a "worm-burner" or "wormkiller." **Origin:** Descriptive.

Baltimore chop: A base hit achieved when the batter chops down on the ball, causing a high bounce that allows the batter to arrive at first base safely before the ball is fielded. **Origin:** Baltimore refers to the home city of the Orioles, for whom Wee Willie Keeler and his mates of the 1890s perfected the art.

Bird-dog: A scout, particularly a freelancing local who alerts regional scouts of finds. **Origin:** Hunting term.

Breaking his dishes: A hard pitch in on the hands. Also called "getting in his kitchen." **Origin:** Descriptive of shattering the bat, like a dropped dish, or the kitchen, where the dishes are kept.

Clutch: A critical situation, or how a player performs in such. **Origin:** Industry. The clutch is a key part of machinery.

Crank: Fan. **Origin:** Common 19th-century word for "fan."

Ducks on the pond: Runners on the bases. **Origin:** Expression favored by Washington announcer Arch McDonald.

Frozen rope: A hard line drive. **Origin:** Descriptive.

Golden sombrero: To strike out four times in one game. **Origin:** An exaggeration of the common sporting phrase "hat trick," which indicates three of something. Originated in cricket, where a bowler who gets three wickets in a row is awarded a hat. A sombrero is a large, gaudy Mexican hat. A player who strikes out five times in a game is said to have a "platinum sombrero."

Hot dog: A flashy player, often a show-off. **Origin:** From the word "hot" and the popular ballpark fare. The term "hot dog," a variation of "dachshund sausage," gained popular usage from concessionaire's calls at ballgames. A player "hot dogging it" is trying to attract the same kind of fan attention a hot dog might command over other refreshments at a ballgame.

Iron Mike: A pitching machine with a mechanical arm. **Origin:** Military slang for a man who's tough and durable.

Junior circuit: The American League. **Origin:** The AL is the newer of the two leagues, founded in 1901. The National League (1876) is referred to as the "senior circuit."

Knock: A hit. **Origin:** Descriptive of the sound of the bat hitting the ball.

Message pitch: An inside pitch used to back a player away from the plate. **Origin:** Descriptive. Sometimes called a "purpose pitch."

Pull the string: To fool a batter with an off-speed pitch. **Origin:** Descriptive of a ball arriving later than the hitter anticipated, as if pulled back by a string.

Rhubarb: A heated argument or fight on the field, usually between manager and umpire. **Origin:** In acting, extras often repeat the word "rhubarb" to one another to simulate audible but indiscernible background talking. Such incessant chatter is often a feature of manager-umpire confrontations.

Stone hands: A poor fielder. **Origin:** Descriptive.

The World Series Earthquake

The real drama at the 1989 World Series between the A's and the Giants had nothing to do with baseball.

It measured 6.9 on the Richter Scale (7.1 surface-wave magnitude), claimed more than 60 lives, and injured thousands. Technically, the earthquake that rocked San Francisco at 5:04 P.M. on October 17, 1989, was the Loma Prieta Earthquake. But it's known as the World Series Earthquake.

Bay Area neighbors Oakland and San Francisco were squaring off for the ultimate prize. While people in the region were affected by the quake no matter what they were doing, the nation experienced the tragedy through the eyes of World Series television cameras. ABC Sports play-by-play announcer Al Michaels was reading taped highlights during the Game 3 pregame show when millions across the country heard him utter the words, "I'll tell you what—we're having an earth..."

Screens went black. When backup power kicked in, the images were powerful. Among them: chunks of concrete falling from an upper-deck section of Candlestick Park; Commissioner Fay Vincent looking dazed after nearly being knocked out of his seat near the Giants' dugout; players from both teams leading their wives and children onto the field, away from the stadium's walls.

Though the old stadium shook, the walls held, and no one inside was seriously hurt. Some players clung to their families on the field, thankful for their safety. Others remained lighthearted, not knowing the severity of the damage outside the stadium. It was only on their way home that many people learned they had just survived the area's strongest quake since the 8.3 monster of 1906.

The Series resumed ten days later with a tribute to those who had lost their lives. A moment of silence was observed at 5:04 P.M., followed by the singing of "San Francisco," an unoffical city anthem. The ceremonial first pitch was thrown by representatives of public safety and volunteer organizations who responded to the disaster. Oakland then completed a bittersweet sweep on a stage that wound up being far more about life than baseball.

The Land of the Rising Major League Star

America's pastime has become the most popular game in Japan, producing some of today's top North American major-leaguers.

It was a question John McLaren had never been asked before. In fact, it was a question the Seattle Mariners bench coach had never *heard* before. It came from members of the enormous Japanese media contingent covering Ichiro Suzuki in their native son's first major-league spring training in 2001.

"I threw Ichiro a lot of batting practice early," McLaren said, referring to the scene before an exhibition game in Arizona. "One day they came up to me and said, 'Yesterday, Ichiro took 214 swings. Today, he took 196. What's wrong?'

"What's wrong? Nothing. I've never known anyone to count batting-practice swings. But they watch absolutely everything he does."

Ichiro arrived in America as Japan's greatest hitter. The same media mayhem took place when that nation's top home run hitter, Hideki Matsui, debuted in the major leagues with the New York Yankees two years later. And when the two squared off in a game for the first time on April 29, 2003, at Yankee Stadium, millions of fans in Japan tuned in at 8:00 A.M. local time to witness what Fuji television announcer Yoshi Fukushima described in the telecast as "the biggest moment in Japanese baseball history, especially [since it occurred] at Yankee Stadium, the House that Ruth Built."

Baseball Fever Begins

In the early part of the 20th century, such a scene would have been difficult to imagine. It was not Japanese players in America who captured headlines, but rather the American stars who made trips to Japan in an effort to globalize the game. Eleven years after Japan's first pro team, the Nihon Undo Kyokai, was formed in 1920, a group of major-leaguers that included Lou Gehrig and Lefty Grove arrived for a tour. In 1934, the great Babe Ruth joined Gehrig, Al Simmons,

Jimmie Foxx, Charlie Gehringer, and Lefty Gomez for a 17-game swing that enthralled Japanese fans. Though the Americans easily won all of the exhibitions, Ruth's 14 home runs and antics in right field—including a memorable inning he played while holding an umbrella—won over a growing nation of baseball enthusiasts.

Superstars of Japanese Ball

It was rarely as easy for major-leaguers to dominate such meetings once the game took hold on Japanese soil. The Japan Pro-Baseball League launched in 1936, and by the 1950s the country was churning out some impressive talent. Tetsuharu Kawakami, known as the "God of Batting" or "Japan's Lou Gehrig," hit .364 in a 1956 exhibition series against the Dodgers that saw the Japanese team claim four games. Shigeo Nagashima won five Japanese MVP Awards, and in 1966 his torrid hitting helped Japan take nine of 17 games against the Dodgers in another major-league exhibition tour. And perhaps the biggest name of all was Sadaharu Oh, the world's all-time home run king. Oh slugged 868 professional home runs in 22 seasons, topping major-league home run champ Barry Bonds by more than 100.

Central vs. Pacific

As Japan's love affair with baseball began to produce these stars on the diamond, the sport grew in the Land of the Rising Sun in much the same way it did in North America. In 1950, two major leagues were formed—the Central and the Pacific. Large stadiums were built, most notably the massive Tokyo Dome in 1988. Salaries soared, and competition for top players became intense. Dynasties emerged, led by the Yomiuri Giants, a team that has captivated fans and earned the unofficial nickname "Japan's Team." Some liken the following the Giants have in Japan to that of the Yankees in the United States, and their championship legacy follows a similar pattern as well: The Giants have won more pennants and Japanese Series Championships than any other team, including nine in a row beginning in 1965. Like the Yankees, they also draw the biggest stars to their lineup, including the likes of Oh and Matsui.

The Silent Treatment

While the Japanese have embraced America's pastime, they have also put their own spin on the game. This is particularly noticeable in the stands. Led by "oendan," or cheerleaders, Japanese fans are known to sing, chant, and make noise using drums, horns, and whistles to root for their teams. They do not boo the opposition, so when the visiting team bats, the stadium goes nearly silent. When the Yankees were in Tokyo playing the Hanshin Tigers in an exhibition series in 2004, Jack Curry of *The New York Times* described it as transforming "from a Metallica concert to a library in seconds." That silence, however, does not mean Japanese fans are not "into" the games. Quite the contrary: Baseball has far outpaced sumo wrestling as the most popular sport in the country, and now it is Japanese players who are helping to raise the caliber of play in North America.

Success in the States

In 1995, Hideo Nomo became the first Japanese-born major-leaguer in 30 years when he took the mound for the Los Angeles Dodgers. Nomo won 123 games and threw a pair of no-hitters during his 12-year big-league career, while position players such as Ichiro and Matsui have followed with great success of their own. Ichiro shattered George Sisler's 84-year-old major-league record for hits in a season when he smacked 262 in 2004, and he is the only player in history to start his big-league career with a run of eight successive 200-hit campaigns. Matsui played in 1,768 consecutive games spanning his career with Yomiuri and New York, and he is just the second player since 1940 to begin his major-league career with three straight 100-RBI seasons. Is it any wonder these guys have a global following?

Overcoming Disabilities

These players overcame physical limitations to make their mark on the game.

In baseball, as in other sports, success is based on individual ability and achievement, and physical shortcomings are routinely exploited by opposing players. Following are profiles of some players who entered the world of Major League Baseball with their own physical limitations.

William Ellsworth "Dummy" Hoy

The day William Hoy made his major-league debut in 1888, his Washington Nationals teammates arrived to find a handwritten note posted on the clubhouse wall.

"Being totally deaf as you know and some of my teammates being unacquainted with my play, I think it is timely to bring about an understanding between myself, the left fielder, the shortstop and the right fielder," the note began. "The main point is to avoid possible collisions with any of these four who surround me when in the field...." Hoy's note went on to explain that, as center fielder, his teammates should listen for him to yell, indicating that he would make the play on a fly ball. "Whenever you don't hear me yell, it is understood I am not after the ball." Though teammates would describe Hoy's yell as more of a squeak, they understood him perfectly.

Rendered deaf and mute as the result of a childhood bout with meningitis, "Dummy" Hoy enjoyed a 14-year career in which he amassed 2,044 hits, 1,426 runs, 40 home runs, 594 stolen bases, 726 RBI, and 273 assists as an outfielder with six teams. As his teammates learned, he was a magnificent fielder and a fine hitter (posting a .287 career batting average)—one of baseball's first stars to overcome a physical handicap.

On May 16, 1902, Hoy came to bat against Luther "Dummy" Taylor of the Giants in the first matchup in baseball history of a deaf pitcher versus a deaf hitter. The opponents exchanged greetings in sign language, then Hoy singled.

Mordecai "Three Finger" Brown

Mordecai Brown turned childhood tragedy into professional success. While growing up on an Indiana farm, Brown lost his right index finger just below the knuckle when he got his hand caught in a corn grinder. Shortly afterward, with his hand still in a cast, he fell and broke the pinky and middle fingers on the same hand. Those fingers grew bent and misshapen.

Brown's deformed hand was an impediment to gripping a baseball, but through ingenuity and practice he developed a unique grip that produced baffling pitches with incredible movement. Not blessed with great velocity, Brown relied on movement, smarts, and remarkable control: He consistently ranked near the top of his league in fewest walks per innings pitched. "The main objective in pitching is to take the power away from the hitter," he told *The Sporting News*. "Keep him from putting too much wood on the ball."

In an era of low scoring, Brown stood out as a run preventer: His ERA was below 2.00 for five straight seasons beginning in 1906. Over a 14-year Hall of Fame career, he won 239 games and fashioned an ERA of 2.06—fourth best in the history of baseball—while leading the Chicago Cubs to two world championships and four National League pennants.

Giants ace Christy Mathewson was one of Brown's toughest opponents. The Hall of Famers faced one another 25 times, with Brown winning 13 of the games, including a stretch of nine victories in a row. After one such game, exasperated Giants manager John McGraw reportedly examined Brown's hand and remarked, "I'm going to have the first finger on the throwing hands of every one of my damned pitchers cut off tomorrow."

Pete Gray

An accidental fall off a wagon when he was six years old cost Pete Gray nearly his entire right arm. Faced with this limitation, he developed a fierce determination to overcome it.

Gray channeled that resolve toward a career in baseball. He taught himself to make solid contact swinging a bat with his left arm only, and he used a customized glove that he would deftly tuck beneath his stub when fielding. He worked his way from semipro ball through the minor leagues, winning over doubters and garnering Southern Association MVP honors with the Memphis Chicks in 1944.

The following year, with many of the best major-league players off to war, Gray was signed by the St. Louis Browns, who saw the addition of a disabled player as both a gate attraction and a message to wounded war veterans. Gray understood this and with a grim resolve made the most of the opportunity, hitting .218 and striking out just 11 times over 253 plate appearances in 77 games.

Bert Shepard

Shepard was a left-handed pitcher for the Bisbee Bees in the Texas–Arizona League when he joined the Army to serve in World War II. He flew 20 combat missions in Europe before his plane was shot down over Berlin in May 1944, and when he awoke in a German hospital he found his right leg had been amputated just below the knee. Needless to say, baseball officials were surprised when Shepard arrived at Washington Senators camp in 1945 anxious to resume his career.

"I had been an athlete all my life," said Shepard, "and I promised myself the day I found my leg was off I would continue to be one."

He made the club as a coach, batting-practice pitcher, and goodwill ambassador, pitching in a series of benefit exhibitions. Shepard's courage and determination were an inspiration to the country at a time when hundreds of young men were returning with injuries like his. On August 4, 1945, after the Red Sox had battered two Washington pitchers for 12 runs in the fourth inning, Shepard entered the game and struck out Catfish Metkovich to end the rally. He followed with five more innings of one-run, three-hit ball in a 15–4 Washington loss. It turned out to be Shepard's one and only appearance in a big-league game, though he continued to pitch in the minors until 1954.

Jim Abbott

"I wanted to be like Nolan Ryan. I didn't want to be like Pete Gray."

Such were the boyhood dreams of Jim Abbott, a Flint, Michigan, native who sought a baseball career despite having a right arm that ended just above the wrist. Abbott didn't want to be accepted into the majors as an oddity, which was the reason many believe one-armed Gray caught on in the war-depleted summer of 1945. Abbott yearned to succeed on his talent alone, and in the end he would do so—but not without becoming a reluctant hero.

Born in 1967, just as his hero, Ryan, was breaking in with the Mets, Abbott taught himself to transfer his glove from his right arm to his left hand by throwing against a brick wall. He later said that his missing hand "wasn't really an issue when I was a kid." By becoming an expert fielder, he kept hitters from using the logical tactic of bunting against him to their advantage. During his college career he racked up a 26–8 record at the University of Michigan, won a gold medal in the 1988 Olympics, and took home the Sullivan Award in 1987 as the nation's best amateur athlete.

After being selected by the California Angels in the first round of the 1988 draft, Abbott became one of a handful of players in history to completely bypass the minor leagues, then overcame a media circus to go 12–12 as a rookie with the 1989 Angels. More great moments would follow—including a 1993 no-hitter for the Yankees—and it wasn't long before he had gotten his wish. He was simply Jim Abbott—pitcher.

⚾ ⚾ ⚾

"God gave me an unusual arm. I've done well with it, and maybe I can keep doing well with it. I certainly don't see anything to be angry about."

—Sandy Koufax's response when asked if he was bitter about having arthritis at age 28, *The Baseball Life of Sandy Koufax*

⚾ ⚾ ⚾

"To know for sure, I'd have to throw with a normal hand, and I've never tried it."

—Mordecai "Three Finger" Brown, when asked if his curveball was aided by the mangled fingers on his pitching hand

All-Time Great

Josh Gibson

This catcher may have been the greatest power hitter of all time.

Born: December 21, 1911; Buena Vista, GA
MLB Career: None. Kept out of the majors by the color line. Played in Negro Leagues 1930–1946.
Hall of Fame Resume: Some say he hit nearly 900 home runs in his career, as many as 75 in one season.
Inside Pitch: Although Gibson was hardly talkative, he did have one famous quote: "A homer a day will boost my pay."

The statistics are sketchy, the stories only hearsay from people who have little documentation to prove their points. The Negro Leagues operated under constraints that made keeping close track of player performance an impossible task, but those who watched these relegated stars usually agreed on one thing: No one hit a baseball farther and with greater frequency than catcher Josh Gibson.

Growing up in Pittsburgh, Gibson began playing semipro ball as a teenager and, as legend has it, was watching the Negro League Homestead Grays in action when he was pulled from the stands and put behind the plate after the Grays catcher hurt his finger. A star on the Grays within a year, the stocky, 6'2" right-handed batter moved on to the Pittsburgh Crawfords in 1934. There, he played alongside fellow future Hall of Famers Judy Johnson, Oscar Charleston, and James "Cool Papa" Bell in black ball's version of "Murderer's Row." On occasion, Gibson also formed half of the most intimidating battery in Negro League history, along with pitching Hall of Fame legend Satchel Paige.

Gibson was fun-loving and popular among his teammates, and he drew high praise from both black and white players for his abilities. In fact, he was known as "the black Babe Ruth." Roy Campanella said Josh was "the greatest ballplayer I ever saw." Walter Johnson claimed he "catches so easy, he might as well be in a rocking chair." Jimmy Powers of the *New York Daily News* wrote in 1939, "I am positive that if Josh Gibson were white, he would be a major-league star," an argument Gibson supported by blasting three homers off Hall of Fame pitcher Dizzy Dean in two exhibition matchups.

One set of partial Negro League statistics credits Gibson with 146 home runs and a .362 average in 501 games spread over 16 seasons (in Negro League games alone). In reality, he may have slugged as many as 84 homers annually playing in more than 200 contests a year in winter (in the Puerto Rican League), spring, and summer combined. Sometimes the Crawfords or Grays (to which Gibson returned for his last five seasons) secured big-league ballparks for their games, and stories abound of Gibson belting homers to the deepest points of Comiskey Park and Yankee Stadium. Hitting home runs farther than 500 feet was reportedly not unusual for Gibson.

Pirates owner William Benswanger and Senators boss Clark Griffith both claimed an interest in bringing Josh to the majors, but the man with an estimated 850 to 900 home runs was still blasting them for the Grays when Jackie Robinson signed with Brooklyn in 1945. Gibson might still have made the big leagues, but struggles with alcohol and illness shrouded his final years, and he died of a brain hemorrhage at age 35 in January 1947—three months before Robinson's debut with the Dodgers.

◎ ◎ ◎

"If they came to Josh Gibson today and he were 17 years old, they would have a blank spot on the contract and they'd say, 'Fill the amount in.' That's how good Josh Gibson was."

—Junior Gilliam

◎ ◎ ◎

"Josh, I wish you and Satchel [Paige] played with me on the Cardinals. Hell, we'd win the pennant by July 4 and go fishin' until World Series time."

It Happened One Day

When the stars aligned for one day of glory,
these players turned in the game of their life.

Some of these men had long and glorious careers; others were journeymen. But what they have in common is that for one day (or night), they put together a game for the ages. Some single-game sensations are detailed elsewhere (like Harvey Haddix's 12-inning no-hitter—see page 17—and Don Larsen's perfect World Series game—see page 118). Here are other highlights.

Jim Abbott

September 4, 1993. Jim Abbott was born without a right hand, but the combination of his athleticism and dogged determination brought him to the bigs. The highlight of his baseball career happened when, as a member of the New York Yankees, he dominated the Cleveland Indians by throwing a no-hitter. Jim walked five batters, but there was never an inning that featured more than one man on base. And the Indians lineup that day featured Albert Belle, Manny Ramirez, and Jim Thome.

Joe Adcock

July 31, 1954. It was a hot, humid day in Brooklyn, so the Milwaukee Braves' Adcock wasn't wasting time taking pitches from Dodger hurlers. He came out swinging, and in five at-bats rapped four homers and a double off four different pitchers, needing only seven pitches to do it. The record he set for total bases in a game (18) wouldn't be broken for 48 years.

Jim Bunning

June 21, 1964. Bunning had seven children, which may be why he pitched his best game on Father's Day. The Phillie hurler faced just 27 Mets that day and struck out ten of them. He also doubled in a pair of runs to add to his 6–0 perfect-game win. Manager Gene Mauch said, "We knew when he was warming up that this was something special."

Ty Cobb

May 5, 1925. Thirty-eight-year-old Cobb, never a power hitter, tired of hearing how super Babe Ruth was, and announced he was going for a home run that day. And did he ever! He swatted three out of the park, tacked on two singles and a double, and set a still-standing AL record for total bases in a game (16). Only two other American Leaguers had ever homered three times in one game. (Ruth wouldn't do it for five more years.)

Ed Delahanty

July 13, 1896. Some historians will tell you that Delahanty was the greatest right-handed hitter ever. They could point to this day as proof. Only one person (Bobby Lowe) had ever homered four times in one game before, and this day at Chicago, Delahanty singled his first time up and then crushed four inside-the-park homers. After the last one, the opposing pitcher was there at home to shake his hand.

Shawn Green

May 23, 2002. It took six Milwaukee Brewer pitchers to get through this Thursday afternoon game at Miller Park, and Dodger Shawn Green was having a lot of fun leading the L.A. attack. He went 6-for-6 with four homers, a double, and a single, and he knocked home seven runs as his team dominated the Brewers 16–3.

Catfish Hunter

May 8, 1968. The 1960s were definitely an era of the pitcher: Hunter's perfect game against the Minnesota Twins on this date was the third perfecto in the decade. He fanned 11 Twins in the game. Hunter's A's won 4–0, and Catfish joined in the batting fun, too, driving in three of the runs himself and hitting one out of the park.

Addie Joss

October 2, 1908. Both the National and American League pennant races were exceptionally tight in 1908. Cleveland, Detroit, and Chicago were within percentage points of each other in the AL when Cleveland's immensely likable Joss faced off against rugged 40-game-winner Ed Walsh of the White Sox. Walsh was excellent, pitching a four-hitter and fanning 15. But Joss was perfect. He faced 27 batters and not one reached first.

Rick Wise

June 23, 1971. The story is told that in 1971, Wise was complaining about the lack of offense from his teammate Phillies' bats and said, "To win around here, you have to pitch a shutout and hit a homer." He did even better than that on this day: He pitched a no-hitter against the Reds (only one batter reached base, on a walk) and slugged two homers. One was a two-run dinger.

Four-Homer Hitters

Including Adcock, Delahanty, and Green mentioned above, only 15 players have hit four homers in one game. It is a rarer feat than pitching a perfect game. Six men have done it on consecutive at-bats: Bobby Lowe for Boston, May 30, 1894; Lou Gehrig for the Yankees, June 3, 1932; Rocky Colavito for Cleveland, June 10, 1959; Mike Schmidt for the Phils, April 17, 1976; Mike Cameron for Seattle, May 2, 2002; and Carlos Delgado for Toronto, September 25, 2003. Schmidt drove in eight runs that day in a windy, 18–16, 10-inning win over the Cubs. Chuck Klein hit four for the Phillies on July 10, 1936, while Pat Seerey of the White Sox did it in 11 innings on July 18, 1948. Dodger Gil Hodges accomplished the feat on August 31, 1950; Giant Willie Mays slugged a quartet on April 30, 1961; and Brave Bob Horner bopped four on July 6, 1986. Mark Whiten slugged four out of the park on September 7, 1993, for the Cardinals and tied the major-league record for single-game RBI with 12.

Magical Moment

Gibson limps to plate, swats walk-off blast.

The Setting: Dodger Stadium; October 15, 1988
The Magic: An injured Kirk Gibson leaves the bench to pinch-hit a game-turning homer that gets the Dodgers rolling in the Series.

When Kirk Gibson, an All-American football star at Michigan State, signed with his hometown Tigers, many people compared him to Mickey Mantle. No one with his combination of speed and power had come along since the great Mick. In his second full season (1984), Gibson helped power the Tigers to a World Series victory, clubbing two upper-deck homers in the decisive Game 5 to seal Detroit's triumph over the San Diego Padres.

As a Dodger in 1988, Gibson was such a critical part of the team's success that he won the National League MVP Award despite posting stats that looked less than sensational. And he was superb in the League Championship Series. But when the World Series started, he wasn't even in the lineup; a bad left hamstring and a swollen left knee had him in street clothes when the game began. But with two out in the last of the ninth and a Dodger on base, Gibbie was called on to hit against Oakland's future Hall of Fame closer Dennis Eckersley. Gibson looked bad on the first two pitches, but he worked the count to 3–2 before reaching out on a backdoor slider and yanking the ball into the right-field seats. He limped around the bases

as the crowd went wild. In his only at-bat of the Series, Gibson gave the Dodgers a win over the favored A's, propelling them to a 4–1 Series win.

Presidential Pitches

The Oval Office is okay, but there's no place like the ballpark.

On April 14, 1910, President William Howard Taft attended the Senators' Opening Day game against the Philadelphia A's at National Park. Seeing him in the stands, umpire Billy Evans called on President Taft to throw out the first ball. Taft's toss began a tradition of first pitches that has been carried on by every American president since then, with the exception of Jimmy Carter.

Presidential first pitches have featured dramatic and comedic highlights—and lowlights. Following are some of the more memorable first-pitch moments.

William H. Taft: When making his trendsetting first pitch in 1910, Taft had a Hall of Fame partner. Washington Senators ace Walter Johnson, who was normally on the pitching end of the baseball battery, received Taft's historic throw. President Taft gave Johnson the ball the next day with the following inscription: "To Walter Johnson with hope that he may continue to be as formidable as in yesterday's game. William H. Taft."

Two years later, Taft missed the opener in Washington while tending to the aftermath of the *Titanic* disaster. Vice President James Sherman filled in for Taft, throwing out the first pitch on April 19 before a scant crowd of just over 10,000 fans.

Woodrow Wilson: Wilson ventured out of the nation's capital to become the first president to attend a World Series game. On October 9, 1915, Wilson threw out the first pitch at Philadelphia's Baker Bowl, moments before Game 2 of the Series matchup between the Boston Red Sox and the Philadelphia Phillies.

Franklin Delano Roosevelt: A true fan of the game, FDR holds the record for most Opening Day first pitches (eight) and overall first pitches (11). In FDR's case, practice didn't make perfect: At the 1940 opener in Washington, Roosevelt made an errant toss, breaking the camera of a *Washington Post* photographer.

Harry Truman: Due to World War II, Roosevelt refrained from visiting major-league ballparks in 1942, '43, and '44. Truman ended the presidential drought when he threw out the first pitch before a game between the Senators and the St. Louis Browns on September 8, 1945. Truman's return to the ballpark signaled that baseball, which had been depleted because of players' involvement in military service, was now back to full strength.

John F. Kennedy: An avid fan of the Boston Red Sox, JFK stayed to watch every inning of the four games he attended while in office. As president, he threw out the first pitch at the newly built D.C. Stadium in 1962. The stadium was later renamed in honor of Kennedy's brother Robert.

Lyndon Johnson: In 1965, Johnson was supposed to throw out the first pitch at the exhibition game that marked the opening of the Houston Astrodome, but he arrived late and missed the opportunity. Three years later, Johnson missed the Opening Day game in Washington, which had been delayed because of the assassination of civil rights leader Martin Luther King, Jr. Vice President Hubert H. Humphrey attended the rescheduled Washington opener in Johnson's absence.

Richard Nixon: Arguably the most knowledgeable baseball fan of all American presidents, Nixon took part in a unique first-pitch ceremony on April 6, 1973. A former POW named Major Luna and Nixon, who was participating in his first ceremonial toss away from the city of Washington, both threw out first pitches before the game at Anaheim Stadium in California. According to Dick Young of the *New York Daily News,* Nixon was not just "a guy that shows up at season openers to take bows and get his picture in the paper and has to have his secretary of state tell him where first base is. This man knows baseball."

Gerald Ford: At the 1976 All-Star Game, the athletic president thrilled fans by doing double duty: throwing out one pitch right-handed to Johnny Bench of the Cincinnati Reds and a second pitch left-handed to Carlton Fisk of the Boston Red Sox.

Jimmy Carter: Carter once told Commissioner Bowie Kuhn that he preferred playing sports to watching them, which explains why he attended only one major-league game while in office—the seventh game of the 1979 World Series between the Orioles and the Pirates. Carter chose not to throw out the first pitch on that occasion, and he remains the only president since Taft who has not thrown one.

Ronald Reagan: A die-hard fan of baseball and a former radio baseball broadcaster, Reagan attended a World Series game between the Baltimore Orioles and Philadelphia Phillies on October 11, 1983, but declined an opportunity to throw out the first pitch due to security reasons. Five years later, Reagan threw out two first pitches at Wrigley Field and then joined the legendary Harry Caray in the broadcast booth to announce the game for an inning and a half. "You know, in a few months, I'm going to be out of work," joked the outgoing president, "and I thought I might as well audition."

George H. W. Bush: The elder Bush became the first sitting president to attend a major-league game north of the border. On April 10, 1990, Bush traveled to Toronto to throw out the first pitch before a matchup between the Blue Jays and his beloved Texas Rangers. Two years later, Bush joined Hall of Fame slugger Ted Williams in throwing out dual first pitches at the All-Star Game in San Diego.

George W. Bush: The younger Bush continued the old tradition into the new millennium, throwing out the first pitch at the first game ever played at Milwaukee's Miller Park on April 6, 2001. Later that year, he became the first president to throw out the first pitch before a World Series game being played at Yankee Stadium.

His visit to New York occurred on October 30, less than two months after the terrorist attacks of September 11, and was part of an effort to restore normalcy to the nation.

President	No. of "First Pitches"	Year(s)
William H. Taft	1	1910
Woodrow Wilson	4	1913–1916
Warren Harding	3	1921–1923
Calvin Coolidge	6	1924–1928
Herbert Hoover	4	1929–1932
Franklin Delano Roosevelt	11	1933–1941
Harry Truman	8	1945–1952
Dwight Eisenhower	7	1953–1960
John F. Kennedy	3	1961–1963
Lyndon Johnson	3	1964–1967
Richard Nixon	3	1969–1973
Gerald Ford	2	1976
Ronald Reagan	3	1984–1988
George H. W. Bush	8	1989–1992
Bill Clinton	3	1993–1996
George W. Bush	6	2001–2008

🏀 🏀 🏀

"Nolan says throw it high because amateurs get out there, no matter how good they are, and throw it in the dirt. You get more of an 'ooooh' [from the crowd] if you heave it over the [catcher's] head instead of going with the fast-breaking deuce into the dirt."

—George H. W. Bush on advice Nolan Ryan gave him on throwing out the first pitch while president

The Wobbly History, and Mystery, of the Knuckleball

The no-spin zone.

The knuckleball is delivered softly so as to limit spin, thus exposing the ball and its seams to vagaries of aerodynamics and wind resistance that physicists have labeled "Bernoulli's principle" and "the Magnus effect." Batters just see the pitch as an unpredictable series of whirls, flutters, and drops.

The pitch has been thrown in various forms since the 19th century but owes its name to infamous junkballer Eddie Cicotte, who unveiled the pitch as a member of the Red Sox in 1908.

Cicotte gripped his pitch by steadying his knuckles against the surface of the ball, a style that is rarely used today. Practitioners of the pitch contend there is no "correct" way to grip a knuckleball: Limiting the ball's rotation is all that matters, which is why there are as many different knuckleball grips as there are knuckleball pitchers. "There are no patents on this delivery," said Cicotte.

Knuckleballers come around at a rate of only a few per generation, in part because the pitch is so difficult to master. "It takes a fanatical dedication that most people don't have," knuckleballer Charlie Hough told *The New York Times*.

The same dedication is required of catchers, who find that receiving a knuckeball is often more difficult than hitting one. Bob Uecker, the broadcaster and former catcher, is fond of saying the best way to catch a knuckleball is to "wait'll it stops rolling, and go to the backstop and pick it up."

Baseball's process of natural selection works against knuckleballers, too: Few teams have the patience or inclination to develop them, and scouts tend to search for attributes in amateur talent—the ability to light up a

radar gun, for example—that simply aren't useful skills when delivering a pitch that rarely exceeds 70 miles per hour.

As a result, many prominent knuckleballers are accidental pitchers. Tim Wakefield was a low-ceiling infield prospect in the Pirates system when a coach caught him fooling around with a knuckleball and subsequently convinced him to give pitching a try.

Others, like Hough and Tom Candiotti, developed knuckleballs only after they were forced to abandon other pitches due to arm injuries or ineffectiveness. And occasionally, a position player who is called in to pitch in a blowout—Todd Zeile and Jose Canseco are two examples—uses the opportunity to experiment with his own knuckler, frequently with disastrous results.

In its purest form, the knuckleball is thrown completely without spin—pushed rather than flung. Its slow flight to home plate is marked by massive turbulence caused by the ball's raised stitches disrupting the flow of air around the sphere. Willie Stargell described it as "a butterfly with hiccups."

Hoyt Wilhelm, who debuted at age 28 and provided relief work until he was 49, and Phil Niekro, who threw knuckleballs almost exclusively throughout his 318-win career, are recognized as baseball's greatest flutterballers. Both are members of the Hall of Fame. Several major-league knuckleballers, including Candiotti and Wakefield, have since worn uniform number 49 as a tribute to Wilhelm.

In 2008, Wakefield was the only knuckleballer pitching regularly in the majors, but don't fret, knuckle fans: Several were working in the minors, and in November 2008, a team in the Japanese League even drafted a 16-year-old schoolgirl, Eri Yoshida, because of her wicked knuckler. When the next great knuckleball artist arrives, he (or she!) will join an exclusive club that includes, among others, Wilbur Wood, Steve Sparks, Eddie Fisher, and Jim Bouton.

◐ ◐ ◐

"There are two theories on hitting the knuckleball. Unfortunately, neither of them work."

—Charlie Lau

Kangaroo Court

Hear Ye! Hear Ye! Kangaroo court is now in session.

The sight of George "Boomer" Scott in a black robe and white wig in the Milwaukee clubhouse in the 1970s could only mean one thing: kangaroo court. Frank Robinson, who later became Major League Baseball's "director of discipline," trained for that job wearing a mophead for a wig in Baltimore's kangaroo court in the 1960s. Such courts in baseball date back to the late 19th century, but the purpose today remains the same: Promote camaraderie, punish stupidity.

The kangaroo court was a fun way for a team to "punish" a player for doing something stupid either on or off the field. It allowed teammates to become more aware of things they were doing wrong, in a way that promoted unity. The "judge" was usually someone with seniority—or an especially good sense of humor. (Don Baylor and Steve Reed both excelled in the role.) The fines imposed were collected and used for a party or given to charity at the end of the season.

Mishaps on the field—throwing to the wrong base, multiple whiffs, missing signs, forgetting the number of outs—ranked high on the list of offenses. Off the field, there were even more ways to get on the court's bad side: making out in public, wearing a hideous outfit (and in the heyday of the kangaroo court in the 1970s, there were lots of questionable clothing decisions), or fraternizing with the "enemy." No one, from batboys to team owners, was safe from the court's watchful eye and imposition of justice.

Kangaroo courts have become rare these days, though they do happen occasionally. Teams today are more of a collection of independents, and they tend to be friendlier with the opposition, thus eliminating one of the major infractions. Some players are just too touchy for the ribbing that goes along with the fines. Many young players aren't even aware of the lore of the kangaroo court. But for those who took part, the court was about more than pointing out mistakes—it was a way to bring the team together (and have a lot of fun in the process!).

Hot Hitting

Some hitters get on a roll and just keep connecting, knocking out hits in game after game. Here are the longest hitting streaks in MLB history.

Joe DiMaggio

1941, New York Yankees

56 games

During his streak, which ran from May 15 until July 17, DiMaggio went 91-for-223, hitting .408. He had 16 doubles, four triples, and 15 home runs, along with 55 RBI. Perhaps most impressive was the fact that DiMaggio's team won 41 of the 56 games. After it ended, DiMaggio hit safely in his next 16 games. After the 41st game, in which DiMaggio tied George Sisler for the AL record, a fan swiped his bat; he had to use Tommy Henrich's in the second game of the doubleheader to move past Sisler. In the middle of the streak, Joe had a hit in the All-Star Game, too.

In front of the largest night game crowd in history to that point—67,468 at Cleveland Municipal Stadium—DiMaggio was stopped, largely due to two sensational plays by Indians third baseman Ken Keltner on hot smashes over the bag.

Even the 56-game streak wasn't DiMaggio's longest—in the minors, he'd had a 61-game streak, which shattered the previous record of 49. Joe's brother Dom had an impressive 34-game streak of his own for the Boston Red Sox in 1949.

Willie Keeler

1897, Baltimore Orioles

45 games

It was the greatest start to any season ever: Keeler hit safely in his first 44 games. Technically, since he had hit in the final game of the 1896 season, he really had a 45-game streak. Throughout his career, Keeler also had two 26-game hitting streaks, and he had 200 or more hits per season eight years in a row, from 1894 to 1901; this record stood for more than a century until Ichiro matched it in 2008.

Pete Rose

1978, Cincinnati Reds

44 games

Pete Rose had banged his 3,000th career hit on May 5, 1978, and most people figured that would be his outstanding accomplishment for the year. But then on June 14, the 37-year-old Rose started a 44-game streak. (DiMaggio was only 26 when he posted his streak in 1941; Keeler was 25 in 1897.) Rose finished that season at .302, with 51 doubles. The closest he came to having his streak snapped early was in its 32nd game on July 19 against Philadelphia. Rose was hitless when he came to bat in the ninth, but he managed a bunt single in the 11th to keep the streak alive. The Atlanta Braves finally held Rose hitless on August 1, after 70 hits over 44 games. The next day he had four hits.

Bill Dahlen

1894, Chicago Colts

42 games

Dahlen was a talented shortstop who also had a knack with the bat. After having his 42-game streak snapped on August 7, he smacked hits in 28 consecutive games, meaning he hit in 70 out of 71 games.

George Sisler

1922, St. Louis Browns

41 games

Sisler had 23 multiple-hit games during his streak, and he batted .460. He had 14 doubles and seven triples but not a single homer during that time. He finished the season with a .420 average, the fourth-highest since 1901, and he was named the American League MVP.

Ty Cobb

1911, Detroit Tigers

40 games

Cobb's bat was on fire during this streak—he batted .476 with 40 runs, 12 doubles, eight triples, and one home run—and so were his feet: He stole home three times. Cobb also had hitting streaks of 35, 25, and 21 games (twice) during his remarkable career.

Paul Molitor
1987, Milwaukee Brewers
39 games

Of all the major-league hitting streaks, Molitor's came to the most bittersweet end. He had gone 0-for-4 against Cleveland rookie John Farrell and was on deck waiting to bat against Doug Jones when his teammate Rick Manning delivered the game-winning hit in the bottom of the tenth.

Jimmy Rollins
2005–06, Philadelphia Phillies
38 games

Some people take issue with this mark since it was accumulated over two seasons. Rollins batted safely in 36 games in 2005, then, seven months later, in two more. But since the official rule for a streak is "consecutive games in which the player appears," Major League Baseball considers it a 38-game streak.

Tommy Holmes
1945, Boston Braves
37 games

This was just the centerpiece of a monster year for Holmes, in which he batted .352 with 117 RBI, scored 125 runs, and had 15 stolen bases. He led the league in hits, homers, and doubles. Unfortunately, the rest of his team wasn't as good, and he finished second in the MVP voting to the first-place Cubs' Phil Cavarretta. Holmes went on to have 20-game streaks in 1946 and 1949.

All-Time Great

Honus Wagner

The only player from his era who is still arguably the all-time greatest at his position.

Born: February 24, 1874; Chartiers (now Carnegie), PA
MLB Career: Louisville Colonels, 1897–99; Pittsburgh Pirates, 1900–17
Hall of Fame Resume: Led NL in batting eight times • Led NL in doubles seven times • Led NL in RBI and steals five times each • Eighth on the all-time hits list
Inside Pitch: His first name is not pronounced "Hoe-nus" but "Hah-nus." He was the first player to have his name inscribed on a Louisville Slugger bat.

Often mentioned alongside Ty Cobb as the greatest dead-ball-era players produced by each league, Johannes Peter Wagner could not have been more different from his AL contemporary. The Pride of the Pirates was a genuine Mr. Nice Guy, as modest and even-tempered as Terrible Ty was vicious and bull-headed. Most famous these days as the guy whose 1910 baseball card could pay for a new house and a college education, "The Flying Dutchman" also happened to be a .327 lifetime hitter with a National League–record eight batting titles and 722 stolen bases. He was also the greatest defensive shortstop this side of Ozzie Smith.

Supposedly discovered by Ed Barrow while he was tossing coal chunks at a boxcar near his tiny Pennsylvania hometown, Honus demolished minor-league pitching for parts of three years before joining Louisville of the NL as an outfielder in 1897. Squat (5′11″, 200 pounds) and bowlegged with a long, beaked nose, Wagner didn't look like a ballplayer—until he got on a field. Once there, the right-handed, barrel-chested slugger with deceptive speed hit .299 and .336 his first two full seasons, with more than 100 RBI per year.

The Louisville franchise shifted to his hometown of Pittsburgh in 1900, and Wagner celebrated by collecting his first National League batting title with a career-high .381 mark. He also led the NL in doubles (45), triples (22), and slugging (.573), despite hitting just four homers. While leading the league in RBI (126 and 91) and stolen bases (49 and 42) each of the next two seasons, he hit .353 and .330 as the Pirates won back-to-back NL pennants.

After playing as many as five positions in a season without one to call his own, Wagner thrived after being made Pittsburgh's starting shortstop in 1903. While becoming the game's best fielder at short, he developed a rifle arm and used his huge hands to scoop up everything hit near him. He also hit .350 with seven batting titles over the next nine seasons, earning the first in '03 when he hit .355 with 101 RBI, 46 steals, and a league-high 19 triples to power the Pirates to their third straight league championship.

Wagner repeated as batting champ in 1904 at .349, and was second at .363 the next year before winning four more crowns in a row. Though he never hit more than ten home runs in a season, he paced the league in slugging six times as the classic dead-ball power hitter— leading the NL seven times in doubles, collecting ten or more triples 13 times (with a high of 20 in 1912), and notching 100 or more RBI on nine occasions (leading the league on five occasions). The five-time stolen-base king swiped 40 or more eight straight years and 20-plus for 18 consecutive seasons.

Retiring at age 43 in 1917 as the National League's career leader in hits (3,415), runs (1,736), doubles (640), and triples (252), the charter Hall of Famer still ranks high on each list. The Flying Dutchman became a Pirates coach at age 59 and stayed on for 18 years, keeping himself young and spinning many a yarn about the good ol' days.

Make Way for the Men in the 'Pen

Relief is just two pitches away.

The idea of a "relief pitcher" being someone who helps *win* the game was unheard of for the first 50 years of baseball. Usually called a "change pitcher," a reliever was brought in to take the beating when the main pitcher was getting wracked.

Frequently during the first several decades of the 20th century, a team's primary starter would be given a chance to protect a lead late in the game. The first "relievers" were players like Mordecai "Three Finger" Brown, Ed Walsh, and Christy Mathewson. The term "relief pitcher" was first mentioned in *Harper's Weekly* in 1914.

Using starters in the clutch remained the rule into the 1930s. Firpo Marberry of Washington was the first pitcher to specialize in relief in the 1920s, and he became the first reliever to register 100 saves. However, this was noted retroactively, because saves didn't become an official stat until decades later.

In 1969, longtime Chicago sportswriter Jerome Holtzman encouraged baseball to adopt the "save" as a formal statistic. This came about and, for the first time in history, a single stat changed the way the game was played on the field. The save gave management a way to measure the performance of their best relievers. Around 1978, closers came to be used for only one full inning and only when their teams were ahead by three runs or less—in other words, when they were in a "save situation." This choice forced managers to create a new job in their bullpens: the "setup man"— that's the person who pitches the inning or two leading up to the ninth. The era of the man who could pitch almost every day had essentially disappeared.

The importance of relief pitchers has increased considerably in the last decade. Today, a reliever is not brought in simply to close the game. There are many types of relief pitchers, such as a long reliever, who comes in any time between the first inning and the fourth inning to get the game under control. There's even a left-handed specialist, a pitcher whose job is to retire left-handed batters.

If anyone doubts that relief pitchers have drastically changed the game, just look at how much (or how little) starting pitchers are being asked to pitch today. In 2004, the National League had 71 complete games. The total was almost twice that five years earlier, and five times that just 25 years before. In 2005, the American League had 85 complete games; in 1980, that number was 549. No pitcher has had ten complete games in a season in either league since 1999.

There are signs that the use of the closer is changing. Although 40 saves is no longer unusual, Bobby Thigpen's 57 for the White Sox in 1990 held as the most saves in one season—until 2008, that is, when Francisco Rodriguez of the Angels racked up 62.

The first reliever to earn 200 career saves was Hoyt Wilhelm. The first with 300 was Rollie Fingers in 1982. Lee Smith landed his 400th save in 1993 and retired as the leader with 478, until Trevor Hoffman passed him in 2006.

⚾ ⚾ ⚾

"When your horse is out there and pitches his butt off, my job is to nail it down."

—Trevor Hoffman

⚾ ⚾ ⚾

"I came into situations that God couldn't get out of, and I got out of them. I'm not blowing my own horn, but this is just fact. Nobody did it like me."

—Goose Gossage

⚾ ⚾ ⚾

"I call [Mariano Rivera] 'the Equalizer.' I mean, I can't tell you how comforting it felt to have him come in when I left the game."

—Roger Clemens

Groundskeeping 101

A soft mound, a swampy outfield, a puddle surrounding first base. These are just some of the tricks groundskeepers have used to help their teams walk away with victories.

"A good groundskeeper can be as valuable as a .300 hitter," Indians' owner Bill Veeck once said. He would have known: Veeck's head groundskeeper was Emil Bossard, who spawned a legacy that has helped keep the "home" in home field advantage.

Bossard had a big job in Cleveland from the 1930s to the 1950s as caretaker for League Park and Municipal Stadium, the two fields used by the Indians at the time. He built the mound tall when fireballer Bob Feller pitched, and he kept the grass on the left side thick, as player-manager Lou Boudreau requested. When slugging clubs like the Yankees came in, the outfield grass was left especially long and wet to turn their doubles into singles. And that's not all. Years later, Roger Bossard confessed that his grandfather used to move the portable fence back 10 to 15 feet against the Yankees to diminish their power. Interestingly enough, Cleveland was the only American League team to win multiple pennants during the Yankees' run from 1941 to '64.

The Bossards branched out. Harold and Marshall took over for their father in Cleveland. Brother Gene followed Veeck to Chicago's Comiskey Park, where, in 1959, the club won its only pennant in 88 years. Gene watered down the field—earning Comiskey the nickname of "Camp Swampy"—and kept baseballs in a freezer to cut down on home runs by slugging opponents. Grandson Roger maintains Comiskey's successor

(U.S. Cellular Field) and claims to be one of the last groundskeepers to know the special maneuvers used by previous generations. "I won't let the tricks die," he told the Sports Turf Managers Association. ESPN listed the Bossard family as seventh on the all-time list of baseball cheaters.

Other groundskeepers took to drowning the field to help ensure victory. During the 1962 best-of-three playoff between the San Francisco Giants and Los Angeles Dodgers, for example, Candlestick Park groundskeeper Matty Schwab stepped in to give his players an edge. At the behest of Giants manager Alvin Dark, the ground around first base was soaked to slow Dodgers speedster Maury Wills. While umpire Jocko Conlan made Schwab work to dry out the right side of the infield, the left side went untouched and remained a sponge to slow down grounders. The Giants won the game (Wills never reached base), and shortstop Joe Pagan fielded eight chances flawlessly. The Giants went on to win the pennant. Schwab, who'd been lured from the Dodgers to the Giants back when the teams were in New York, received a full World Series share. Dark would forever retain the nickname "Swamp Fox."

But Schwab was not alone in his tactics, nor was he alone throughout baseball history. The Tigers grounds crew regularly drenched the area around home plate so Ty Cobb's bunts would stay fair. The Indians' crew watered down third base to protect Al Rosen, who broke his nose nine times while fielding ground balls. Kansas City groundskeeper George Toma, among others, wet the mound and then let it bake in the sun when the opposing pitcher was Catfish Hunter, who preferred a soft mound. If a team wants to use every possible advantage, they might as well start with the ground beneath their feet.

◎ ◎ ◎

"Fenway Park in Boston is a lyric little bandbox of a ballpark. Everything is painted green and seems in curiously sharp focus, like the inside of an old-fashioned peeping-type Easter egg."

—John Updike, *The New Yorker*

Larry Doby:
First in the AL

Recognition for a man who often found himself overshadowed.

Larry Doby must have resigned himself to finishing second. In 1947, he made his debut for the Cleveland Indians, becoming the second African American to play major-league baseball in the 20th century. Three decades later, Doby became the second black man to manage a major-league team. (Frank Robinson was the first, for the Cleveland Indians in 1975.) Yet, Doby never publicly complained about being a bridesmaid. He handled his role as a secondary baseball pioneer with dignity and grace, thereby advancing the cause for other African Americans who would succeed him.

Doby starred in the Negro Leagues from 1942 to 1947, though he did lose some of that time to service in World War II. His abilities as a hard-hitting second baseman caught the attention of Cleveland Indians owner Bill Veeck, who was aggressively seeking black talent for his major-league team in 1947. In the early days of July, Veeck arranged to purchase Doby's contract from the Newark Eagles. Veeck paid $15,000 to Eagles owner Effa Manley for Doby, who was hitting .414 at the time.

Jackie Robinson had broken the game's color barrier only 11 weeks earlier, making his Brooklyn Dodgers debut on April 15. Unlike Robinson, Doby did not receive the benefit of playing minor-league ball, which would have allowed him to make a gradual transition to the majors. Instead, Veeck brought Doby directly from the Negro Leagues to the Indians.

Veeck also laid out some ground rules. "He sat me down and told me some of the do's and don'ts," Doby recalled. "Don't even turn around at a bad call at the plate, and no dissertations with opposing players—either of those might start a race riot."

On July 5, Veeck personally escorted Doby to Comiskey Park, where the Indians were playing the Chicago White Sox. Doby didn't start the game but would immediately find himself tested. He was called upon to pinch-hit in the seventh inning with two men on base, but he struck out, swinging and missing badly at the third strike. It didn't matter. In the larger scheme, Doby had arrived—second overall, but the first black player in American League history.

Over the years, historians have carefully examined the racism that Jackie Robinson faced from teammates, opponents, and fans during his early days in the majors, but the similar obstacles that Doby faced have not received nearly as much scrutiny. Like Robinson, Doby heard insults from opposing players and taunts from fans who didn't want a black man sharing the diamond with his white counterparts. Most of Doby's teammates showed him a cold indifference, but a few were outright nasty and rude; some even refused to shake Doby's hand before his first game. On one occasion, an opposing player spit on Doby as he slid into second base, but he chose not to retaliate. "I couldn't react to [prejudicial] situations from a physical standpoint," Doby once said. "My reaction was to hit the ball as far as I could."

Doby's debut season did not unfold as dramatically as Robinson's. While Robinson played well enough to win the National League Rookie of the Year Award and helped the Dodgers advance to the World Series, Doby played sparingly and flailed at the plate, hitting only .156 in 32 at-bats. But Doby rebounded in 1948: He became the Indians' regular center fielder, hit .301 with 14 home runs, and helped Cleveland clinch the AL pennant.

Although baseball's color barrier had delayed his major-league career, Doby diligently overcame the late start. By the time his career ended, he had qualified for seven All-Star teams, led the American League in home runs twice, and finished second in MVP voting in 1954. In 1978, he was again hired by Veeck, this time to manage the White Sox.

Doby didn't always end up in second place. He was the first African American to lead his league in home runs, the first to hit a homer in the World Series, and the first to be on a Series-winning team (the Indians in 1948). Coupled with his performance in the Negro Leagues, Doby's many pioneering accomplishments helped earn him election and induction to the National Baseball Hall of Fame in 1998. Always a man of great strength and dignity, Doby passed away in 2003 at the age of 79.

Greatest Games of All Time

1986 NLCS, Game 6

Mets 7, Astros 6

The Setting: The Astrodome, Houston, TX

The Drama: Three runs by the Astros in the first, three by the Mets in the ninth, one each in the 14th, then five total in the 16th—the longest postseason game in history was also one of the most dramatic.

Some call this the greatest game ever played. That may be true, considering the game's length (4:42) and its importance. Had the Mets lost, they would have been forced to face Astros ace Mike Scott again. Scott had held them to one run in two complete-game victories in the series while striking out 19.

These were the first two NL expansion teams, both born in 1962. This was the Mets' third trip to the postseason—they had won the NLCS in 1969 and again in '73. The Astros' only previous postseason appearance had been in 1980, when they lost in five games to Philadelphia in the NLCS.

The Mets lost Game 1 of this series to Scott, with Glenn Davis's second-inning homer accounting for the game's only run. Bob Ojeda pitched a complete game in Game 2 to get the Mets even. After the Mets scored four times in the sixth inning of Game 3 to tie the score, the Astros took a one-run lead in the seventh. But in the bottom of the ninth, Wally Backman bunted himself on and Lenny Dykstra slugged a homer to win it for New York. Game 4 was another Scott victory.

Game 5 went 12 innings, as 39-year-old legend Nolan Ryan faced 21-year-old superstar Dwight Gooden. The two clubs were knotted at one run each after nine innings, but Backman singled in the 12th, then scored the winning run on a Gary Carter single.

The Mets hoped to get off to a good start in Game 6, but it was the Astros who jumped ahead. They scored three times off Ojeda and would have had more but for a bungled suicide squeeze attempt. Another baserunning blunder cost Houston a scoring chance in the fifth. But it didn't matter to Bob Knepper, who held the Mets to two hits through eight innings.

Dykstra led off for the Mets in the ninth, pinch-hitting for Rick Aguilera, and promptly whistled a triple into center field. Mookie Wilson followed with a hard single, and one batter later Keith Hernandez belted a double that brought Wilson home. The Mets were within one run.

Dave Smith replaced Knepper on the mound, but his control was erratic. Consecutive walks to Carter and Darryl Strawberry loaded the bases, and Ray Knight stroked a long fly to right to bring Hernandez home. The Mets had fought their way back to a tie.

Neither team could push across any more runs through the 13th inning, as Roger McDowell held the Astros in check and Smith and Larry Andersen teamed up to stifle the Mets.

In the top of the 14th, Carter singled and Strawberry walked. A too-hard bunt by Knight forced Carter at third, but Backman came through again, singling in the lead run. As the Mets took their one-run lead into the bottom of the ninth, they turned to their relief ace, Jesse Orosco, to close the door. Orosco retired the first hitter in the bottom of the 14th, but next up was clutch hitter Billy Hatcher, who knocked a home run into the foul-pole screen in left. The Astros had dramatically retied the game.

The Mets came rolling back again, scoring three times in the top of the 16th thanks in part to some sloppy Astros play. Hatcher misplayed a Strawberry pop-fly into a double, then Knight singled him home. A walk to Backman and two wild pitches by Jeff Calhoun, followed by another Dykstra base hit, sent New York into the last of the 16th up by three. The Astros were backed into a corner.

But again the Astros came back with a roar. With one out, pinch hitter Davey Lopes reached base with a walk. Both Bill Doran and Hatcher singled to bring one run home. After a force-out at second, Davis—the hero of Game 1—also came through with a single. The score was 7–6, with two out and two on.

Orosco and Kevin Bass battled it out to a 3–2 count before Bass chased an Orosco slider and missed. The Mets jubilantly stormed to the mound and mobbed Orosco at the end of the longest post-season game ever played.

Below the Mendoza Line

These guys believed Ted Williams when he said that hitting was the hardest thing to do in professional sports.

Great hitters receive the fans' adulation and respect. It's not an easy thing to hit a baseball, much less do it with power and precision. In fact, there are plenty of men who make a career of professional baseball but never quite master what seems to be such a basic skill.

Bill Bergen, Catcher
947 games • 3,028 ABs • 2 HRs • 193 RBI • .170 BA • .194 OBP
    Most notoriously weak hitters don't maintain careers for as many as 900 games; Bergen, who played for Cincinnati and Brooklyn from 1901 to 1911, was one of the exceptions. He set a record in 1909 for the lowest season batting average by a player with enough plate appearances to qualify for the batting title when he hit .139 in 346 at-bats. But what he lacked in hitting skills, he made up for behind the plate. Considered an exceptional catcher and handler of pitchers, Bergen caught a majority of his teams' games for more than half his career.

John Vukovich, Third Base
277 games • 559 ABs • 6 HRs • 44 RBI • .161 BA • .203 OBP
    During a ten-year career with the Philadelphia Phillies, Milwaukee Brewers, and Cincinnati Reds, Vukovich had 559 at-bats—roughly equivalent to one season's worth. He batted .161 with six home runs, 44 RBI, and 29 walks while striking out 109 times. In spite of those numbers, Vukovich managed to last a decade in the majors because of his slick fielding at third base, a willingness to play anywhere on the infield, and a professional work ethic that helped him become a highly respected coach.

Doug Flynn, Second Base
1,308 games • 3,853 ABs • 7 HRs • 284 RBI • .238 BA • .266 OBP
    Flynn is best remembered for being one of the players the New York Mets acquired in 1977 as part of the Tom Seaver trade with

the Cincinnati Reds. Well, Flynn didn't make anyone forget "Tom Terrific." Although an adept fielder, which kept him in the starting lineup for some weak Mets teams, Flynn finished his career with a batting average, on-base percentage, and slugging percentage all below .300. In a total of 1,308 games, Flynn hit a mere seven home runs, with four of those coming during the 1979 season.

Mario Mendoza, Shortstop
686 games • 1,337 ABs • 4 HRs • 101 RBI • .215 BA • .245 OBP
Mendoza was a brilliant defensive shortstop who would have been better off bringing his glove to the plate. His hitting futility in the 1970s gave birth to a brand-new baseball term: the "Mendoza Line." Since Mendoza rarely hit above .215 (his career average) for the Pittsburgh Pirates, Seattle Mariners, and Texas Rangers, anyone who hit below that figure was said to be hitting "below the Mendoza Line." Some baseball observers have adjusted the line to the .200 mark, making the Mendoza club even more exclusive (though not a club players are anxious to join).

Darrel Chaney, Shortstop
915 games • 2,113 ABs • 14 HRs • 190 RBI • .217 BA • .296 OBP
Chaney was a switch-hitter, but that didn't help him much. He struggled to hit against both left-handers and right-handers. Managing to last 11 seasons with the Cincinnati Reds and Atlanta Braves because of his versatility and slick glove, Chaney swatted a grand total of 14 home runs and posted a pathetic lifetime slugging percentage of .288. He never hit higher than .252 in any one season (1976 was his best year), but he did hit .201 or worse six times in his career (with a low of .125 in 10 games in 1971).

Bob Gilks, Outfield
339 games • 1,385 ABs • 1 HR • 142 RBI • .231 BA • .265 OBP
A 19th-century outfielder who played with Cleveland in the American Association before joining the National League, Gilks was a smart player who used to cleverly trap balls in the outfield and then start double plays against unsuspecting baserunners. Unfortunately, smarts didn't help Gilks at the plate. Playing with

the Cleveland Spiders and Baltimore Orioles of the National League, Gilks had no power and wasn't good at getting on base (a lifetime on-base percentage of .265). He also never managed to hit higher than .238 in a full major-league season.

Jack McGeachy, Outfield

608 games • 2,464 ABs • 9 HRs • 276 RBI • .245 BA • .265 OBP

Another 19th-century player who unskillfully swung a bat, McGeachy compiled a lifetime batting average of .245 with only nine home runs over six seasons in the dead-ball era. A veteran of the National League, the Players League, and the American Association, McGeachy didn't draw many walks, either; he reached base just 26.5 percent of the time.

Ted Beard, Outfield

194 games • 474 ABs • 6 HRs • 35 RBI • .198 BA • .315 OBP

Formally known by his birth name of Cramer Theodore Beard, this Pittsburgh Pirate and Chicago White Sox of the 1940s and '50s might have been the worst-hitting outfielder of all time. Gifted with the glove, Beard managed to last seven seasons in the majors, but his lack of hitting limited his playing time. He had little power, compiling a career slugging percentage of .285 while batting just .198. A look at these statistics explains why he never had more than 177 at-bats in a single season.

Ron Herbel, Pitcher

332 games • 206 ABs • 0 HRs • 3 RBI • .029 BA • .065 OBP

This right-hander for the San Francisco Giants, San Diego Padres, New York Mets, and Atlanta Braves was a moderately successful reliever, but he faced a monumental struggle each time he strode to the plate with a bat in his hand. In his 206 major-league at-bats, Herbel collected a total of just six hits. Of those, none were home runs. His lifetime average? A miniscule .029—the lowest batting average ever for a player with at least 100 at-bats. If ever a pitcher needed a designated hitter, it was Herbel; unfortunately, he had already retired by the time the American League adopted the DH rule in 1973.

Who in the Hall?

1) Which two future Hall of Fame second basemen were traded for each other in 1926?

A: Rogers Hornsby and Frankie Frisch

2) Which Hall of Famers are the only three pitchers inducted with a losing record in the major leagues?

A: Satchel Paige, Rollie Fingers, and Bruce Sutter

3) Who in the Hall is also a member of the Mexican and Cuban halls of fame?

A: Martin Dihigo

4) Who once pitched two nine-inning complete games on the same day three times in the same month?

A: "Iron" Joe McGinnity (winning all six)

5) Who in the Hall of Fame stole second, third, and home in the same inning four times?

A: Ty Cobb

6) Which Hall of Famer is the only player to play every inning of every game in a season, straight through the World Series?

A: Cal Ripken, Jr. (of course!) in 1983

7) Whose 81-year-old, NL-record 44-game hitting streak did Pete Rose break in 1978?

A: Willie Keeler

8) Who holds the major-league record with 24 consecutive pitching wins?

A: Carl Hubbell

9) Who is the Hall's only pitcher never to have started a game?

A: Bruce Sutter

Money Talks

Who was worth more: Babe Ruth or Todd Hollandsworth?

The following numbers, when dragged from the years of Cobb and Ruth into the present and adjusted for inflation, seem both remarkable and absurd. Babe Ruth making less than Todd Hollandsworth? Wagner, Cobb, and Gehrig all earning less than Ryan Vogelsong, a right-handed hurler with an ERA of 5.86 who played only three full seasons in the majors? Or high-priced pitcher Kris Benson, who tore his rotator cuff and didn't pitch a game in 2007 or 2008? What's going on here?

The difference, of course, is the amount of money baseball takes in nowadays as opposed to the days of old. Back then there was no television revenue, very little radio, and almost no merchandising. Teams had to make do with ticket sales, the profit on the hot dogs and sodas they sold, and what they could make selling players. Today we include stadium naming rights and plush skyboxes, parking revenues, and shares of merchandise earnings. George Steinbrenner bought the Yankees in 1973 for $10 million; today, some estimates put the team's value at $1 billion.

Year	Player	Annual pay	Inflation-adjusted value today
1900	NL salary limit	$2,400	$57,700
1910	Nap Lajoie	$12,000	$267,000
1910	Honus Wagner	$18,000	$401,000
1915	Ty Cobb	$20,000	$395,900
1930	Babe Ruth	$80,000	$938,000
1934	Dizzy Dean	$3,000	$46,400
1936	Lou Gehrig	$36,000	$526,100
1939	Joe DiMaggio	$26,500	$712,000
1946	MLB minimum	$5,000	$55,700
1957	Don Newcombe	$30,000	$224,600

Year	Player	Annual pay	Inflation-adjusted value today
1958	MLB minimum	$7,000	$49,900
1959	Ted Williams	$125,000	$866,500
1968	MLB minimum	$10,000	$60,000
1969	Willie Mays	$145,000	$836,600
1970	MLB minimum	$12,000	$65,600
1980	Nolan Ryan	$1,000,000	$2,756,500
1981	Dave Winfield	$2,000,000	$4,856,400
1988	StL Cardinals median	$240,000	$422,600
1989	MLB average	$512,000	$866,000
1990	Mark Davis	$2,125,000	$5,164,600
1992	MLB average	$1,084,000	$1,469,400
1994	Cal Ripken, Jr.	$5,500,000	$7,480,500
1996	StL Cardinals median	$625,000	$822,600
2001	Todd Hollandsworth	$1,450,000	$1,782,000
2001	MLB average	$2,264,000	$2,659,600
2005	Alex Rodriguez	$26,000,000	$29,126,300
2006	MLB minimum	$327,000	$354,900
2006	Ryan Vogelsong	$555,000	$602,300
2006	StL Cardinals median	$1,000,000	$1,085,200
2006	Kris Benson	$8,333,000	$9,043,000
2008	Brad Lidge	$11,500,000	$11,500,000

The Founding Father Fallacy

It's a great story that's been passed from one generation to the next. It's also a work of fiction.

"The first scheme for playing Baseball, according to the best evidence available to date, was devised by Abner Doubleday at Cooperstown, N.Y. in 1839."

That finding, announced after a three-year study by the Mills Commission in 1907, is the main reason the tiny central New York hamlet was chosen to be the home of the National Baseball Hall of Fame and Museum. This "creation myth" has since been debunked from so many angles that it seems positively ridiculous now, but it was accepted as truth back then.

Had Abner Doubleday truly invented baseball in 1839 in Cooperstown, New York, as so many generations of children have been told over the years, pundits could answer the question "Why Cooperstown?" in far fewer words. As it stands, the response requires a little more explanation.

So why Cooperstown? "The answer involves a commission, a tattered baseball, a philanthropist, and a centennial celebration," says the Hall of Fame in its official statement. The commission was the brainchild of sporting goods tycoon Albert G. Spalding in 1905, in response to a story that baseball had evolved from the British game of rounders.

The baseball in question was an old, tattered, homemade ball that had been discovered in a dusty attic trunk in a farmhouse near Cooperstown in 1934. It became known as the "Doubleday Ball," and it served to support the commission's 1907 findings. Singer sewing machine magnate Stephen C. Clark purchased the "Doubleday Ball" for $5 in 1935 and pushed for the construction of the Hall of Fame in Cooperstown. The museum's opening was planned to coincide with a "century of baseball" celebration set to take place in Cooperstown in 1939. Thanks largely to Clark and his family, the Hall of Fame opened its doors in June of that year.

Even before the Hall of Fame opened, many people questioned the findings of the Mills Commission, which said that

Doubleday, a West Point cadet and Union general in the Civil War, had set down rules for a game of "town ball," in which a group of Cooperstown boys were going to take on a group from a neighboring town. The tale was based largely on the testimony of Abner Graves, a retired mining engineer who claimed to have witnessed the event. But historians later learned that Graves's testimony was questionable at best and that baseball's presumed "founding father" was likely not in or even near Cooperstown in 1839.

Abner Doubleday's credibility as the inventor of baseball wasn't helped by the dozens of diaries he wrote after retiring from the United States Army in 1873. None of the diaries include any mention of baseball, and neither did the Abner Doubleday obituary that was published in *The New York Times* 20 years later.

In fact, the Hall of Fame plaque of Alexander Cartwright credits *him* as the "Father of Modern Base Ball." Cartwright, a New York bank teller and a talented draftsman, organized the first regular team, which he called the New York Knickerbockers. Rather than play "town ball," where team scores could top 100, Cartwright devised rules for a game that would feature bases that were 90 feet apart on a diamond-shape infield, nine players per side, a three-strikes-and-you're-out policy, and "force outs" at first base if the ball got to the infielder before the runner—all rules that have stood the test of time. The first game played under Cartwright's rules took place at the Elysian Fields in Hoboken, New Jersey, on June 19, 1846.

⚾ ⚾ ⚾

"Two hours is about as long as an American can wait for the close of a baseball game—or anything else, for that matter."

—Albert Spalding

These Pitchers Can Hit

Easy outs? Think again!

Nowadays a "good-hitting pitcher" is one who knows how to bunt, but the game has nearly always had one or two folks who, while they earned their salary on the mound, were stalwarts with the stick as well. Many of them even served as pinch-hitters for their team.

Jack Bentley

They were calling Bentley "the next Babe Ruth" in 1922, when he hit .349, second in the International League, in 153 games for the Baltimore Orioles (which was Ruth's first team, too). In 1923, he won 13 games for the pennant-winning New York Giants and hit .427 in 52 games. He also had two pinch hits in that year's World Series. In Game 5 of the 1924 Series, he slugged a two-run homer off Walter Johnson and pitched in three games, winning one. His lifetime batting average was .291; his ERA 4.01, with a 46–33 record.

Doc Crandall

Crandall was one of the game's first true relief pitchers, and his ability with the stick made him a valuable pinch hitter as well. He swatted the ball at a .285 clip for his career while posting a 2.92 ERA. He had a sensational season in 1910, when he won 17 games for the New York Giants, lost just four, and slugged his way to a .342 average while fashioning an impressive 2.56 ERA.

Wes Ferrell

Ferrell's 38 homers outdistance the career mark of any other pitcher, and his nine in 1931 are best for a pitcher in a single season. In 1935, he won back-to-back games with homers: one as a pinch hitter and one for himself. At age 40, he managed and played in the minors, where he won the batting title with a .425 average.

Mike Hampton

Mike Hampton didn't hit his first double until his third season in the majors, but before long he was topping the leader board for hitting by pitchers. In fact, he won the Silver Slugger Award for his position five years in a row. One year he had three doubles and three triples and knocked home ten runs. When he became a free agent, he moved to the hitter's paradise of Colorado, where in 2001 he slugged seven homers and drove in 16 runs.

Don Newcombe

In 1955, Newcombe had quite a year. Not only was he 20–5 for the pennant-winning Dodgers, but he hit .359 and set a National League record for homers by a pitcher in a season, with seven. Twice that season he hit two homers in one game. He even stole home once. His .271 lifetime average ranks among the best in major-league history for a pitcher.

Al Orth

This turn-of-the-20th-century pitcher banged out 389 career hits and was used as a pinch hitter 78 times. His lifetime average of .273 is one of the best marks ever for a pitcher, and he hit .290 or better seven times. Oh, and he also won 204 games.

Schoolboy Rowe

Rowe was more than just a pitcher who occasionally pinch-hit; he was counted on off the bench. In 1943, while playing for Philadelphia, he led the NL in pinch-hit appearances and pinch hits, going 15-for-49. He is one of just five pitchers ever to slug a pinch-hit grand slam.

George Uhle

In 1923, slider pitcher Uhle tore the American League apart. He won 26 games, threw 29 complete games, and pitched 357 innings, leading the league in all three categories. He also batted .361 that year, one of the highest marks ever for a pitcher. He hit a grand slam off Dutch Leonard in 1921, and he holds the highest career batting average (.289) of 20th-century pitchers (minimum 1,000 at-bats).

Managers Sound Off

"I believe in rules. I also believe I have a right to test the rules by seeing how far they can be bent."

—Leo Durocher, *Nice Guys Finish Last*

"Managing is never fun. If you pull off something big, it's expected. If you fail, you're a bum."

—Paul Richards, *Baseball's Greatest Managers*

"If you have to begin fining them, it's time to get rid of them."

—Hughie Jennings's managerial theory

"Show me a good loser, and I'll show you an idiot."

—Leo Durocher

"Don't pull that stuff on me. How can a pipsqueak like you be Babe Ruth's manager?"

—Doorman to Yankees skipper Miller Huggins

"I never questioned the integrity of an umpire. Their eyesight, yes."

—Leo Durocher

"You do things my way, or meet me after the game."

—Manager Frank Chance's supposed warning to his Cubs players

"Just give me a happy ballclub, and we'll be hard to beat."

—Billy Southworth, *Baseball's Greatest Managers*

On-Field Brawls

Baseball players might not rival hockey players as fighters, but there have been some memorable scraps on the diamond.

A lack of boxing or wrestling skills has not prevented several epic, dugout-clearing brawls in the majors. As former player and skipper Bill Rigney once said, "Baseball players are the worst fighters I've seen in my entire life."

Senators vs. Yankees (July 4, 1932)
This historic scrap did not take long to settle after Senators outfielder Carl Reynolds collided hard with Yankees catcher Bill Dickey on a play at the plate. As Dickey would later describe: "It was hot, the games had been close, and I had been banged around for days. When Reynolds came at me, I just had to hit somebody." So Dickey slugged Reynolds, breaking his jaw with one punch. The star catcher was fined $1,000 and suspended for 30 days.

Dodgers vs. Giants (August 22, 1965)
As these archrivals battled it out for the NL pennant, tensions ran high. Giants ace Juan Marichal had been backing the Dodgers off the plate all day, and Dodgers catcher John Roseboro had had enough. Putting a new twist on brushback pitches, he tried to fire the ball as close to Giants hitters as possible on his throws back to pitcher Sandy Koufax. Finally, after a Roseboro throw whizzed a little too close for comfort past his head, Marichal turned and bashed the Dodgers catcher on the head with his bat, opening a gash that required 14 stitches to close. It also triggered a 14-minute brawl and resulted in an eight-game suspension and $1,750 fine for Marichal.

Reds vs. Mets (October 8, 1973)
Pete Rose was never shy about playing physically, and in this NLCS game, with the Reds trailing 9–2, he tried to break up a fifth-inning double play by taking out Bud Harrelson at second base. Rose's hard slide started a scrap between the two players,

clearing the benches for a brawl that lasted ten minutes and saw Reds reliever Pedro Borbon tearing up a Mets cap with his teeth.

Shea Stadium fans showered Rose with trash when he took his place in left field in the top of the sixth inning, and Reds manager Sparky Anderson pulled his team from the field when a bottle nearly hit Rose. The umps finally succeeded in settling everyone down, and the game was eventually completed. The 9–2 score held up as the final, and the Mets took the series in five games.

Braves vs. Padres (August 12, 1984)

Some contend this game set baseball back 50 years. Braves starter Pascual Perez beaned Padre Alan Wiggins with the first pitch of the game; the Padres retaliated by throwing at Perez every time he came to bat. When Perez waved his bat at San Diego pitcher Ed Whitson after a fastball whizzed behind his helmet in the second inning, the fight-fest began. It started with a bench-clearing melee—the first of two in that inning. More brawling broke out in the fifth, eighth, and ninth frames. In the later innings, even the fans jumped onto the field to participate in the fray.

Eventually, five of those fans, one of whom had poured a beer over Kurt Bevacqua's head, and 14 game participants were ejected, managers Joe Torre and Dick Williams among them. After the game, Torre called Williams an idiot and compared his actions to those of Hitler. While Torre took some criticism for that comment, it was Williams who absorbed the worst punishment for his role in the altercation—a $10,000 fine and ten-day suspension.

Blue Jays vs. Red Sox (June 23, 1985)

Toronto's George Bell set the standard by which all "mound charges" are compared—if the goal is comedy, that is. Boston starter Bruce Kison beaned Bell and, instead of throwing a punch or trying to wrestle Kison, Bell charged the mound and tried a ridiculous karate kick. Kison easily avoided it, then dropped Bell with a nifty left hook. The laughs kept coming as the benches cleared: Blue Jays reliever Bill Caudill got into the action wearing an undershirt and unbuttoned pants.

Orioles vs. Yankees (May 19, 1998)

After Orioles closer Armando Benitez gave up an eighth-inning, go-ahead home run to Yankee Bernie Williams, he put a fastball between the shoulder blades of the next batter, Tino Martinez. Rather than waiting to get revenge when the Orioles came to bat, reliever Graeme Lloyd came charging from the bullpen to take a swing at Benitez. Yankee Darryl Strawberry took a swing at Benitez with what many called a sucker punch; it caused Strawberry to spill into the Baltimore dugout, where he was roundly pummeled by Alan Mills.

White Sox vs. Tigers (April 22, 2000)

Even hockey players were entertained by this one: "It was a pretty vicious fight for a baseball game," Chris Osgood of the Detroit Red Wings noted. It started when Tigers pitcher Jeff Weaver plunked Carlos Lee in the sixth inning. Chicago's Jim Parque retaliated against Dean Palmer in the seventh, prompting Palmer to throw his helmet at the pitcher. What followed was some of the best "real" fighting to ever take place on a baseball diamond. Sox pitcher Keith Foulke suffered a cut that required stitches. When Major League Baseball reviewed tapes of the bench-clearing incidents, they suspended 16 players—five more than the number ejected from the game.

Red Sox vs. Yankees (July 24, 2004)

The Red Sox and Yankees have scrapped no less than six times since 1938. This incident was the most notable. After being hit by a pitch in the third inning at Fenway Park, Yank Alex Rodriguez had words for Boston starter Bronson Arroyo as he made his way to first base. Red Sox catcher Jason Varitek stepped between the two, giving A-Rod a faceful of catcher's mitt before Rodriguez put him in a headlock. The benches cleared, and Yankees pitcher Tanyon Sturtze had his face bloodied in the fracas. Four players were ejected. The Red Sox had the last laugh, however: They heated up down the stretch and won the first World Series title for the franchise since 1918.

Learning the Lingo

To live in the world of baseball, one must speak the language.

Angler: A ballplayer who looks for endorsement opportunities.
Origin: Descriptive, from fishing.

Aspirin: A baseball, particularly when thrown hard. Also: *pill, pea.*
Origin: Descriptive. A ball resembles an aspirin when it's thrown
so fast it appears to the batter to shrink.

Bag: Base. **Origin:** From 19th-century equipment guides describing a base as a sack of sand or sawdust.

Balloon: A pitch that's easy to hit. **Origin:** Descriptive of a sphere
that's larger than a baseball.

Blue: An umpire. **Origin:** Historically, the color of their uniforms.

Brass: Team management. **Origin:** Military. Refers to insignias
on the uniforms of officers.

Bush: Unprofessional. **Origin:** Refers to "bush leagues."

Bush leagues: Minor leagues. **Origin:** Bushes indicate remoteness, as in, "Out there, where the bushes grow."

Can of corn: An easy basket catch. **Origin:** Refers to a grocer
retrieving canned goods from high shelves by pushing them with a
stick and allowing them to drop into his smock.

Cheese: A fastball, usually the pitcher's best pitch. Also "cheddar." **Origin:** British expression meaning "top quality."

Daisy cutter: A low line drive. **Origin:** Descriptive.

Fungo: Fielding practice retrieving hit balls, and the special bat used to hit those practice balls. **Origin:** Numerous theories, ranging from a combination of the words "fun" and "go," to the cricket expression "fun goes," to the German word "fungen," or catch.

Goose egg: Zero. **Origin:** Descriptive of the numeral. A pitcher who is throwing a shutout is said to be "throwing goose eggs."

Hose: An arm, usually a pitcher's. **Origin:** Descriptive.

Irregular: A bench player. **Origin:** Opposite of "regulars," or everyday players.

Junk: Pitches with movement but not velocity. **Origin:** Descriptive of the repertoire of a pitcher who doesn't have a good fastball.

Moneyball: An economic approach to team-building that exploits market inefficiencies that are revealed by advanced statistical analysis. **Origin:** The title of Michael Lewis's bestselling book about the Oakland A's and Billy Beane, their general manager.

Payoff pitch: A pitch delivered on a 3-and-2 count. **Origin:** Descriptive in that the pitch has potential to "pay off" for the batter (a walk) or the pitcher (a strikeout).

Stepping in the bucket: When a batter pulls away from a pitch with his front foot. **Origin:** Probably refers to the dugout, which often contains a bucket of water.

Texas Leaguer: A bloop single, similar to a dying quail or ducksnort. **Origin:** Named for the Texas League, where minor-leaguers of dubious skill might play.

Uncle Charley: A curveball. **Origin:** Unknown, but "uncle" suggests warm familiarity. An especially good curveball can be referred to as "Lord Charles." Occasionally called "Aunt Susie."

Magical Moment

Mac outslugs Sammy in the Great Home Run Chase.

The Setting: Busch Stadium, St. Louis; September 8, 1998
The Magic: Mark McGwire breaks Roger Maris's home run record, set in 1961.

Mark McGwire was a big home run hitter while he was still in college, and in his first full big-league season (1987) he broke the record for homers by a rookie (49)—a record, set by Boston Brave Wally Berger, that had stood for 57 years. McGwire slugged 52 homers in 1996, making him just the second man to top 50 since 1977. Dealt from Oakland to St. Louis in July 1997, McGwire finished the season with 58 homers, setting the record for most dingers hit without winning a home run title (he hit 34 in the AL and 24 in the NL).

Sammy Sosa, who had begun his career in 1989 with the Rangers and played for just over two seasons with the White Sox, was traded to the Cubs in 1992, where he came into his own as a power hitter. Through 1997, he hit 201 home runs.

Next up: the great home run derby of 1998. McGwire and Sosa put on a summer-long homer fest that kept the nation enthralled. McGwire started off the season by homering in March, then kept rolling with 10 in April, 16 in May, and 10 more in June. That month Sosa swatted a record-setting 20, and the race was on. It seemed that every fan in America chose one of the two sluggers to root for. McGwire slugged his 60th on September 5, his 61st two days later, and on the night of September 8, against Sosa's Cubs and with a national TV audience watching, Big Mac lined a Steve Trachsel fastball just over the left-field fence (it was his shortest homer of the year, but no one cared). Maris's record, which had stood for 37 years (three years longer than Babe Ruth's), had bitten the dust. McGwire finished the season with 70 homers; Sosa, 66. Three years later Barry Bonds would raise the single-season record to 73.

Baseball's Best Broadcasters

Besides being excellent announcers, each of these men became the living, breathing connection between a team and its town.

Mel Allen

New York Giants and Yankees, 1939–43
New York Yankees, 1946–64

After being fired by the Yankees (after 24 years!), Allen returned to the air a decade later on the national TV show *This Week in Baseball.* His voice was warm and mellifluous, and his signature phrase was "How 'bout that?" He nicknamed Joe DiMaggio "The Yankee Clipper" and Phil Rizzuto "Scooter," and his home run call was the simply perfect "Going, going, gone!"

Red Barber

Cincinnati Reds, 1934–38
Brooklyn Dodgers, 1939–53
New York Yankees, 1954–66

Red was first and foremost a reporter, yet his easy Southern tone and rural phrases were a big hit in Brooklyn. Among the expressions he helped introduce to baseball's lexicon were "rhubarb" (a real battle) and "catbird seat" (sitting pretty). When his Dodgers rallied, Barber said, "The boys are tearin' up the pea patch." He also trained two other broadcasting greats: Ernie Harwell and Vin Scully.

Jack Buck

St. Louis Cardinals, 1954–2001

Buck was so vital to the St. Louis baseball scene that Busch Stadium sports a statue of him behind a microphone. His trademark tag line, "That's a winner," was also the title of his autobiography. But his most famous call for the Cards came when non-slugger Ozzie Smith belted a homer to win Game 5 of the 1985 National League Championship Series. Buck hollered, "Go crazy, folks, go crazy!"

Harry Caray

St. Louis Cardinals, 1945–69
Oakland A's, 1970
Chicago White Sox, 1971–81
Chicago Cubs, 1982–97

He supposedly talked his way into his first interview and was told by the owner of St. Louis's largest station, "Your voice has an exciting timbre." Caray went on to share that excitement with fans for more than five decades, most notably in Wrigley Field. He was known for saying "Holy Cow!" and singing "Take Me Out to the Ball Game" during the seventh-inning stretch. His signature home run call was "It might be, it could be, it is!"

Ernie Harwell

Brooklyn Dodgers, 1948–49
New York Giants, 1950–53
Baltimore Orioles, 1954–59
Detroit Tigers, 1960–91, 1993–2002

His calm, intelligent style came about because he started his baseball career as a writer. For Harwell, who became known as "the voice of the Tigers," each game was a mini-seminar on baseball personalities, tactics, and history. One sports columnist said he had "authenticity."

Russ Hodges

Cincinnati Reds, 1932–33
Chicago Cubs and White Sox, 1935–37
Washington Senators, 1938–45
New York Yankees, 1946–48
New York/San Francisco Giants, 1949–70

He was the Giants' announcer in both New York and San Francisco, and his home run call was "Bye bye, baby!" But Hodges's spot in broadcasting history was secured after his famous call of the "Shot Heard 'Round the World"—Bobby Thomson's three-run homer in the last of the ninth of a playoff game against the Dodgers, which won the 1951 pennant for the men from New York. "The Giants win the pennant!" Hodges hollered . . . nine times.

Waite Hoyt
Cincinnati Reds, 1942–65

His style was described as "casual, sincere, matter of fact." Fellow broadcaster Russ Hodges said the result was an authoritative tone: "When Hoyt says it's so, the Cincinnati public goes by what he says." Radio listeners were entertained by the anecdotal stories Hoyt shared during rain delays; fans loved the stories so much that two record albums of "Hoyt's best" were released.

Bob Prince
Pittsburgh Pirates, 1948–75, 1982–85
Houston Astros, 1976

There was no more outrageous phrase-turner and home-team cheerleader than Pittsburgh's Bob Prince. If the Pirates were down by a run he'd announce, "All we need is a bloop and a blast." On a Bucco homer, Prince would roar, "You can kiss it good-bye." After every victory, he bellowed, "We had 'em all the way!"

Vin Scully
Brooklyn/Los Angeles Dodgers, 1950–present

In 1976, Dodger fans voted Scully the Most Memorable Personality in Dodger history. His tone and style are absolutely one-of-a-kind, and he always matches the rhythm of his perfectly parsed sentences to the action on the field. Some of his game calls are so notable, they have been transcribed and anthologized in books of baseball literature.

⚾ ⚾ ⚾

"The first rule for sports announcers might well hold true for the patrons in the park: Follow the ball. But this rule should be broken, or modified, to suit the occasion."

—Hall of Fame broadcaster Red Barber

All-Time Great

Roger Clemens

Only the Rocket has won seven Cy Young Awards (two more than anyone else), racking them up with four different teams, and in both leagues.

Born: August 4, 1962; Dayton, OH
MLB Career: Boston Red Sox, 1984–96; Toronto Blue Jays, 1997–98; New York Yankees, 1999–2003, 2007; Houston Astros, 2004–06
Hall of Fame Resume: 354 career wins (ninth all time) • 4,672 strikeouts (third all-time) • 46 career shutouts
Inside Pitch: Clemens was chosen by a panel of baseball experts as one of the six best pitchers of all time.

The burly right-hander first showed he was something special in college, where he sported a 25–7 record in two All-American seasons with the Texas Longhorns. His first two big-league seasons were pretty average, but his talent exploded in 1986, and Clemens became the dominant pitcher in the American League. On April 29, 1986, he struck out 20 Mariners, becoming the first pitcher ever to fan that many in a nine-inning game. His 24–4 record equaled a winning percentage of .857, and he also led the league in earned run average and opposing batting average. He took home both the Cy Young and MVP Awards and helped put his team in the World Series. This would become typical of the Clemens style—not just to be one of the best, but to dominate.

After that sensational 1986 season, Clemens followed up with another 20-win year that included 18 complete games and seven shutouts, which put another Cy Young Award on his mantel. The next five seasons he won 18, 17, 21, 18, and 18 games, respectively; won two strikeout crowns; and piled up 24 shutouts.

But something slipped out of gear for Clemens after that; starting in 1993, he had four seasons with no more than 11 wins each.

When Clemens became eligible for free agency, the Red Sox let him go, with the team's general manager uttering the now-notorious quote that Roger was "in the twilight of his career." Clemens signed with the Toronto Blue Jays and kicked things back into high gear, winning 21 and 20 games in 1997 and '98, respectively, and earning back-to-back pitching "Triple Crowns" (league leadership in wins, strikeouts, and ERA).

After two years with the Blue Jays, Clemens wanted out, so the Jays traded him to the Yankees in 1999. With New York, Clemens notched his first World Series victory as the Yanks swept Atlanta. In 2001, he started the season 20–1, the first pitcher ever to do that, and finished 20–3, which earned him his sixth Cy Young Award. That year, he also won his 300th game and netted his 4,000th strikeout on the same night—Friday, June 13. In 2003, Clemens announced his imminent retirement and was feted by teams around the league throughout the season, but when the Houston Astros made him an offer he couldn't refuse, he signed with them for 2004. Clemens and longtime pal Andy Pettitte formed a dangerous pitching duo that helped secure the NL wild card for the Astros. That season, Clemens went 18–4 with a 2.98 ERA, and he brought home his seventh Cy Young Award.

In 2005, Clemens won 13 games and two in the postseason as he helped the Astros reach the World Series. He didn't sign for the 2006 season until relatively late, and he appeared in just 113 innings, the second-fewest of his career.

In May 2007, 44-year-old Clemens signed a prorated $28 million deal with the Yankees that allowed him go home to Texas between starts. Appearing in 18 games, he finished the season 6–6, in the process becoming the first pitcher since Warren Spahn (1963) to reach 350 wins.

Clemens retired—again—after the 2007 season and did not play in 2008. Though his reputation has been marred by his implication in baseball's steroid scandal, Clemens will nonetheless go down in the history books as one of the most dominant pitchers the game has ever seen.

Wait Until Next Year. Again.

We know all about their postseason travails, but for Cubs fans, suffering happens throughout the entire season.

In failing to win a World Series since 1908 or even make it to the fall classic since just after World War II, the Chicago Cubs have suffered enough late-season collapses to leave their loyal fans feeling as lost as a ball in the ivy-covered walls of Wrigley Field. Then again, dramatic losses are not just a September/October habit for the lovable Cubbies—they've perfected the art in April and May as well.

On April 17, 1976, Chicago held a 13–2 lead over Philadelphia after just four innings at Wrigley, but the Phillies stormed back to take a 15–13 lead on three home runs by third baseman Mike Schmidt. The Cubs evened things up in the ninth, but Schmidt unleashed his record-tying fourth homer in the tenth, giving Philadelphia an 18–16 victory.

The Phillies were the visitors once again on May 17, 1979, when Chicago went down 7–0 in the top of the first, answered with six runs in the bottom of the inning, then fell behind 17–6 in the fourth before improbably knotting the game 22–22 in the eighth. Such a comeback deserved a win, but, being the Cubs, they lost 23–22 in the tenth on a homer by—who else?—Mike Schmidt.

A bit less energy—but no less frustration—was issued on April 21, 1991, when Chicago traveled to Pittsburgh and led a fairly routine game,

3–2, through seven. The Cubs went up 7–2 with four runs in the eighth, but the Pirates countered with four in the bottom of the frame and then scored once more in the ninth to send the game to extra innings. After an Andre Dawson grand slam and five runs in the 11th, the Cubs seemingly had the game locked up, but the Pirates scored six of their own in a steady drizzle to win 13–12.

The new century has brought no relief. In 2006, the 98th season since the Cubs' last World Series title, the club presented a prime example of why it would be yet another case of "Wait until next year" at Wrigley Field. Up 4–1 after one inning against the Braves on May 28, they fell behind 11–5 in the sixth before eventually rallying to tie the game with four ninth-inning runs. In the 11th, however, a pop-up by Atlanta's Ryan Langerhans hit third baseman Aramis Ramirez in the head for a two-base error, and Marcus Giles stroked a two-out single for a 13–12 Braves victory. "You think you've seen everything and wonder what else can happen, and something else happens," Chicago manager Dusty Baker said after the game.

Cubs fans everywhere know just what he was talking about.

◖◗ ◖◗ ◖◗

"I am a fan because [the Cubs] are always the underdogs. That may be why I bought a Studebaker 30 years after the company went out of business."

—Roger Ebert

◖◗ ◖◗ ◖◗

"Sad to say, but the history of the Cubs is synonymous with losing. The team hasn't won the World Series in a century. So no matter how well the Cubs might be playing at the moment, pessimism is always one loss away."

—Jim Peltz, *Los Angeles Times* (latimes.com)

Babe Didrikson Zaharias

Perhaps the greatest female athlete of all time, Babe Didrikson Zaharias left her mark on baseball.

It was the most unusual of baseball showdowns. Two of the 20th century's greatest sports icons stared each other down across a distance of 60 feet, 6 inches. At the plate: Joe DiMaggio, the Yankee legend whose Hall of Fame plaque would one day show three American League MVP Awards, two batting titles, and a record 56-game hitting streak. On the mound: a woman.

But this was no ordinary woman. She was, perhaps, the greatest female athlete of all time. Babe Didrikson (later Zaharias) had been throwing harder, running faster, and playing better than the boys since she was a girl in Port Arthur, Texas. On this day, she was pitching for the barnstorming House of David men's team, a club whose other players wore long beards. Babe's arm had impressed the team enough that her lack of a beard was easily overlooked.

The details of this legendary face-off between DiMaggio and Didrikson have grown cloudy over time. However, DiMaggio once described it to writer Bert Sugar. "Struck him out on three pitches," Sugar reported; the clincher was an overhand fastball.

Born Mildred Ella Didrikson, Babe earned her nickname after a Ruthian feat: She smashed five home runs during a childhood game. Truth is, baseball was not even her best sport. She set Olympic records at the 1932 Games in Los Angeles, winning the javelin and the 80-meter hurdles and breaking a world record in the latter. She was also a basketball star, a world-class swimmer, and—above all else—a brilliant, big-hitting golfer whose titles included the 1948, 1950, and 1954 United States Women's Opens.

In 1934, Babe pitched in two major-league spring training games in Florida. She threw the first inning of a Philadelphia Athletics game against Brooklyn, walking one batter but not allowing a hit. Two days later, she pitched an inning for the Cardinals against the Red Sox, yielding her first runs. She did not bat in either game, but in warm-ups she reportedly chucked a baseball from center field to home plate—a distance of 313 feet.

Chatter

"A hot dog at the ballpark is better than steak at the Ritz."

—Humphrey Bogart in a film ad for organized baseball

"In baseball you're with every guy on your club and you're against every player on the other club from the time the game starts until it's over. You've got your whole club with you, too, but you're all alone sometimes where they can't help you."

—Joe Garagiola, *Baseball Is a Funny Game*

"I don't care if half the league strikes. This is the United States of America and one citizen has as much right to play as another."

—Commissioner Ford Frick to Cardinals players, who had been planning to strike when the Dodgers and Jackie Robinson came to St. Louis in 1947, *The Summer Game*

"I'd walk through hell in a gasoline suit to play baseball."

—Pete Rose

"Baseball's unique possession, the real source of our strength, is the fan's memory of the times his daddy took him to the game to see the great players of his youth."

—Bill Veeck, *The Hustler's Handbook*

"Allen Sutton Sothoron pitched his initials off today."

—Lead in St. Louis newspaper, 1920s, quoted in *The Pitcher*

"If you're not having fun [in baseball], you miss the point of every-thing."

—Chris Chambliss

Pet Peeves

Rarely do animals and baseball go hand-in-hand, but some key moments on the field have made these critters the stars of the show.

Ballplayers know to expect the unexpected, to try to be prepared for whatever they might encounter. But sometimes the unexpected arrives in a different package—a furry or feathered one—when an animal makes a surprise appearance on the field.

Fowl Balls

Even the best batters admit that hitting Randy Johnson's fastball isn't easy, but a dove flying a bit too close to the action at a 2001 spring-training game certainly made solid, if not tragic, contact. Johnson's seventh-inning delivery, intended for Giants outfielder Calvin Murray, hit the bird instead. Feathers erupted, and the ball—and what was left of the bird—ricocheted into foul territory behind the first base line. The delivery was ruled a non-pitch.

On August 4, 1983, Dave Winfield of the Yankees had a similar "fowl" incident, but with more dramatic consequences. Between innings of a game against the Blue Jays at Exhibition Stadium, Winfield struck and killed a seagull while throwing in the outfield. He was arrested after the game on a charge of cruelty to animals. He posted $500 bail and was scheduled for a court date the next time the Yankees visited Toronto, but the charges were later dropped. If convicted, Winfield could have faced up to six months in jail. "They say he hit the gull on purpose," remarked Yankees manager Billy Martin. "They wouldn't say that if they'd seen the throws he'd been making all year."

The Curse of the Cat?

Occasionally in player–animal matchups, it's the players who fall victim. A stray black cat made an eerie appearance in a critical Mets–Cubs game on September 9, 1969. Just as Billy Williams dug into the batter's box in the first inning, the cat darted out from beneath the Shea Stadium stands, stopped briefly to consider Williams, slinked past Ron Santo in the on-deck circle, then headed for the visitor's dugout, where Mets fans believe he hissed at Cubs manager Leo Durocher.

Was it an omen? It marked the last night of the season that the Cubs went to bed in first place. Despite holding a divisional lead of ten games over the Mets as late as August 13, the Cubs' 7–1 loss on the night the cat appeared reduced their lead to a half-game, which the surging Mets erased the next night. Like the cat, the Cubs weren't heard from again.

Her Dogs Called the Schotts

Marge Schott, the brash one-time owner of the Reds, was known for her inappropriate behavior and comments, and also for her love of animals. Her beloved St. Bernards, Schottzie and Schottzie 02, like several of her struggling Reds teams, were known to leave a mess on the Riverfront Stadium field. However, it was the dogs, not the players, who graced the covers of the team's media guides.

In September 1998, Mark McGwire arrived in Cincinnati fresh from breaking Roger Maris's home run record, only to be humiliated when Schott forced him to pet Schottzie and rub the dog's hair on his Cardinals jersey for good luck. Unfortunately, this brought McGwire no luck at all: He's allergic to dogs.

Fleeing the Bees

In March 2005, a spring-training game between the Rockies and the Diamondbacks was called after a swarm of bees invaded the field. Darren Oliver, who was pitching for Colorado, was literally chased off the mound by the swarm. He suspected that the coconut-scented gel in his hair was to blame. However, after he fled, the bees chased Arizona shortstop Sergio Santos out to deep center field before umpires stepped in. "I guess we've got to call that a 'bee' game," joked Arizona manager Bob Melvin.

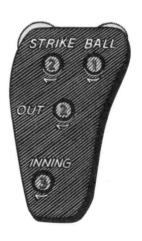

The Bad Boys of Summer

Some major-leaguers have become infamous not for their play but for their antics on and off the diamond.

Baseball has its share of good guys, to be sure, but there have been some not-so-good-guy counterparts as well.

Roberto Alomar: Splish Splash

It was one reactionary smudge on Roberto Alomar's otherwise clean resumé, but it was a wet one. After being called out on strikes by ump John Hirschbeck in a 1996 game in Toronto, an enraged Alomar argued the call to no avail, then spit in the umpire's face in disgust. The act, which was caught by TV cameras and replayed over and over, earned the Orioles infielder a five-game suspension and the ire of fans. Years later, Alomar and Hirschbeck became friends, and the player helped the ump raise money to support research of a rare brain disease that had claimed the life of Hirschbeck's eight-year-old son in 1993.

Albert Belle: His Tricks Were No Treat

Albert Belle's drinking and run-ins with fans and media were well-documented, making him one of baseball's least loved players. October 1995 was a particularly bad month for Belle: First, he was caught on camera shouting obscenities at NBC reporter Hannah Storm. On Halloween a week later, Belle jumped into his truck to chase some teenagers who had thrown eggs at his home. He was fined $50,000 by MLB for the Storm incident and $100 by a judge for turning a trick-or-treat stunt into a potentially dangerous pursuit.

Hal Chase: Dollars, Not Sense

Hal Chase was one of the best defensive first basemen of all time. It makes perfect sense, as he was generally on the defensive regarding his vices. He was accused as early as 1910 of throwing games and betting against his own team. Chase beat such charges until 1918, when Reds skipper Christy Mathewson grew suspicious and suspended him for "indifferent play." Two years later, Chase was indicted on bribery charges related to the Black Sox scandal and was eventually banned from baseball for life by Commissioner Kenesaw Mountain Landis.

Vince Coleman: An Explosive Personality

After a loss at Dodger Stadium in 1993, Mets outfielder Vince Coleman threw a firecracker out of a car window toward a group of fans in the parking lot. The explosion injured two children and a woman. Coleman, who later said he was not aware that throwing firecrackers at people could result in injury, avoided felony charges by pleading guilty to a misdemeanor charge of possession of an explosive device. He received three years' probation, 200 hours of community service, and a $1,000 fine.

Dave Kingman: That Dirty Rat

Slugger Dave Kingman never got along well with the media. No matter how much of a nuisance reporters can be, though, none deserve the nasty trick Kingman played on the *Sacramento Bee's* Susan Fornoff in 1986. Kingman, playing for Oakland late in his career, sent a package to the press box addressed to Fornoff, with a tag that read, "My name is Sue." Inside the package was a live rat. When asked if he planned to apologize to Fornoff, Kingman answered, "I've pulled practical jokes on other people, and I didn't apologize to them." The incident earned Kingman a $3,500 fine and furthered his reputation as a troublemaker, which didn't help his chances of signing a free-agent deal later.

John Rocker: Big Stats, Bigger Mouth

John Rocker saved 38 games for the Atlanta Braves in 1999. The biggest news he made that year, however, was not with his arm, but with his mouth. A December 1999 *Sports Illustrated* article quoted the Macon, Georgia, native as saying he would never play for a New York team because he might find himself on the train next to "some queer with AIDS" or "some 20-year-old mom with four kids." He added that he was "not a very big fan of foreigners" and mocked Asian women. Needless to say, Rocker was not greeted warmly when the Braves played in New York—or anywhere else, for that matter.

The Black Sox Scandal

Baseball's Golden Age was preceded by its darkest hour: the 1919 World Series scandal in which "Shoeless" Joe Jackson emerged as a shameful symbol. Though acquitted by a jury, Jackson and his alleged coconspirators were convicted in the court of public opinion and banned from baseball for life.

The *Chicago Herald and Examiner* described the young lad who emerged from the crowd outside a Chicago courthouse on a September day in 1920 as "a little urchin." The child was said to have grabbed Joe Jackson by the coat sleeve. The newspaper's report of the exchange went on:

"It ain't true, is it?" the lad asked.

"Yes, kid, I'm afraid it is," Jackson replied.

"Well, I'd never have thought it," the boy exclaimed.

Nowhere did the newspaper report that the boy demanded, "Say it ain't so, Joe," although this version of the story became the one that was passed down through the years among generations of baseball fans. Almost three decades later, a few years before his 1951 death, Jackson told *Sport Magazine* that the entire story was a fictional account, made up by a sportswriter. He said the only words exchanged on the way out of the courthouse that day were between himself and a law enforcement officer. Had there been such a boy, Jackson added, he would have told him, "It ain't so, all right, just like I'm saying it now."

What is so is this: Members of the 1919 Chicago White Sox committed baseball's cardinal sin, deliberately losing the World Series to the Cincinnati Reds for pay. Eight members of that team, including the great and graceful "Shoeless" Joe Jackson, ended up banned from baseball for life for their parts in the scandal.

Two years after their 1917 world championship, the 1919 White Sox fielded a powerful team that took the American League pennant. The Sox were favored to defeat Cincinnati in the World Series—heavily favored, in some gambling circles.

By all accounts, Sox infielder Chick Gandil was the ringleader of the "Black Sox"—he was the man who made contact with known gamblers and indicated that, for a price, the Series could be thrown. He immediately involved 29-game-winner Eddie Cicotte, and others followed: Jackson, pitcher Claude Williams, infielders Buck Weaver and Swede Risberg, outfielder Oscar "Happy" Felsch, and utility man Fred McMullin. Some of the players would play lead parts in the fixing of games. Others, notably Weaver and, some say, Jackson, had knowledge of the plan but were not active participants.

When the Series began, the players were promised a total of $100,000 to throw the games. But by the time the Reds won the Series in eight games, the payout was considerably less, and whispers about what had taken place began swelling to a roar. Sportswriters speculated in print about a possible fix even before Cincinnati wrapped up the Series, but nobody wanted to believe it could be true. No official action was taken, however, until the following September.

The 1920 season began with rumors of gambling in other big-league dugouts. Something had to be done, and in September a grand jury convened to examine allegations of instances of gambling in the game—and they soon looked at the 1919 World Series. Eight White Sox players were called to testify, and several, including Jackson, admitted knowledge of the fix. All eight were indicted for conspiracy to defraud the public and injure "the business of Charles Comiskey and the American League." Although the group was acquitted due to lack of evidence when Jackson and Cicotte's testimony "disappeared," the damage had already been done in the form of huge headlines across the country. Baseball, America's game, was facing its darkest hour.

The Black Sox were not as fortunate on the scales of baseball justice as they had been in the court of law. Kenesaw Mountain Landis, baseball's newly appointed commissioner, suspended all eight players for life in an effort to restore credibility to the game. It was a crushing blow for Chicago, and for Weaver and Jackson in particular. While Gandil had received $35,000 and Cicotte $10,000 for the fix, Weaver received nothing. Actually, it was proven that he had turned down an invitation to participate in the scam. And Jackson, who was considered one of the greatest outfielders and hitters—and certainly one of the most sympathetic figures—in the history of the game, hit .375 with six RBI in the 1919 Series while playing errorless defense.

Many still clamor for Shoeless Joe to be enshrined in the Hall of Fame, arguing that the numbers support his claim that he did nothing to contribute to the fixing of the 1919 World Series. The $5,000 he accepted from the gamblers, however, nearly matched his 1919 salary of $6,000 and sealed his fate as a tragic figure in baseball's most infamous 20th-century scandal.

Say it ain't so, Joe.

⚾ ⚾ ⚾

"(Shoeless Joe) Jackson's fall from grace is one of the real tragedies of baseball. I always thought he was more sinned against than sinning."

—Connie Mack

⚾ ⚾ ⚾

"Regardless of the verdict of juries, no player who throws a ballgame, no player that undertakes or promises to throw a ballgame, no player that sits in conference with a bunch of crooked players and gamblers where the ways and means of throwing a game are discussed and does not promptly tell his club about it, will ever play professional baseball."

—Judge Kenesaw Mountain Landis, August 4, 1921

⚾ ⚾ ⚾

"I copied [Shoeless Joe] Jackson's style because I thought he was the greatest hitter I had ever seen, the greatest natural hitter I ever saw. He's the guy who made me a hitter."

—Babe Ruth

The Miracle Mets

*The Mets went from lovable losers to world champs—
and did it in heroic fashion.*

The New York Mets, one of the first two National League expansion clubs, set an all-time modern record for losses during their first season (120 in 1962). They improved some, but not a lot, garnering at least 100 defeats in five of their first six years. Some wags said, "A man will walk on the moon before the Mets win a pennant." In 1968, they lost "only" 89 games. But this was a talented group at the core, led by superstar pitchers Tom Seaver and Jerry Koosman and able batters Cleon Jones and Tommie Agee.

In 1969, the National League expanded again and split into two six-team divisions. The Mets were picked to finish near the bottom  of the NL East, but they stayed surprisingly competitive and were second behind the Cubs on June 15 when they pulled off a miraculous deal, obtaining 33-year-old first baseman Donn Clendenon from the Montreal Expos. At least it turned out to be miraculous: In his first 16 games as a Met, Clendenon knocked home either the lead run or the winning run four times. But the Cubs hung tough, and they led the Mets by five games on July 19. That day, two Americans walked on the moon.

Some might say an even bigger miracle happened when the Mets fell 9½ games back in August and then went on a tear, winning 22 of their last 27 games as the Cubs collapsed down the stretch. The Mets' magic continued as they swept the Braves in the first National League Championship Series and then toppled the powerful Baltimore Orioles in five games to win the World Series. The Miracle Mets had pulled off one of the biggest upsets in baseball history.

All-Time Great

Ted Williams

*He wanted to be known as "the greatest hitter who ever lived,"
and most would agree he got his wish.*

Born: August 30, 1918; San Diego, CA
MLB Career: Boston Red Sox, 1939–42, 1946–60
Hall of Fame Resume: Last man to bat .400 for a season (1941)
• Hit more than 30 homers eight times • Led league in runs six
times • Led league in walks eight times • Led league in homers
and RBI four times each
Inside Pitch: He is the only person enshrined in both the
Baseball and Fishing Halls of Fame.

He struck out in his first major-league at-bat, homered in his
last, and, during the 21 years in between, made the art of hitting
his personal quest. Ted Williams looked at the goal of wood meeting ball in a scientific way, and if grades were awarded instead of
statistics, his achievements—a .344 lifetime average, 521 homers,
and a slugging percentage (.634) second only to Babe Ruth—
would rank him at the head of his class.

The lessons started early: swings taken before, after, and sometimes during school as a pencil-thin teen in San Diego. He signed
with the Red Sox in the summer of 1937, and although Williams
didn't make the big club the following spring, his parting shot to
Boston's starting outfielders who had ridiculed him—"I'll be back
and make more money than the three of you combined"—would
prove dead-on. A year later, he returned for good.

The major leagues were packed with sluggers in the years just
prior to World War II, but rookie Ted was able to distinguish
himself in 1939 with a .327 average, 31 homers, and a rookie-
record 145 RBI. In '41, Joe DiMaggio captured the attention
of the nation with a 56-game hitting streak, but Ted out-hit him
.412 to .408 over the course of the streak and finished the season

with 37 homers, 120 RBI, and a .406 batting mark—the last time a major-leaguer has reached the charmed .400 level. But sportswriters awarded the MVP Award to DiMaggio in what turned out to be the first of many times the outspoken Williams (a two-time MVP) would be snubbed due to friction with the press.

Williams was a decent left fielder, but when he said he lived for his next at-bat it was no exaggeration. His goal was perfection at the plate; he sought the same from pitchers, and his careful eye enabled him to lead the American League in walks seven times in his first nine full seasons (each time with more than 125). He was criticized for not swinging enough and not hitting in the clutch—this despite

posting an incredible .482 career on-base percentage (the best in history) and a .359 lifetime batting average in September (his best month).

The winner of Triple Crowns in 1942 and '47 (he missed a third in 1949 by .0002 on his batting average), Ted led the American League nine times in slugging, seven times in batting, six times in runs scored, and four times each in homers and RBI. The Player of the Decade of the 1950s hit .388 with 38 homers at age 38 in 1957, won his final batting title (.328) a year later, and slugged 29 long ones in just 310 at-bats in his final season in 1960. Despite missing nearly five full seasons as a Navy and Marine flyer and parts of two more due to injury, Williams retired as third on the all-time homer list—and first in many never-ending debates regarding the greatest hitter of all time.

The Game's Off

Postponements: They're not just about rainouts anymore.

Rain has been the cause of 99 percent of all cancellations and post-ponements in major-league history. But what about snow? Hurricanes? Bugs? Military invasion? Let's just say you might need more than an umbrella at the ballpark.

Snowed Out
Baseball games have been canceled because of snow many times, but the worst instance came in April 1982: Heavy snow wiped out Opening Day in New York, Detroit, Chicago, Milwaukee, Cleveland, Pittsburgh, and Philadelphia. Fortunately, Minnesota debuted the enclosed Metrodome on the day the storm hit.

A Roof Doesn't Matter If the Streets Are Flooded
While the typical rainout is common in outdoor baseball, what about an indoor rainout? The first one in major-league history took place in Houston on June 15, 1976. The Astros and the Pirates both made it to the Astrodome, as did a handful of fans, but the flooded streets made it impossible for the umpires to reach the covered stadium.

That Blows!
When Hurricane Ike made landfall in September 2008, it wreaked havoc throughout Texas and the islands of the Carib-bean. Consequently, it also forced the Astros to transfer two home games from Houston to Milwaukee's Miller Park against the division-leading Chicago Cubs, handing them an unwanted break and halting their late-season surge.

Well, at Least the Roof Isn't on Fire
The Montreal Expos had no choice but to cancel a game at Olympic Stadium on July 13, 1991, when the luckless facility's retractable roof couldn't keep the rain out. Less than two months later, a 55-ton concrete beam crashed onto a walkway, and the Expos had to play their final 13 home games on the road. The

Kingdome in Seattle had a similar problem on July 19, 1994, when four ceiling tiles fell, causing a game against the Orioles to be canceled. The strike came along in August to prevent the spectacle of Seattle spending three months on the road.

That was followed by the collapse of a piece of masonry at Yankee Stadium in April 1998, which forced the Yankees to cancel two games against the Angels, play a third game at Shea Stadium, and transfer a weekend series from New York to Detroit.

Buzz Off!

Swarms of bugs have caused many delays, but pesky gnats actually forced the crowd to be sent home from Ebbets Field in the fifth inning on September 15, 1946. With Brooklyn battling for a pennant, the umpires decided that the large number of fans waving scorecards at the bugs made it too difficult for players to see the ball. The Dodgers buzzed off with a 2–0 win over the Cubs.

Riotous Crowds

Riots have resulted in several forfeits, including the final Washington Senators game in 1971. With two outs in the ninth inning, the Senators, who were up 7–5, were forced to end the game after unruly fans stormed the field. And on August 10, 1995, fans at normally laid-back Dodger Stadium pelted the field with souvenir baseballs, resulting in the first National League forfeit in 41 years.

World Events

On a far more somber note, four events have led to the cancellation of the complete schedule of major-league games for one or more days: the death of President Warren Harding in August 1923; the D-Day invasion on June 6, 1944; President Franklin D. Roosevelt's death in April 1945; and the terrorist attacks on New York's World Trade Center on September 11, 2001, after which the schedule was postponed for six days. Games might have been canceled after the assassinations of Martin Luther King, Jr., and Senator Robert F. Kennedy in 1968, but Commissioner William Eckert wavered in his decisions, angering players and fans.

Hitting the Books

Priceless tips from the master batsmen.

Of course there's some innate talent involved, as well as a bit of luck. But for the most part, great hitting comes down to hard work and lots of practice.

Ted Williams: "Hit only strikes."

Ty Cobb: "Keep your left elbow cocked on a level with your hands or higher. And keep your hands well away from your body."

Willie Keeler: "Hit 'em where they ain't."

Cal Ripken: "Choose the right bat. Repetitive practice is essential."

Mike Piazza: "Try to spread your feet a little wider than shoulder width for balance."

Tony Gwynn: "For me the most effective way to practice hitting is to use a batting tee and a bag of Wiffle balls. The sooner you can hit a Wiffle ball cleanly off a tee, the sooner you will become a better hitter."

Manny Mota: "The most valuable advice that I can give a young hitter is to think about hitting the ball up the middle. If you think about hitting up the middle, you can adjust to hit the ball wherever it is pitched."

Ted Williams again: "Hitting is 50 percent above the shoulders."

And some general advice: Never speak to the catcher. And no matter what the count, always expect fastballs, but be prepared to adjust to other pitches.

33 Innings to History

A look at the longest professional game of all time.

The longest game in professional baseball history took 33 innings and parts of three days to complete, and while many of the players who suited up for the Class-AAA epic between the Pawtucket Red Sox and Rochester Red Wings on April 18, 1981, later saw action in the majors, this is one minor-league contest they would never forget. The scorecard is in the Hall of Fame, as, incidentally, are the plaques of both starting third basemen.

The "PawSox"—Boston's top farm club, led by third baseman Wade Boggs—played host for the game, which began on a cold and windy Rhode Island night before 1,740 fans at McCoy Stadium. They watched the visitors (affiliates of the Baltimore Orioles) take a 1–0 lead in the seventh, but Pawtucket knotted the score in the ninth. And there the seemingly endless string of zeroes on the scoreboard began, interrupted only by matching "1s" when both teams scored in the 21st.

Conditions grew so frigid after midnight that pitchers broke up benches and lit fires in the bullpen. Umpires could not find a rule about International League curfews, so action continued until league president Harold Cooper was reached by phone and suspended play after 32 innings at 4:07 A.M. on Easter Sunday. At that time only 19 fans remained, and Red Wings third baseman Cal Ripken, Jr., (like Boggs, destined for Cooperstown) later remembered that it was the only time in his distinguished career that his postgame meal consisted of breakfast.

The 2–2 contest made national headlines, both in the days that followed and when it resumed on June 23. By then Major League Baseball players were on strike, so reporters descended 140 strong on Pawtucket. They were joined by a sellout crowd of 5,746, who waited just 18 minutes before Dave Koza singled in Marty Barrett to give Pawtucket a 3–2 victory in the bottom of the 33rd. All told, 41 players saw action over 8 hours, 25 minutes of play, but only one stat mattered to Pawtucket center fielder Dallas Williams: 0-for-13, the worst single-game batting line ever.

Colorful Characters

It was always a laugh when any of these characters were around.

People complain that today's game, with its stratospheric payrolls and second-by-second analysis, has lost the sense of good fun and genuine silliness it once had. No one did more to keep things humorous than this gaggle of goofies.

Yogi Berra

This popular Hall of Fame catcher had a unique way with words. His marvelous, sometimes uproarious, nearly Zen (but not quite) "Berra-isms" are inextricably intertwined with baseball lore, and they often reveal a mind with a keen understanding of the game. His malapropisms made people scratch their heads, but they also coaxed a chuckle.

Dizzy Dean

No ballplayer has ever had a more accurate nickname. Horrible English ("there is a lot of people in the United States who say 'isn't,' and they ain't eating") and a genuine boyish love of the game characterized Dizzy's personality. After a short but highly successful pitching career in the 1930s and '40s, he was a broadcaster for more than 20 years.

Arlie Latham

A song written about Latham called him the "freshest man on Earth," and the fans of the late 1800s loved him for his roaring enthusiasm. Latham would lead the fans in cheers and heckle the opposition without mercy. Then, just to show them all how much fun he was having, he'd somersault his way out to his position. In the off-season, fans would turn out around the country for his stage act.

Bill Lee

"The Ace from Outer Space," Bill Lee, marched to the beat of a different drummer—or two or three. Saying outrageous things was as natural to him as breathing. The first time he saw Fenway Park's Green Monster, he asked, "Do they leave it up during games?" After Game 4 of the 1975 World Series, a reporter asked his impression of the Series so far; Lee answered, "Tied."

Rabbit Maranville

It may be that no one had more fun playing baseball than the Rabbit—the eternal puckish clown, the one with the funniest faces and the loudest pratfalls. As a defensive player in the 1910s, '20s, and '30s, this longtime Brave was a superstar. As an on-the-field entertainer and practical joker, he was a genius. The fans couldn't take their eyes off him.

Germany Schaefer

Schaefer's famous steal of first base—from second—was not a joke: He was trying to get a run home from third by drawing a throw from the catcher. When the catcher didn't bite (and the umpire ruled there was nothing illegal about the act), Schaefer set out from first to re-steal second. The catcher threw; the run scored. It worked.

Casey Stengel

"Stengelese" was the way this colorful manager dealt with the pestering questions of the press. "Best thing wrong with Jack Fisher is nothing," said Case. But Stengel was a beloved, fun-loving player long before he became a manager. After being traded from Brooklyn to Pittsburgh in 1918, he returned to Ebbets Field by tipping his cap to the crowd and having a bird fly out.

Rube Waddell

A colorful oddball, Waddell possessed a childlike sense of life and baseball—an endearing trait that was attached to a sensational left arm. He loved fire trucks and fishing trips, he wrestled alligators, and his roommate had it written in his contract that Rube was forbidden to eat crackers in bed.

Greatest Games of All Time

1960 World Series, Game 7

Pirates 10, Yankees 9

The Setting: Forbes Field, Pittsburgh

The Drama: Five lead changes, three clutch home runs, bizarre fielding, baserunning genius—this has to be the greatest seventh game of all time.

Out of 102 World Series, only 35 have gone to the limit. Most of those final games were not terrifically close, nor very exciting. Only 13 were decided by one run. Of those 13, one stands out for having the least likely script of all: Game 7 of the 1960 Series between the New York Yankees and Pittsburgh Pirates.

When Rocky Nelson homered for Pittsburgh with Bob Skinner on first in the bottom of the first inning, Pirates fans may have seemed relieved, but they couldn't get too cocky. They knew this Yankee club could score. (In their three Series wins, the Yanks had pulverized the Pirates 16–3, 10–0, and 12–0.) The Bucs tacked on two more in the second for a 4–0 lead, but the hair-raising roller-coaster ride was just getting started.

Through the first four innings, Pirates starter—and NL Cy Young Award winner—Vern Law allowed only two singles. A fifth-inning homer by Bill Skowron put the Yanks on the board. Yankee power exploded in the sixth. After a single and a walk, Law was replaced by Roy Face. With one out, Mickey Mantle stroked an RBI single and Yogi Berra crushed a three-run homer. The Yankees had taken the lead, 5–4.

Face disposed of the first two Yankees in the top of the eighth, then walked Berra. Two singles and a double later, the New Yorkers had extended their lead to 7–4. The Pirates were three runs down with just six outs to go, but a leadoff single by pinch-hitter Gino Cimoli got the eighth off and rolling for Pittsburgh. The next batter, Bill Virdon, chopped down on a pitch and grounded it toward short, a likely double-play ball. But Yank shortstop Tony

Kubek, uncertain how to play the wicked hops of the notorious Forbes Field infield, hesitated, moved back, then in, and the ball hit him in the throat. Both runners were safe with nobody out.

Dick Groat, National League batting champ and MVP, rapped a single to left, scoring Cimoli. Yanks hurler Bobby Shantz was replaced by Jim Coates. A sacrifice bunt moved runners to second and third, and then Nelson hit a short fly-out. The Bucs' last chance was Roberto Clemente, hitless in the game thus far. Clemente chopped one to first, where Skowron gloved it and waited to toss to Coates for the third out. But Clemente was in full flight, and he out-hustled the pitcher to the bag. The Bucs had pulled to within one.

Hal Smith, a former Yankees farmhand, got around on a pitch from Coates and powered it over the left-field wall. Three Pirates scored, and the Bucs had turned the tide once again. Pittsburgh took a 9–7 lead into the top of the ninth.

But the Yankees weren't done, either. Bucs manager Danny Murtaugh brought in Bob Friend, a burly right-hander who had won 18 games in the regular season but who had been no puzzle for Yank batters; they had swatted him around for 11 hits and eight runs in just six innings of work in the Series. Bobby Richardson and former Pirates slugger Dale Long quickly rapped singles, and Harvey Haddix entered the game in relief.

With one out, Mantle singled in Richardson, making it 9–8 Bucs. Then Mantle provided one of the most electrifying moments in World Series history. Berra lined a one-hopper down the first base line that Nelson speared. He stepped on first and raised his arm to throw to second for the tag on Mantle that would end the Series. But Mantle had not gone to second; his remarkable instincts sent him back to first, where his diving dance-step kept him away from Nelson's attempted tag. This allowed the runner on third to score, and the Yanks had improbably tied the score at nine runs each.

But the Pirates would have the final say. Second baseman Bill Mazeroski, leading off the bottom of the ninth, smashed a climactic game-winning homer over the left-field fence, bringing the players and Pittsburgh fans to their feet. Jubilant fans poured onto the field to celebrate the first World Series–ending homer in major-league history.

Ballplayers Go to War

Several baseball players sacrificed for their country during World War II.

When World War II broke out, many baseball players stepped up to the plate to serve. Some were drafted, some volunteered, and some were called to bring America's pastime to the soldiers in order to provide an outlet during the interminable downtime of the military. No matter what their call to duty, all emerged changed men. Two major-leaguers—Elmer Gedeon and Harry O'Neill—as well as 40 minor-leaguers were killed. What follows are stories of just some of the survivors.

Zeke Bonura

Bonura drove in 100 runs four times in seven seasons with the White Sox, Senators, Giants, and Cubs and was a .307 career hitter. As an inactive duty Army master sergeant playing minor-league ball in 1941, he was recalled to the service after Pearl Harbor. Driven by his passion for baseball, Bonura was an expert organizer of players, games, ball fields, and equipment from Mississippi to Algeria. He organized games even as German planes strafed overhead. Soldiers referred to him as the "Judge Landis of North Africa." General Dwight D. Eisenhower presented Bonura with a Legion of Merit medal in October 1943 for his contributions to military athletics. Subsequent orders brought him (and baseball) to Italy and France. There Bonura continued his mission while editing a military sports periodical, offering personal instruction, and keeping an eye out for talent as a scout for the minor-league Minneapolis Millers.

Bob Feller

Although many of the game's top stars avoided combat, Bullet Bob was an exception. Despite being his mother's sole supporter with no chance of being drafted, Feller enlisted in the Navy the day after Pearl Harbor. He became an antiaircraft gunner on the USS *Alabama* in 1942 and served in the treacherous, U-boat–infested North Atlantic before heading to the South Pacific Theater. There

he saw plenty of combat duty in Kwajalein and the Marshall Islands as well as in the "Marianas Turkey Shoot" that destroyed much of Japan's remaining air force. Feller, who'd won 25 games in his last season before the war, won 26 in his first full season back with the Indians in 1946.

Hank Greenberg

By age 29, Greenberg had won the American League MVP Award twice and placed third the year he hit 58 home runs. Yet a high draft number led him to join the Army Air Corps early in the war. Greenberg had actually been honorably discharged on December 5, 1941 (after being drafted in 1940), but he reenlisted immediately after Pearl Harbor and was put in charge of a bomber squadron in China. After serving for nearly five years, Greenberg was among the first baseball stars to return to the game. His home run clinched the 1945 pennant for the Tigers, and he hit .304 and clubbed Detroit's only two home runs in its World Series triumph.

Ted Lyons

Lyons joined the Marines in 1942, 20 years after his major-league debut. Though three years past the maximum draft age of 38, Lyons signed up anyway and was assigned mostly athletic duties. He returned to pitch for the White Sox in 1946 as the game's oldest player at that time (45). He then spent three years managing the Chicago team.

Bert Shepard

Shepard was a minor-leaguer whose plane was shot down during a bombing mission in 1944. A German doctor amputated his leg, but he pitched with a prosthesis and received a tryout with the Senators the next year. He threw 5⅓ innings, allowing just one run, in his lone major-league outing.

Warren Spahn

Spahn was 21 years old when he debuted for the Boston Braves in 1942. He made just two starts before spending more than three years in the army as a combat engineer. He took part in the Battle of the Bulge and received a rare battlefield commission for helping take the crucial Remagen Bridge in Germany. Spahn received a Bronze Star as well as a Purple Heart after he was hit with shrapnel. He served another six months in the service after the war, then went on to become the winningest left-hander in major-league history.

Cecil Travis
An excellent hitter before the war, Travis suffered severe frostbite in his legs during the Battle of the Bulge. The Senators were thankful to get the three-time All-Star shortstop back, but he wasn't the same; he mostly played third base because of his diminished speed. Before World War II, he was a .327 hitter over nine seasons; after the war, he hit .241 and didn't last through 1947.

Ted Williams
Teddy Ballgame had already batted .406, won two batting titles, and averaged 32 home runs and 129 RBI over his first four seasons when he became a Marine pilot. Williams served as an instructor and did not see action in World War II, but he later saw extensive combat and was shot down in Korea. He gave almost five full years to the military and was still among the greatest hitters ever to play the game.

"I honestly feel that it would be best for the country to keep baseball going…if 300 teams use 5,000 or 6,000 players, these players are a definite asset to at least 20,000,000 of their fellow citizens—and that in my judgement is thoroughly worthwhile."

—President Franklin Delano Roosevelt's "green light" letter to
Judge Kenesaw Mountain Landis, January 15, 1942

"May the sun never set on American baseball."

—President Harry Truman marking the 75th anniversary
of the major leagues, February 2, 1951

The Seventh-Inning Stretch

The history (and lore) behind a seventh-inning tradition.

The seventh-inning stretch, a ritual practiced today at ballparks throughout the major and minor leagues and beyond, was long rumored to have originated at a 1910 Washington Senators game attended by President William Howard Taft. Seeking relief from his confining seat at American League Park, the 300-pound chief executive rose in the seventh. Fans, thinking he was leaving, did likewise as a sign of respect, and when he wound up sitting back down they did the same.

Thus a rite of fandom was born—or so it was thought.

Turns out this tale of President Taft might have stretched the truth just a bit. Researchers found evidence of a seventh-inning stretch all the way back in 1882. During an exhibition game between Manhattan College and the semipro New York Metropolitans, Manhattan's coach, a prefect named Brother Jasper of Mary, noticed the student fans growing fidgety. Calling time, he asked them to stand and unwind, and when the break proved to have restorative powers, he called for it to occur at the same time—the seventh inning—in all subsequent games. When the New York Giants squared off with Manhattan and saw Brother Jasper's practice, they took it back to the majors and started its spread.

Even this may not be the earliest incidence of the trend, however. A letter written in 1869 by player-manager and future Hall of Famer Harry Wright of the Cincinnati Red Stockings—baseball's first acknowledged professional club—makes mention that at games of that era, "The spectators all arise between halves of the seventh inning, extend their arms and legs, and sometimes walk about. In so doing they enjoy the relief afforded by relaxation from a long posture on hard benches."

Harry sounds like he's on the level, but wouldn't it be great if we really *could* give President Taft the credit?

All-Time Great

Lou Gehrig

Despite playing in Babe Ruth's shadow, and doomed to an early death, he was a powerful batter who dominated slugging for years.

Born: June 19, 1903; New York, NY
MLB Career: New York Yankees, 1923–39
Hall of Fame Resume: Led league in games seven times • Led in RBI five times • Led in home runs three times • Led in runs four times • 184 RBI in 1931 is still American League record • Had more than 400 total bases per season five times
Inside Pitch: Gehrig was banned from intercollegiate sports his first year at Columbia University because he had played professionally (under a phony name) the summer before. The person who recommended he do that was New York Giants manager John McGraw.

Now that his incredible streak of 2,130 consecutive games played has been topped by Cal Ripken, Jr., there is a new opportunity to examine the career of Lou Gehrig. The record that was once thought unbreakable no longer stands, but what Gehrig accomplished in the seasons comprising his string remains remarkable—and only his own Yankee teammate Babe Ruth can claim a more prodigious level of sustained offensive excellence.

It seems fitting that a player of Ripken's disposition toppled Gehrig's mark; Gehrig was himself a wise and modest man who drew far more solace from family than from nightclubs. A native New Yorker and left-handed slugger who attended Columbia University, the sturdy six-footer joined the Yanks at age 20 in 1923 and saw limited duty backing up star first baseman Wally Pipp for two seasons. The first game of Gehrig's streak saw him pinch-hit on May 31, 1925, and when he started the next day after Pipp com-

plained of a headache, nobody thought much of it. In the end, Pipp was out of a job as Gehrig played the final 126 games of the season, finishing at .295 with 20 homers.

As the cleanup hitter for the Yankee pennant-winners of 1926, Lou paced the American League with 20 triples while adding 47 doubles, 16 homers, and 112 RBI. He also hit .348 in the Yanks' World Series loss to St. Louis, but Ruth (who preceded him in the New York batting order) remained the team's main man, with 47 homers and four more in the Series. "The Iron Horse" stepped it up in '27, finishing with 47 dingers. Ruth set the world afire by smashing a record 60 homers for the world champs, but Gehrig was AL MVP with astounding totals of 218 hits, a .373 average, a league-best 175 RBI, and 52 doubles, 18 triples, and a .765 slugging percentage never topped by anyone not named Babe or Barry.

Lou upped his batting average to .374 in 1928, leading the league with 47 doubles and 142 RBI. Similar stats followed each of the next nine years. Over 11 full seasons from 1927 to '37, Lou averaged .350 with 39 homers and 153 RBI (including an AL-record 184 in '31) while playing on five world champions. His numbers fell off to a still-impressive .295–29–114 when the Yanks took their third straight Series in '38, and some said the streak was getting to him. In fact, the problem was actually a rare and incurable disease called amyotrophic lateral sclerosis—now known as Lou Gehrig's disease—that was slowly eating away at his body.

On May 2, 1939, with a .143 average, the suddenly sluggish and feeble-footed star took himself out of the lineup. Shortly thereafter, his doctors informed him he would never play again. On July 4, Lou Gehrig Day at Yankee Stadium, more than 60,000 fans honored a classy man who told the hushed crowd, "I have an awful lot to live for." Gehrig died less than two years later at age 37.

Out of the Limelight

You might be surprised to learn what interesting twists some players' lives took when their baseball careers ended.

Sometimes, the name gives it away. Hi Jasper, an early-20th-century pitcher for the White Sox, Cardinals, and Indians, had the perfect first name with which to greet patrons in his second career as a bartender. Others, like Happy Finneran, might have considered a name change once their playing days were over—Finneran went from the pitcher's mound to the funeral home, where he worked as a funeral director and embalmer.

Joe Quinn: Undertaker
The first Australian to reach the major leagues played second base sporadically for 17 years, through 1901. He played on five championship teams but was also a player/manager with the 1899 Cleveland Spiders, whose 20–134 record remains the worst in history.

Having been involved with that club must have made Quinn's "other" job a little easier to bear. This colorful character spent his off-seasons and part of his post-playing career serving as an undertaker in St. Louis, where he first took up U.S. residence.

Lu Blue: Chicken Farmer
A switch-hitting first baseman with a terrific eye at the plate, Blue spent most of his 13-year career with the Detroit Tigers. In 1929, he finished first in the American League in total times on base, and he finished second in the AL in walks four times in his career.

His life after baseball was unusually productive. In 1941, he retired to a career as a chicken farmer in Virginia, dabbled in chinchilla farming, and later owned a chicken hatchery in Maryland. A World War I veteran, Blue is perhaps the best-known former big-leaguer buried in Arlington National Cemetery.

Grover Cleveland Alexander: Performer in a Flea Circus
One of the greatest pitchers of all time, Alexander won 373 career games, led St. Louis to a World Series title with his famous 1926

strikeout of Yankee Tony Lazzeri, and was enshrined in the Hall of Fame in 1938. Alexander ranks third among pitchers in career wins (he's tied with Christy Mathewson), trailing only Cy Young and Walter Johnson.

Out of uniform, Alexander experienced many struggles in life, such as epilepsy, hearing loss, and double vision. Within a year of his induction to the Hall, Alexander could be found working for Hubert's Museum and Flea Circus on 42nd Street in Manhattan. For $100 a week, Alexander would stand on a small wooden platform and recount tales of his career at 30-minute intervals.

Rocky Colavito: Mushroom Farmer

Rocky Colavito was one of the most popular players—and people—in Cleveland early in his career. He was a skilled fielder and powerhouse hitter, with 41- and 42-homer seasons. In 1959, he hit home runs in four consecutive at-bats in a single game. He was traded to Detroit before the 1960 season for Harvey Kuenn, an act that Tribe fans blame for cursing their club.

Colavito finished his career with 374 home runs, a .266 batting average, 1,159 RBI, and one season with a perfect 1.000 fielding percentage. Then he slipped away into an unusual post-baseball job. Rocky went from big-slugging outfielder to mushroom farmer, a gig that kept him well out of the limelight that his sometimes tumultuous playing career had attracted.

Mark Fidrych: Pig Farmer

On the mound, he was "The Bird." Fidrych's animated wiggles, gyrations, and head bob made him one of baseball's marquee players. His mastery of opposing hitters helped him win the 1976 AL Rookie of the Year Award and finish second in Cy Young Award voting. He was the definitive one-year wonder, compiling a 19–9 record and 2.34 ERA before winning just ten times over the remainder of his career.

A torn rotator cuff forced Fidrych to retire at the age of 29. He moved to a 107-acre pig farm near his hometown of Northborough, Massachusetts, where he cared for the animals, hauled gravel, and worked as a licensed commercial truck driver.

Babe Ruth's Called Shot

Whether Ruth called a home run in the 1932 World Series remains one of baseball's greatest mysteries.

This much is known. The Yankees had already won the first two games of the '32 fall classic when they met the Cubs at Wrigley Field for Game 3. Although Chicago players were understandably frustrated, there was bad blood between the teams that extended beyond the norm. In August, the Cubs had picked up former Yankee shortstop Mark Koenig from the Pacific Coast League to replace injured starter Billy Jurges, and Koenig hit .353 the rest of the season. Despite these heroics, his new teammates had only voted him a half-share of their World Series bonus money—a slight that enraged his old colleagues. The Yanks engaged in furious bench-jockeying with their "cheapskate" opponents the entire series; Chicago players and fans shouted back, jeering that Ruth was old, fat, and washed-up.

Up to bat. When Ruth stepped up to bat in the fifth inning of Game 3, the taunts started as usual. A few people threw lemons at Babe from the stands, and he gestured toward the crowd before settling in at the plate. Charlie Root's first pitch was a called strike, and Ruth, looking over at the Chicago dugout, appeared to hold up one finger—as if to say, "That's only one." He did the same thing with two fingers after taking the second pitch, another strike. Then, some eyewitnesses recalled, he pointed toward dead center field. Others didn't remember this act, but there was no mistaking what happened next: Ruth slammed Root's third offering deep into the right-field bleachers. Onlookers recalled him chuckling as he rounded the bases, and he and on-deck batter Lou Gehrig laughed and shook hands back at home plate.

What really happened? Here is where the facts end and speculation begins. Those among the 49,986 fans on hand who noticed Ruth's display likely assumed it was just another round in the ongoing feud between the two clubs, and most sportswriters made nothing out of it in their accounts of New York's 7–5 victory. The homer was not a game-winner; it was just one (in fact, the last) of 15 home runs Ruth hit in World Series play during his career. He had already taken Root deep earlier in the same contest, and Gehrig also had two blasts in the game. The Yanks finished their four-game sweep the next day.

This being Babe Ruth, however, it only took a few speculative accounts from among the many reporters present to get the ball rolling. "Ruth Calls Shot" read the headline in the next day's *New York World Telegram,* and soon sports fans everywhere were wondering. Gehrig claimed he heard Ruth yell to Root, "I'm going to knock the next one down your goddamned throat" before the fateful pitch, while Cubs catcher Gabby Hartnett recalled the remark as "It only takes one to hit." Root and Cubs second baseman Billy Herman denied any gesture to the outfield, and grainy film footage that surfaced in 1999 was unclear either way. Ever the diplomat, Ruth himself granted some interviews in which he substantiated the claim, and others in which he denied it.

So did he or didn't he? We may never know for sure, but perhaps it's better that way. When the subject is Babe Ruth, facts are only half the fun.

ⓒ ⓒ ⓒ

"One of the secrets of the Babe's greatness was that he never lost any of his enthusiasm for playing ball, and especially for hitting home runs. To him a homer was a homer, whether he hit it in a regular game, a World Series game, or an exhibition game."

—Sportswriter Frank Graham, *The New York Yankees*

Magical Moment

Mr. October turns it on.

The Setting: Yankee Stadium; October 18, 1977
The Magic: Reggie Jackson earns the title "Mr. October" with three homers on consecutive pitches in the Yankees' World Series victory-clinching game.

Reggie Jackson didn't just crave the spotlight—he hogged it. Before he signed with the Yankees, he announced of New York: "If I played there they'd name a candy bar after me." (When he got there, they did.) Upon his arrival in 1977 he told a reporter, "I'm the straw that stirs the drink." And he proved it with one night of amazing power.

The Yankees had returned to the Series in 1976 for the first time in 12 years (a mighty long stretch for the Yanks), only to get stomped in four games. In '77, they led the Series 3–2 over the Dodgers, but Los Angeles had the lead in Game 6 on a solo homer by "the other Reggie," Reggie Smith. With one on and none out in the fourth, Jackson stepped up to the plate and swatted the first pitch he saw from Burt Hooton over the right-field fence. Just like that, the Yanks were up 4–3. When Jackson came to bat again in the fifth, there was a Yank on first and two down. He crushed the first pitch he saw from Elias Sosa even farther back into the right-field stands. Two pitches, two homers for Reggie; Yanks up 7–3. Jackson batted again in the eighth, this time against Charlie Hough. Hough's first offering was his famous knuckleball, and Reggie creamed it. This made three homers on three swings. Jackson became only the second player to crack three dingers in one Series game (Babe Ruth was the other). On that night, Mr. October didn't just stir the drink—he shook it.

Talking Trash

"We had a lot of triple-threat guys—slip, fumble, and fall."

—Pittsburgh catcher Joe Garagiola on the awful Pirate teams
of the early 1950s

*"It was a cross between a screwball and a changeup. It was a
screw-up."*

—Cubs reliever Bob Patterson on a lousy pitch hit by Cincinnati's
Barry Larkin off him for a game-winning homer, from *The Wall
Street Journal,* quoted in *Parade,* December 29, 1996

"Well, you can't win them all."

—Connie Mack on his 1916 A's, who went 36–117

"Shall I get you a net, or do you want a basket?"

—Red Sox shortstop Heinie Wagner needling Giants shortstop
Art Fletcher during the second game of the 1912 World Series;
Fletcher had made three errors in the contest

*"I have always maintained that the best remedy for a batting
slump is two wads of cotton. One for each ear."*

—Bill Veeck, *The Hustler's Handboook*

*"People found humor in the way the Mets lost or—rarely—won. I
suppose it would have been gentler for that team to play in privacy."*

—Tom Seaver on the '62 Mets, *Baseball Is My Life*

*"With this batting slump I'm in, I was so happy to hit a double that
I did a tap dance on second base. They tagged me between taps."*

—Frenchy Bordagaray of the Dodgers

Life Before Jackie

Integration? Not if baseball's big boys could help it.

In the history of baseball, nothing is more shameful than what Jackie Robinson had to endure as the major leagues' first African American player. He was brought to the majors over vigorous protest, but once he reached the spotlight at Brooklyn's Ebbets Field in 1947, his emotions courageously in check, he was there to stay. As he continued to be snubbed and demeaned, newspapers, magazines, radio, and newsreels followed his every move. As Jackie succeeded, and then excelled, more African Americans followed. And the rest, as they say, is history.

In the previous century, though, progress for players of color on the diamond had been stopped dead in its tracks.

African Americans were barred from the newly formed National League as early as 1876, when owners came to a backroom "gentleman's agreement" that was not challenged outright until Robinson's debut 71 years later. The minor leagues, however, were a different story: Anywhere from 25 to 50 African Americans found spots on minor-league teams in the 1870s and 1880s. Bud Fowler and Frank Grant were probably the best of this group, but neither man was able to make the jump to the majors, despite competing against white players deemed to be of big-league caliber.

But Moses Fleetwood Walker did make it. He and his brother Welday had helped launch the Oberlin College baseball team in 1881, and both later played at the University of Michigan. In 1883, "Fleet" joined the Toledo Blue Stockings of the Northwestern League. When Toledo joined the American Association, which was then a major league that was competing with the National League, the club brought along all its top players.

On May 1, 1884, the Toledo Blue Stockings debuted in the major leagues, with Walker a proud member. A barehanded catcher, Fleet teamed with Tony Mullane to form an intimidating battery. But he wasn't exactly welcomed into the league with open arms: He was hit with six pitches in one game alone. Fleet batted

.263 in 42 games before a broken rib from a foul tip essentially ended his season. Welday, who had joined him in Toledo in July, appeared in five games as an outfielder and batted .222. At the end of the season, Toledo exited the AA and the Walker brothers' major-league careers came to an end.

Recent research has shown that the Walkers may not have been the first African Americans to play in the majors, however. Research shows that Brown University student William Edward White, who played one game for the major-league Providence Grays in 1879, may have been a light-skinned African American— possibly a former slave.

In 1887, six of ten International League teams fielded African American players, with Fleet Walker and George Stovey forming a formidable "colored battery" for the Newark Little Giants. But Cap Anson, player-manager of the NL Chicago White Stockings, refused to take the field for an exhibition against the Little Giants. Anson had tried to do the same in 1883 against Walker in Toledo, but when the Blue Stockings threatened not to pay Anson, he relented, unhappily. This time, Anson got his way, and leagues voted to ban new contracts with African Americans. In 1889, Fleet Walker became the last African American in the International League until Jackie Robinson debuted with the Montreal Royals in 1946.

Even the new American League, which was at war with the established National League, fell in with the same unwritten agreement. In 1901, the AL's first year, Baltimore Orioles manager John McGraw tried to pass off Negro Leaguer Charlie Grant as a Native American named Chief Tokohama, but Chicago White Sox owner Charlie Comiskey foiled the plan when he recognized Grant as the catcher from the Columbia Giants. The AL would not integrate until Larry Doby joined the Cleveland Indians in 1947.

◖ ◖ ◖

"If Judy Johnson were white, he could name his price."

—Connie Mack on the top third baseman of the Negro League during the 1920s and '30s

Greatest Games of All Time

1975 World Series, Game 6

Red Sox 7, Reds 6

The Setting: Fenway Park, Boston

The Drama: The seemingly down-and-out Red Sox engineer a comeback for the ages that ends on one of the game's indelible images—Carlton Fisk waving the ball fair.

When it comes to exciting comebacks and thrilling plays, there have been more great sixth games in World Series history than seventh games. But this one in 1975 earned itself the honorific title, now and forever, of "Game 6."

Cincinnati was the "Big Red Machine," a high-scoring attack with brilliant defense, excellent speed, and a manager (Sparky Anderson) who was willing to substitute for a pitching advantage on a moment's notice. Three of its starters—Joe Morgan, Tony Perez, and Johnny Bench—are in the Hall of Fame. A fourth, the great Pete Rose, is considered by many to deserve a spot there, too.

The Red Sox, on the other hand, looked like a team that had been stitched together. Spectacular rookie Jim Rice was hurt. Elder statesman Carl Yastrzemski was now a first baseman. But on the plus side, the whole team played "Yaz-style," making heady plays when they had to: sometimes a great catch, sometimes a great throw, sometimes a key hit or homer. The issue was timing, and the 1975 Red Sox had it in spades.

Game 6 was delayed three days by a steady Boston rain. It was as if the gods were mercifully forestalling the inevitable; Boston had reached the World Series only twice since 1918 and had lost both times. They trailed in this Series 3–2.

But soon after the game began on October 21, Lynn pounded a two-out Gary Nolan pitch into Fenway's center-field bleachers, and the Sox took a 3–0 lead. But pitching magician Luis Tiant gave up the lead to the Reds in the fifth when Lynn banged hard

against the wall in pursuit of a Ken Griffey triple, crumpling against the fence as two runs scored.

In the seventh, a two-out double by George Foster sent Griffey and Morgan home, and the Reds' lead increased to 5–3. Cesar Geronimo's solo homer added the sixth run in the top of the eighth. The spirits of Bostonians were flagging.

Lynn opened up the last of the eighth with a single off the leg of relief pitcher Pedro Borbon, and Rico Petrocelli drew a walk. Anderson called for his bullpen ace, Rawly Eastwick, who got two outs. Bernie Carbo was sent to hit for pitcher Roger Moret; Carbo had belted a pinch homer in Game 3, but Eastwick seemed to have his number on this night. Carbo barely stayed alive by getting the slightest amount of bat on a 2–2 pitch to send it foul.

But then Eastwick made a mistake, and Carbo crushed it into the center-field stands, a hit one sportswriter described as "a giant electric jolt." Fenway Park was rocking; the Red Sox had miraculously tied the game. The Sox seemed seconds away from winning it when they loaded the bases with none out in the last of the ninth. But a fly ball down the left-field line by Lynn was grabbed by Foster, and the outfielder made a perfect throw home to double up Denny Doyle, who was trying to score from third. In the top of the 11th, Rose was hit by a pitch and forced at second. Morgan then smacked a ball into right field that looked like a sure home run, but Sox outfielder Dwight Evans went dashing back, made a sensational twisting, turning catch, and doubled off the runner who had left first.

At 12:30 A.M., Fisk led off the bottom of the 12th. He got under a Pat Darcy sinker and lifted a high fly ball down the left-field line. As it traveled, Fisk frantically tried to wave it fair, jumping up and down at the plate and pleading with the ball to stay in. Almost unbelievably, it hit the foul pole and bounced up and over the Green Monster to win the game in thrilling style.

Perhaps even more important was the impact this game had on baseball. Experts of the time who had written off baseball as too slow and dull were proven wrong. Game 6 was watched by 62 million people; 75 million tuned in to Game 7. The joy in Boston lasted just that one day, however, as the Reds prevailed in Game 7.

All-Time Great

Willie Mays

No player ever combined such high levels of skill in every category with such natural exuberance for the game.

Born: May 6, 1931; Westfield, AL
MLB Career: New York/San Francisco Giants, 1951–52, 1954–72; New York Mets, 1972–73
Hall of Fame Resume: 660 home runs (fourth all time)
• 63 games with two or more homers (third all time in the NL)
• 22 extra-inning homers (first all time) • All-time leader in outfield putouts and chances • 12 Gold Gloves
Inside Pitch: Mays was batting .477 for AAA Minneapolis when he was called up to the bigs in May 1951. When he was hitless after 12 at-bats, he asked to be sent back down, but manager Leo Durocher refused. And the next day Willie got his first hit—a home run off Warren Spahn.

It is becoming increasingly difficult to judge players of more recent vintage against those of days gone by, but among careers still remembered by a great many fans, no ballplayer has been more glowingly praised than Willie Mays. Mickey Mantle may have represented pure power, Ted Williams precision at the plate, and Roberto Clemente grace in the field, but for overall ability the vote usually goes to the Say Hey Kid.

Mays, who was among the last Negro Leaguers to make the majors, was a strapping young Alabaman who could hit with power, run with style and speed, and catch anything struck in the direction of center field when he emerged as a 20-year-old in 1951. After winning the Rookie of the Year Award (.274, 20 homers) on the National League champions, he missed most of the next two years fulfilling military obligations. He returned in '54 rippling with new muscle and ready to wreak havoc. He didn't disappoint, hitting a career-high .345 that year to win his only batting title and his first of two MVP Awards. His candidacy was augmented by totals of 41 homers, 119 runs, and 110 RBI.

In coming years, those types of numbers would seem almost commonplace for Mays, as from 1954 to '66 he accomplished the following for the Giants in New York and San Francisco: slugged at least 29 homers each season, averaging 40 a year; scored 100 or more runs 12 times, averaging 117; and notched 100 or more RBI on ten occasions, averaging 109. He won four stolen-base titles during this time, and he once swiped 58 of 68 over a two-year span.

Willie's over-the-shoulder catch of Vic Wertz's 430-foot smash to deep center in the '54 World Series has been called the greatest grab of all time, and it brought into national focus another key aspect of Mays's game: his defense. He won a Gold Glove in each of the first 12 years the trophy for fielding excellence was awarded. Mays patented a flashy, one-handed basket catch, and—even with runners around the league wary of testing his arm—he recorded 12 or more assists on nine occasions.

For most of his career, Mays was viewed alongside Mantle as one of the two men most likely to break Ruth's all-time record of 714 home runs. After Willie slugged 52 to take home his second MVP Award in 1965, he had 505 and, at age 34, appeared to be within striking distance. But by 1967, the man who was named Player of the Decade for the '60s had seemingly aged overnight. His flashes of brilliance grew increasingly less frequent, and by 1973 he was a slow-moving benchwarmer for the Mets. He never caught the Babe and was eventually passed on the home-run leaderboard by Hank Aaron and Barry Bonds (his godson), but no one would question that his 660 home runs, 2,062 runs, 1,903 RBI, .302 average, and 338 steals qualify him as an all-time great.

Sealing the Deal

When the game is on the line, these are the guys to call.

Dennis Eckersley

Eck was a starter during his first 12 years in the majors, but alcohol problems kept him from stardom. He put his demons behind him when he moved into the bullpen, where he became one of the greatest closers ever. From 1988 to '92, his record was 24–9 with 220 saves, and he struck out 378 while walking only 38. In 1989–90, he had more saves (81) than hits (73) and walks allowed (7) combined. He was inducted into the Hall of Fame in 2004.

Rollie Fingers

In 1972, Oakland owner Charlie Finley asked his players to grow mustaches. Fingers's handlebar became his trademark, along with his deadly efficiency. He was one of the first pitchers to refuse to pitch more than two innings at a time (so he could be effective several days in a row). The AL MVP and Cy Young Award winner in 1981 had the major-league record for saves upon his retirement (341), six World Series saves, and a spot in the Hall of Fame.

Goose Gossage

Gossage looked every inch the flamethrower, firing the ball with his powerful build and appearing as if every bone in his body would pop out of his skin. He was the captain of the Yankee bullpen during their 1978 world championship season, and he helped the Padres make it to the Series in 1984. He notched 310 career saves and was elected to the Hall of Fame in 2008.

Trevor Hoffman

Hoffman took over the all-time saves leadership in 2006, moving past Lee Smith; by the end of the 2008 season, he'd amassed 554 career saves. You don't get to that level without being consistent, but Hoffman has had truly spectacular seasons as well. In 1998, he converted 53 of 54 save opportunities, with a teeny ERA of 1.48. Not surprisingly, his Padres played in the World Series that year.

Mariano Rivera

Every closer thrives on pressure; Rivera thrives on the most intense pressure—postseason pressure, when championships are on the line. He has appeared in 76 postseason games and has an 8–1 record, with 34 saves and an ERA of 0.77. He is second on the all-time saves leaderboard. And he does it all with an impossibly calm demeanor, never getting flustered on the mound, no matter what.

Lee Smith

Like 1960s closer Dick Radatz, Smith was one big dude. But unlike "The Monster," Smith had a long and productive career. He threw hard and stared at the batter even harder. But for some reason, GMs kept trading him; he pitched for eight different clubs. Smith retired in 1997 as the all-time saves leader, with 478. (He's now third.)

Bruce Sutter

When Sutter began throwing his split-fingered fastball, every opposing manager was sure he was loading it up; it just dropped too far too fast to be anything but a spitter, they reasoned. Sutter used it to dominate National League batters for nearly a decade. He led the Cardinals to the World Series in 1982 and rang up two saves in the Series itself. He won one Cy Young Award and four Fireman of the Year Awards. He was elected to the Hall of Fame in 2006.

Hoyt Wilhelm

Wilhelm was 29 when he first pitched in the big leagues, but he stuck around long enough after that to appear in more major-league games than any other pitcher (1,070) at the time of his retirement. (He is currently fifth.) His secret was the dazzling dance of his knuckleball, which was so daunting that catchers turned to extra-large gloves to snag it. He had an ERA under 2.00 each year from 1964 to '68 and earned a spot in the Hall of Fame.

I Went to a Fight and a Ballgame Broke Out

Sometimes players and fans cross the line that separates participants from spectators—and end up with ugly results.

Don't Mess with Babe
Senators at Yankees, 1922

Mired in a slump, Babe Ruth tried to stretch a single into a double at the Polo Grounds. When he was called out at second base, he threw dirt in the face of umpire George Hildebrand. The Babe was ejected and booed by the home fans. When one called the Yankees slugger a bum and, according to Ruth, "other names that got me mad," Ruth went after the heckler in the stands. Once the man ran out of reach, Babe returned to the top of the dugout and screamed, "Anyone who wants to fight, come down on the field! Ah, you're all alike, you're all yellow!"

Rocky, Outside the Ring
Tigers at Yankees, 1961

Although many Rockys have graced the boxing ring over the years, it was baseball's Rocky Colavito who did some of the most notable battling. In 1961, the former Indians slugger, who'd been very popular with Cleveland fans, wasn't as well received as a Tiger, and the pressure apparently got to him. He once went after an official scorer who charged him with a controversial error. When a drunken fan heckled him at Yankee Stadium, the outfielder climbed into the stands to attack the man, earning an ejection.

Getting His Kicks
Indians at Yankees, 1961

A few weeks after Jimmy Piersall kicked a fan who approached him at Yankee Stadium (Piersall said he thought the man might have been wielding a knife), two teenage fans charged the Indians outfielder in the first game of a doubleheader at the same site. He dropped the first one with a punch, then chased the other, but he was too far away to land a kick. No matter; Piersall's teammates and the police helped out. Asked if he wanted to press charges against the fans, Piersall refused, saying, "I've had 117 fights, and that's the first time I've ever won."

Jekyll or Hyde? Hard to Tell
Dodgers at Giants, 1981

Reggie Smith, a normally even-tempered man, could only take so much harassment. Giants fan Michael Dooley had been taunting the Dodgers outfielder from behind the Giants dugout. "You stink! You have no class!" Smith recalled the heckler saying. Smith could tolerate the verbal barbs, even tossing a few back. However, when the fan threw a souvenir batting helmet at him in the sixth inning, Smith climbed into the stands and landed a solid punch on Dooley that triggered a five-minute fracas between Dodgers players and Giants fans. Eight fans were taken into custody, and Dooley was treated for injuries at a nearby hospital.

Belle's Bull's-Eye
Angels at Indians, 1991

An Angels fan taunted Cleveland outfielder Albert Belle from the left-field stands, sarcastically inviting the recovering alcoholic to a keg party. In response, the Indians slugger picked up a foul ball in the seventh inning, turned, and unleashed a laser into the fan's chest from 15 feet away. Belle's one-week suspension was reduced to six games upon appeal, but he was also ordered to pay $3,846—one week's salary—to a charity of his choice.

"Nasty Boy" Scores Takedown
Astros at Cubs, 1995

Reliever Randy Myers comprised one-third of the Cincinnati Reds' "Nasty Boys" pitching trio in the '90s before he wound up pitching for the Chicago Cubs. At least one Chicago fan forgot Myers's reputation for nastiness, however, when he charged the mound at Wrigley Field after Myers gave up an eighth-inning, two-run homer. Myers used his martial arts background to deliver a crushing blow. "He reached for his pocket, and I thought it could be for a knife or a gun, so I dropped him with a forearm," Myers said. He expertly kept the fan pinned to the ground until teammates rushed to his aid.

Unhappy Homecoming
Astros at Brewers, 1999

Bill Spiers, a former Brewer, was back in Milwaukee as an Astro when a fan ran onto the field and jumped him. Said Spiers, "I looked down and saw blue jeans wrapped around my neck. I couldn't move, so I fell down backwards trying to get him off me." Mike Hampton and other teammates came to the rescue. Hampton delivered some hard kicks to the instigator, who was arrested and held on $250,000 bail. Spiers tried to stay in the game despite scrapes, bruises, and whiplash but was removed in the next inning.

Hats Off, But Dodgers Object
Dodgers at Cubs, 2000

In the ninth inning of a game at Wrigley Field, a Cubs fan swiped rival catcher Chad Kreuter's cap and may have hit him as well. At the same time, others doused the Dodgers bullpen with beer. When Kreuter went after the main offender, his teammates followed. Chaos ensued for several minutes. Nine days after the Dodgers' 6–5 win, Major League Baseball suspended 16 players and three coaches for their involvement, though some of the suspensions were reduced on appeal. The moral of the story? "If you wanted a hat that bad, be polite and ask for one," said Dodger Todd Hundley.

Not One of His Best Pitches
Rangers at Athletics, 2004

After Oakland fans taunted the Rangers bullpen, pitcher Frank Francisco decided to take matters into his own hands. More specifically, he took a plastic folding chair and threw it toward the hecklers. The chair hit a man in the head, then a woman in the face, breaking her nose. Francisco pleaded no contest to a misdemeanor assault charge and was sentenced to a work program and anger management classes.

Who in the Hall?

1) When Whitey Ford pitched 33⅓ consecutive scoreless World Series innings, whose 43-year-old record of 29⅔ did he break?

A: *Babe Ruth's*

2) Who captured more league strikeout crowns than any other pitcher?

A: *Walter Johnson (12)*

3) Who became the first former major-league non-pitcher to play professionally in Japan?

A: *Larry Doby, with Chunichi in 1962*

4) Which future Hall of Famers comprised two-ninths of baseball's first entirely non-white starting lineup on September 1, 1971?

A: *Roberto Clemente and Willie Stargell of the Pirates*

5) Who pitched no-hitters during the terms of three different U.S. presidents?

A: *Cy Young*

6) Who are the only two players in history to steal a base in four different decades?

A: *Ted Williams and Rickey Henderson*

7) Which player graced the cover of the first edition of *Sports Illustrated?*

A: *Eddie Mathews*

8) Which Hall of Famer is the only grandfather ever to hit a major-league home run?

A: *Stan Musial, at age 42, hours after the birth of his grandson*

9) Who hit his first home run inside the park and the remaining 510 of his career over the wall?

A: *Mel Ott*

Magic at the Plate

Get ready for some eye-bulging stats. These are the greatest season-long hitting performances in MLB history.

Baseball is a numbers game, and over the course of a long season those numbers tend to even out. A batter might hit over .400 for a month or even two, but over the course of a long season, that average is bound to drop. A great hitter might slump for a few weeks, but eventually that average will creep back up to where it belongs.

Every now and then, however, something special happens: pure magic at the plate. Fans come to expect steady greatness from certain players, but over the years even some of the most consistent stars have reached dizzying heights at the plate, exceeding the expectations of even their biggest fans.

Nap Lajoie, 1901, Philadelphia Athletics

The Numbers: .426 BA, 14 HR, 125 RBI, 145 R, 232 H, .463 OBP, .643 SLG

The Dominance: More than a century later, the batting average Lajoie posted in the American League's inaugural season remains the best in league history. The batting race wasn't much of a contest: Second-place Mike Donlin hit .340. Nap took home the Triple Crown, leading the AL in—among other categories—home runs, RBI, hits, total bases, slugging percentage, and on-base percentage. His contributions to the AL helped legitimize the junior circuit.

Ty Cobb, 1911, Detroit Tigers

The Numbers: .420 BA, 8 HR, 127 RBI, 147 R, 248 H, .467 OBP, .621 SLG, 83 SB

The Dominance: In the midst of the "dead-ball era," the Georgia Peach found all kinds of ways to create offense. His average was the best in the major leagues, and he stole 25 more bases than his nearest AL pursuer. He paced the league in singles, doubles, triples, runs, RBI, and slugging, and his eight home runs ranked second. The result was perhaps the greatest offensive campaign since Nap Lajoie's a decade earlier.

Babe Ruth, 1920, New York Yankees

The Numbers: .376 BA, 54 HR, 137 RBI, 158 R, .532 OBP, .847 SLG, 150 BB

The Dominance: Ruth enjoyed several colossal seasons, but this was one of the best. He had set the major-league season home run record a year before, socking 29 in his final year in Boston; in 1920, he matched that number in his home stadium alone. The Babe's total homer output (54) topped that of every other *team* in the AL, and he outslugged every NL club save Philadelphia. The Browns' George Sisler, with 19 homers, was baseball's second-leading long-ball hitter.

Babe Ruth, 1921, New York Yankees

The Numbers: .378 BA, 59 HR, 171 RBI, 177 R, 457 TB, .512 OBP, .846 SLG

The Dominance: Yes, Ruth broke his own home run record, and that garnered the headlines of the day. Looking back, however, it was his remarkable total base standard that set this season apart. It was 92 sacks superior to his nearest AL competitor, and to this day it remains a major-league record. Ruth also led the league in RBI and runs by 32 and 45, respectively, posting career-high totals in each.

Rogers Hornsby, 1922, St. Louis Cardinals

The Numbers: .401 BA, 42 HR, 152 RBI, 141 R, 250 H, 450 TB, .722 SLG

The Dominance: Hornsby's batting average was 47 points higher than his nearest National League pursuer. His home run and RBI totals also led the league, giving him the first of his two Triple Crowns. He racked up 136 more bases than anyone else in the NL; his total has not been matched by any major-leaguer since. What's more, Hornsby shattered the previous NL season home run record of 27.

Fans...or Fanatics?

Love is strange ... and noisy, too.

Some fans skim through the daily game reports and nod at the stats. Some pore over articles and numbers from across the country. And then there are the ultimate devotees—the ones whose lives would scarcely seem to exist without their team.

Hilda Chester—Brooklyn Dodgers
Famous for ringing her cowbell from the center-field bleachers in Ebbets Field, Chester was the epitome of the raucous Dodger fan. She carried not just one cowbell but two—one to ring out in celebration and the other to toll in mourning. (One of the bells is now in Cooperstown.) She also carried a large sign that let everyone know "Hilda Is Here."

Wild Bill Hagy—Baltimore Orioles
From Section 34 of Baltimore's Memorial Stadium in the late 1970s arose a large, long-haired, full-bearded, well-beered cab driver who spelled out O-R-I-O-L-E-S with his body, and the crowd went bonkers. One writer said Hagy had "a voice that sounds like a cement mixer in action." When told he was "amazing," Wild Bill responded, "There ain't nothing amazing about it. They could do the same thing if they drank a case of beer every night."

Lolly Hopkins—Boston Red Sox
Lolly was a Boston fan of the pre–World War II era who would never think of hollering: She used a megaphone. And, in polite New England style, she was  perfectly willing to cheer for good play on the part of either team.

Bruce "Screech Owl" McAllister—Pittsburgh Pirates
It wasn't a pleasant sound, but it was memorable. When Bruce McAllister let go one of his patented screams back in the 1930s, no

one sitting in Forbes Field could miss it. Of course, with KDKA beaming Pirate games all over the East and Midwest, Bruce would often be heard in Connecticut and Missouri, too.

Mike "'Nuf Ced" McGreevy—Boston Red Sox

The man's moniker came about because he was the ultimate authority on any sports question you threw at him. Bartender McGreevy headed the Royal Rooters, a raucous group of Boston fans who drove the Pirates wacky in the 1903 World Series with their pronounced singing of "Tessie" (with words altered to hassle the Pirates players). In 1912, when a front-office blunder shut the Rooters out of Game 6 of the World Series, they just broke down the gates and marched around the field.

Mary Ott—St. Louis Cardinals

One writer called Ott's voice "a neigh known to cause stampedes in Kansas City stockyards." That's particularly impressive when you realize Mary lived in St. Louis! Ott's voice carried, but she testified to her love of what she called "scientific rooting," the art of getting the other team's goat with her scornful laugh. The "Horse Lady of St. Louis" first came to national attention when revered umpire Bill Klem threatened to throw her out of a game in 1926.

Patsy O'Toole—Detroit Tigers

In 1930s Detroit, the fan who made the most noise was Patsy, who rightfully earned his nickname as the "All-American earache." Opposing players got the full brunt of a Patsy attack, and he was especially tough on the hated Yankees.

Jack Pierce—Brooklyn Dodgers

Pierce's fandom bordered on obsession. He was sure that Dodger infielder Cookie Lavagetto was the greatest player ever. So to honor his idol, Pierce showed up at Ebbets Field every day, bought ten seats, and—using containers of gas he brought along— blew up dozens of balloons with "Cookie" written on them. He released them throughout the game. He even continued this ritual in 1942, when Cookie was in the Army, not in Brooklyn.

From Bad to Worse

The integrity of the game is of utmost importance in baseball.
Unfortunately, that honor has not always been upheld.

Money to Be Made? You Bet.

Game-fixing didn't start with the 1919 White Sox, although the
Black Sox scandal has come to define this crime. It actually began
when the National League was barely a year old.

The first-place 1877 Louisville Grays made a number of suspicious errors during an Eastern road trip that caused them to lose
seven games and tie one. This prompted speculation that players
dumped games—and the pennant—intentionally. It turned out
they did. Western Union telegrams linked players with a known
gambler, and four men—Bill Craver, Jim Devlin, Al Nichols, and
George Hall (who confessed)—were banned from baseball for life.

The first two decades of the 20th century were also filled with
baseball corruption. First baseman Hal Chase served as its poster
boy, having been linked to several "thrown" games before earning
a ban for his role in the Black Sox scandal. Additionally, there were
attempts to bribe umpires (Bill Klem in 1908) and even official
scorers (a 1910 attempt to get Cleveland's Nap Lajoie a batting
title over the unpopular Ty Cobb). Suspicions that the 1914, 1917,
and 1918 World Series were fixed were never proven; if they had
been, perhaps the drama of 1919 would have been avoided. As it
was, banning the eight White Sox players for life served notice that
baseball was serious about keeping its games on the up-and-up.

Charlie "Hustle"

If the 1919 White Sox are Exhibit A in the argument against game-
fixing, Pete Rose holds the same distinction when it comes to the
dangers of gambling. In 1989, the all-time major-league hits king
was banned from baseball (and, subsequently, from becoming
eligible for Hall of Fame election) for making baseball bets while
managing the Cincinnati Reds.

Initially, Rose vehemently denied having bet on the game. In
his 2003 book *My Prison Without Bars*, however, he admitted

to placing as many as five wagers per week on Reds games while serving as the team's manager. He insists he never bet *against* the Reds as he continues to plead his case for reinstatement, but thus far the commissioner's office has held its ground.

Rose wrote: "I've consistently heard the statement: 'If Pete Rose came clean, all would be forgiven.' Well, I've done what you've asked. The rest is up to the commissioner and the big umpire in the sky."

Colluding with the "Enemy"

Collusion is defined as a secret agreement, particularly one used for treacherous purposes. Baseball fans learned the word in the 1980s, when owners apparently worked together to keep player salaries down at a time when the game was thriving financially.

From 1984 to 1987, baseball attendance soared, as did licensing revenues and profit margins, yet free-agent salaries did not keep pace. For example, in 1985 more than half of all players who filed for free agency wound up signing with other clubs. The following year, however, only four of 33 signed deals with new teams; the rest re-signed with their old clubs—some for less money than they'd made before. Furthermore, most were only offered one-year contracts.

The players' union filed a grievance in February 1986 called *Collusion I.*, and 19 months later an arbitrator ruled in their favor. Team owners were forced to pay damages for their decision not to outbid one another for players, thus stifling salary growth. Collusion grievances were brought twice more against owners during this period. Arbitrators sided with players on those occasions, too. In all, owners were found to owe more than $100 million in the 1980s collusion cases.

Cocaine Crackdown

Celebrating wins or drowning the sorrow of a loss into the early morning hours can be traced back to baseball's inception. And some of the game's greatest players were also among its legendary carousers. Somewhere along the line, however, instances of illegal and dangerous off-field behavior became no innocent matter.

Texas pitcher Fergie Jenkins was arrested in 1980 and charged with possession of marijuana, hashish, and cocaine. What followed was a rapid-fire succession of drug-related incidents. Padres rookie Alan Wiggins was arrested for cocaine possession in 1982. That year also marked the first of several rehab attempts by Dodgers pitcher Steve Howe, who was repeatedly suspended. Kansas City teammates Willie Aikens, Vida Blue, Jerry Martin, and Willie Wilson pleaded guilty in 1983 to attempting to purchase cocaine.

In 1985, a federal grand jury in Pittsburgh heard testimony from 11 active big-leaguers. The result: An indictment of seven drug dealers who were linked to players between 1979 and '85. During the "Pittsburgh Drug Trials," Mets first baseman Keith Hernandez estimated that 40 percent of players had used cocaine. Soon after, some of his teammates—most notably Dwight Gooden and Darryl Strawberry—were counted among that number.

Steroid Scandals

Throughout the past decade, the game's longstanding home run records have fallen in rapid succession as several players made enormous gains in strength and stature. Few would argue that some of those gains have not been natural ones. In fact, in his 2004 State of the Union address, President George W. Bush called for "strong steps" to be taken to rid baseball of performance-enhancing drugs.

While the "steroid scandal" has been highlighted by far more speculation than fact, grand jury testimony in a highly publicized case against the San Francisco–area laboratory BALCO did produce some compelling information about the use of these drugs. As a result of the same case, Barry Bonds admitted to using two types of performance enhancers—the "clear" and the "cream"—but said it was without knowledge of what those substances contained; as of 2009, Bonds is under federal indictment for perjury.

Bob Sheppard:
The Voice of Yankee Stadium

With a voice as familiar to fans as any player in Yankees history, Bob Sheppard became a baseball legend in his own right.

Reggie Jackson called announcer Bob Sheppard's vocals "The Voice of God." A plaque in Yankee Stadium's Monument Park, displayed next to those of Jackson, Ruth, DiMaggio, and other pinstriped legends, deems him "The Voice of Yankee Stadium."

Whatever one calls the incomparable Sheppard is inconsequential compared to the way *he* called batters to the plate in the Bronx. His first lineups included Joe DiMaggio, Mickey Mantle, and Yogi Berra for the Yankees and Ted Williams for the visiting Red Sox.

Sheppard's perfect diction, deliberate pace, and classy style are impossible to convey on paper, but those who have heard him would not have a hard time believing he once taught speech at St. John's University or that he serves as a lector at his church.

Since his debut on April 17, 1951, when he first boomed the words, "Ladies and gentlemen, welcome to Yankee Stadium," Sheppard delighted crowds at more than 4,500 major-league games, including 22 World Series. He also served for nearly 50 years as the voice of the New York Giants football team. Well into his 90s, he could still roam the corridors of Yankee Stadium and be recognized only occasionally.

His voice, however, is a different story—few lovers of America's pastime would have a hard time placing that deep, distinguished tone. It belongs to a man who prefers unique names like Melky Cabrera to easy ones like Steve Sax, who went about his job in the same hardworking manner for more than 55 years, and who is so irreplaceable that some Yankees consider a digital recording of Sheppard as his only viable replacement. Sheppard once noted, "Most men go to work. I go to a game. Not a bad life, is it?"

All-Time Great

Barry Bonds

He leaped from excellence to true greatness at an age when many others are hanging it up.

Born: July 24, 1964; Riverside, CA
MLB Career: Pittsburgh Pirates, 1986–1992; San Francisco Giants, 1992–2007
Hall of Fame Resume: 73 homers, 2001 • All-time home run leader • Seven-time league MVP • Three-time MLB Player of the Year • 762 home runs, lifetime (through 2007)
Inside Pitch: Barry and his father, Bobby, are the only players who've each had five 30-homer/30-steal seasons.

If you're looking for truly dramatic proof of what a sensational hitter Barry Bonds is, you'll find it in his stats for walks received. No hitter ever intimidated pitchers and managers into giving up a free base like Barry did. Consider this: Babe Ruth was walked 170 times in 1923. For the next 77 years, no one came close to that figure. Then Barry Bonds garnered 177 walks in 2001. Three years later, he was passed an unbelievable 232 times. A record that had held for three-quarters of a century was leapfrogged by 36 percent. It's the equivalent of someone breaking Hack Wilson's RBI record of 191 by knocking in 260 runs!

Because his father was a highly talented star, Barry Bonds grew up in major-league locker rooms. His godfather was Willie Mays. So he was never intimidated by the atmosphere or the attention of the big leagues. When he began his career with the Pirates in 1986, his cocky attitude showed that he knew he belonged. Bonds was at the center of a developing team that canny GM Syd Thrift was building slowly but surely. In 1990, it all came together: The team won the NL East, and Bonds led the way with a .301 average, 33 homers, and a league-leading slugging percentage. He also drove in 114 runs, stole 52 bases, and won his first MVP Award. The Pirates took their division the next two seasons, as well, with

Bonds winning another MVP Award in 1992. After that season, the brash Bonds made it clear he was looking for big money, and if Pittsburgh couldn't deliver, he'd move on.

He made good on his promise when he signed with the San Francisco Giants in December 1992 for $43 million over six years. San Fran fans were pleased, and Bonds won his third MVP Award that year, belting 46 home runs. For the next three years, Bonds put up big numbers, but his teams were subpar. He routinely hit 30 to 45 home runs and tallied more than 100 RBI. The Giants rebounded to win their division in 1997 and 2000, but the post-season, in which Bonds always faltered, continued to be a struggle. They lost in the first round both times, with Barry collecting just six hits in those seven games.

Meanwhile Bonds was undertaking an intensive strength-building program. He'd always had a quick bat, but the combination of eye surgery and newly bulked-up muscles (perhaps due to steroid use, many have speculated) turned him into an incredibly disciplined home run hitter, the likes of which the game had never seen before. The result was that in 2001, Bonds blew past the record of 70 home runs set by Mark McGwire  in 1998, pounding out a total of 73. That, along with his .863 slugging percentage (breaking Ruth's 81-year-old record), firmly established Bonds as one of the most elite sluggers in baseball history.

His performance in the 2002 postseason finally knocked that particular monkey off his back, as he batted .471 in the World Series and hit eight home runs in 17 postseason games. In 2006, he moved past Babe Ruth for second-most homers lifetime, and a year later, he broke Hank Aaron's all-time record.

ERA on the Mound

The women who brought new meaning to "ERA" in baseball.

The year was 1931, and the New York Yankees were making their way north from spring training, stopping to play exhibition games along the way. Facing the Chattanooga Lookouts, they must have been surprised when they saw their mound opponent was a 17-year-old girl named Jackie Mitchell. Was she serious? She certainly thought she was, and she bent off several wicked curveballs, striking out Babe Ruth and Lou Gehrig consecutively on only seven pitches. A few days later, Commissioner Kenesaw Mountain Landis voided her contract, insisting that baseball was "too strenuous" for a woman. Mitchell began barnstorming with the House of David team, but after a few years she grew tired of the sideshow antics and retired to work at her father's optometry office. Although she continued to play with local teams from time to time, Mitchell did not play professional baseball again.

It would be 66 years until another woman played in a professional game. Her name was Ila Borders, and she got her chance with the St. Paul Saints of the independent Northern League after being signed by Mike Veeck, son of the legendary Bill Veeck, Jr., in 1997. One month into the regular season, Borders was traded to the Duluth-Superior Dukes, where she saw limited use. In all, she had 15 appearances, a 7.53 ERA, and no decisions for the season. She was back with the Dukes for 1998, however, and in her third appearance of the season, she became the first woman to win a men's pro game—a 3–1 victory in which she pitched six scoreless innings.

Borders was praised for her nearly perfect mechanics, "a curve with a variety of breaks, a changeup that worked like a screwball," her control, and her "pitching smarts." However, her fastball just wasn't strong enough to allow her to compete consistently. Although *Sports Illustrated* named her one of the top 100 female athletes of all time while she was still active, and she had a 1.67 ERA in 15 appearances in 1999 for the Madison Black Wolf of the Northern League, she retired after the 2000 season.

Hall of Fame Talk

"To Johnny Bench, a Hall of Famer for sure."

—Inscription on ball signed by Ted Williams for Cincinnati's 20-year-old rookie catcher, spring training 1968

"I hope so, just as I hope someone will come along and break all my records. I wouldn't want my records to just stay in the books all the time. I'd like to see someone break them. It means there's improvement."

—Hank Aaron, when asked in 1971 if he felt he could break Babe Ruth's career home run record, *Hammerin' Hank of the Braves*

"Here lies a man who batted .300."

—What Cap Anson wanted on his tombstone; his lifetime average was .329

"I never had to be lonely behind the plate, where I could talk to hitters. I also learned that by engaging them in conversation, I could sometimes distract them."

—Catcher Roy Campanella, *It's Good to Be Alive*

"My favorite umpire is a dead one."

—Johnny Evers

"...the perfect hitter. Joe's swing was purely magical."

—Ty Cobb on Shoeless Joe Jackson, *Baseball Digest*, July 1973

Forgotten Shots

Some of baseball's most crucial home runs were overshadowed by a moment that proved even more magical.

Memorable home run: Bill Mazeroski's ninth-inning solo home run off Ralph Terry, Game 7 of the 1960 World Series
Forgotten dinger: Hal Smith's eighth-inning three-run home run off Jim Coates

Mazeroski's shot, the first ever to end a World Series, put a stunning cap on a wild victory for the Pirates that would have been impossible were it not for Hal Smith's one and only plate appearance in the game. Smith, a reserve catcher, entered the game in the eighth inning after Smoky Burgess, the Pirates starting catcher, was pulled for a pinch runner. Smith's two-out, three-run homer off Jim Coates capped a five-run rally, giving Pittsburgh a 9–7 lead that the Yankees erased with two runs of their own in the ninth.

Smith's three-run homer, which had spurred his team to the position they were in, fell by the wayside when Mazeroski deposited Ralph Terry's second pitch over the left-field wall at Forbes Field, winning the World Series for the Pirates despite the team having been outscored 55–27.

Memorable home run: Carlton Fisk's 12th-inning solo home run off Pat Darcy, Game 6 of the 1975 World Series
Forgotten dinger: Bernie Carbo's eighth-inning three-run home run off Rawly Eastwick

If Carlton Fisk provided the dramatic climax, Bernie Carbo supplied the surprise plot twist.

Batting for Rogelio Moret with two on and two out in the eighth and the Red Sox trailing 6–3, Carbo faced the Reds' Rawly Eastwick in what looked like a mismatch. Eastwick had already won two games and saved a third in the Series, and Carbo, some believed, was sent up to hit merely to tempt manager Sparky Anderson's famous hook. However, after working the count to 2–2, Carbo hacked at a waist-high inside fastball and sent it over the center-field fence. The hit set the stage for Fisk's 12th-inning shot off the foul pole, which tied the 1975 World Series at three games apiece. (The Reds won Game 7.)

Memorable home run: Kirk Gibson's ninth-inning two-run home run off Dennis Eckersley, Game 1 of the 1988 World Series
Forgotten dinger: Mickey Hatcher's first-inning two-run homer off Dave Stewart

The Dodgers' status as heavy underdogs to the mighty Oakland A's in the 1988 World Series was made more acute due to an injury to left fielder and NL MVP Kirk Gibson. His replacement, veteran Mickey Hatcher, who had hit only a single home run all year, connected for a two-run shot against A's ace Dave Stewart to open the scoring. Gibson eventually limped into action and hit the decisive shot off closer Dennis Eckersley in his only appearance of the Series. But Hatcher wasn't finished. He hit another home run in the Dodgers' five-game upset and finished the Series with a .368 average.

Memorable home run: Aaron Boone's 11th-inning solo home run off Tim Wakefield, Game 7 of the 2003 ALCS
Forgotten dingers: Jason Giambi's fifth- and seventh-inning solo home runs off Pedro Martinez

Grady Little's lazy trigger finger and Aaron Boone's game-ending home run are the lasting images of one of the cruelest heartbreakers in Red Sox history. Boston starter Pedro Martinez was magnificent through the first seven innings but faltered in the eighth. Red Sox manager Little waited to lift Martinez until after the Yankees had erased a three-run lead on four straight hits. To that point, the only blemishes on Martinez's game were solo home runs by Jason Giambi in the fifth and seventh innings that put the previously scoreless Yankees on the board and kept them alive. By the end of the eighth, the game was an even 5–5.

In the bottom of the 11th, with the game still tied, Boone launched Tim Wakefield's first delivery into the left-field stands at Yankee Stadium, ending the game and the Series in favor of New York—and also ending Little's employment with the crestfallen Red Sox.

Learning the Lingo

To live in the world of baseball, one must speak the language.

Annie Oakley: A walk. **Origin:** Named for the riflewoman who could shoot holes in a playing card, making the card resemble a punched ticket, or free pass.

Bases drunk: Bases "loaded." **Origin:** Euphemism.

Bean: A player's head. A "beanball" is a pitch aimed at it. **Origin:** Descriptive.

Bonehead, Boner: A mistake-prone player or a botched play. **Origin:** Descriptive of a head that contains no brain, just a bone. Popularized by journalists writing of Fred Merkle's costly base-running blunder in 1908.

Cakewalk: An easy win or easy opponent. **Origin:** Dance contests that offered a cake as the prize.

Chin music: Inside brushback pitch close to the jaw. Also: "a close shave." **Origin:** Descriptive. "Music" is the whooshing of the ball.

Clubhouse lawyer: A player who frequently talks about and/or undermines a manager or teammate. **Origin:** Descriptive of verbose prosecutors or defense attorneys. Probably began with sportswriters alarmed at "Bolshevik" views among early attempts at unionization.

Collar: Going hitless in a game. **Origin:** Descriptive. The shape of a collar resembles the number zero.

Cup of coffee: A brief stay in the majors or with one team. **Origin:** Hyperbole, suggesting a player was there only long enough to have a cup of coffee.

Gas: An especially quick fastball. **Origin:** The automobile. Stepping on the gas to accelerate.

Gopher ball: A pitch hit well, often for a long home run. **Origin:** A pun on "go for," as in a hit that will "go for extra bases," or a pitch a batter will "go for."

Handcuff: An inside pitch at the hands, or a ball batted directly at a fielder that's difficult to field. Also: "shackle." **Origin:** Descriptive.

Hot Stove League: The baseball off-season. **Origin:** Descriptive of winter gatherings around a stove.

Mendoza Line: A batting average of .200, marking the threshold between a below-average hitter and an extremely poor one. **Origin:** A remark by George Brett (some accounts say Bruce Botche or Tom Paciorek) referring to his batting average relative to that of Mario Mendoza, the light-hitting infielder and career .215 hitter of the 1970s and '80s.

Muffin: An unskilled player. **Origin:** Common in the 19th century, probably descriptive of something new like a freshly baked muffin. A muffin is prone to "muff," or make a foolish mistake.

Paint the black: A pitch on the inside or outside corners of the strike zone. **Origin:** Descriptive of the black outline of home plate.

Pickle: A rundown play. **Origin:** Dates back to Shakespeare, as a description for a compromising position.

The Show: The major leagues, often from the perspective of a minor-leaguer. **Origin:** Descriptive of larger crowds, parks, and more media and amenities relative to the minors.

Squeezed: When an umpire calls a tight strike zone. **Origin:** Descriptive.

The Game That Wouldn't End

A 1985 Mets–Braves game lasted nearly seven hours and featured 29 runs and 46 hits over 19 innings.

It was getting late on July 4, 1985, at Atlanta's Fulton County Stadium. Rick Aguilera was scheduled to start for the New York Mets the following night against the Braves, so the pitcher returned to his hotel room for some rest. When he woke up at 3:00 A.M. and saw Braves–Mets baseball on his TV, Aguilera assumed it was highlights from the game and went back to sleep. Never in his wildest dreams would he have imagined his teammates were still playing. But they were.

It was the game that wouldn't end, which was a shame for those among the 44,947 in attendance who were there mainly for the Independence Day fireworks after the game. First, there were two rain delays. Then, after the Mets took a 10–8 lead in the 13th and it appeared the end was at hand, the Braves scored twice in the bottom of the inning. New York scored another run in the 18th, but a home run by Braves reliever Rick Camp extended what had already become one of the longest games in major-league history.

Camp, however, gave up five runs in the top of the 19th. Atlanta managed two runs in the bottom of the frame, but the time had come to surrender. The Mets won 16–13, recording the final out at 3:53 A.M. after six hours and ten minutes of play.

New York's Keith Hernandez hit for the cycle. The Mets pounded out a club-record 28 hits. Only one position player, third-string Mets catcher Ronn Reynolds, did not get in the game. New York's Darryl Strawberry and manager Davey Johnson were ejected in the 17th inning for arguing balls and strikes; they were outlasted by about 8,000 fans.

As a reward to those who stuck it out, the Braves decided to go ahead with the fireworks—to the dismay of those who lived near the ballpark. Many Atlanta residents awoke to what they thought were gunshots at just past 4:00 A.M.

"It probably wasn't the best game I ever played in," said Braves third baseman Ken Oberkfell, "but it certainly was the oddest."

"The Catch"

The catch that made 111 wins irrelevant.

The Setting: Polo Grounds, New York; September 29, 1954
The Magic: Willie Mays hauls down Vic Wertz's drive and changes the World Series.

The 1954 World Series was unusual primarily because of the absence of the Yankees, who had won the championship the previous five years. The Giants and Indians teams that faced each other that year had a lot in common: Both had led their leagues in home runs and runs scored, and each boasted that year's league batting champion (Willie Mays of the Giants and Bobby Avila of the Indians). Mays was in the top five in on-base percentage and slugging percentage, as was the Tribe's Al Rosen. Both teams' pitching staffs led their leagues in fewest hits allowed, earned run average, and opponent batting average. But those who set the odds made Cleveland the favorite for two reasons: The Indians had set an American League record with 111 wins, and the AL was considered the stronger league by far. (The Yankees had won 103 games that year.) But the oddsmakers hadn't counted on Willie.

It was the first game of the Series, tied at two in the eighth inning, when two Indians reached with nobody out. Indians first baseman Vic Wertz slugged a ball into the vast expanse of the Polo Grounds' right center field. But Mays zoomed out there, made the catch with his back to the plate, then spun and fired an immense strike to second, making the runner on first return. The catch was sensational; the throw otherworldly. The Giants won in ten innings, and the Indians never got back into the Series—New York swept them, and it was a dose of Mays Magic that made the difference.

◍ ◍ ◍

"I don't rate 'em, I just catch 'em."

—Willie Mays, when asked if he had a favorite among his defensive gems, *The Baseball Life of Willie Mays*

The Clown Princes of Baseball

Cracking up the fans by being goofy, wacky, and zany—such was the job of the baseball clown.

Before there were stadium video screens; T-shirt launchers; and PA systems that blared rock, rap, and reggae between pitches, there was the baseball clown. Forerunners of Mr. Met, the San Diego Chicken, the Phillie Phanatic, and every other major-league mascot, clowns used a brand of slapstick and pantomime that was sometimes more entertaining than the game.

Nick Altrock
Nick Altrock was the star pitcher of the 1906 "Hitless Wonder" White Sox and was instrumental in the team's World Series win. But an arm injury essentially ruined his career, and he was traded to the Washington Senators, where he became a coach in 1912. There, he started a clown act with infielder Germany Schaefer, until Schaefer defected to the Federal League. Altrock then teamed up with Al Schacht, the "Clown Prince of Baseball." Their antics kept Altrock in a Senators uniform for more than 40 years. He played up his oversized ears and mouth with exaggerated gestures, and he goofed around with a huge baseball glove. The fans also loved Altrock's one-man shadowboxing routine. He even made a joke of the record book, batting randomly in games until the age of 57.

Al Schacht
Born on the site that eventually became Yankee Stadium, Al Schacht once fanned Babe Ruth three times in a game in 1920. Schacht found his calling the following year, working with Nick Altrock in a clown act in the World Series. Schacht worked 25 World Series and 18 All-Star Games. Like Altrock, Schacht was hired by the Senators as a coach, but he gained fame for his signature tattered frock coat and crumpled top hat. He toured with the USO on three continents during World War II, opened a restaurant, and penned the cleverly titled tome *G.I. Had Fun*.

Jackie Price

Jackie Price showed potential as a ballplayer, but when his career seemed to be languishing, he incorporated his playing skills into entertaining performances as a way to stay in the game. Indians owner—and master showman—Bill Veeck hired Price in 1946 to perform for the crowd before games. Price even ended up playing in seven games that year, but mostly he kept the fans amazed and delighted by antics such as taking batting practice while hanging upside down. As part of his act, Price would sometimes wrap himself in live snakes; unfortunately, during a train ride with the team in 1947, Price let some of the snakes loose, and they frightened several passengers to the point that the conductor had to stop the train. Manager Lou Boudreau ordered him off the train, and that was the end of Price's career with the Indians. However, he did appear in short films and continued to travel with his act.

Max Patkin

Another player-turned-clown was Max Patkin, whose athletic skill petered out at the minor-league level. But when he served up a home run to Joe DiMaggio in a 1944 military exhibition and then chased DiMaggio around the bases, imitating his every move, a hilariously goofy star was born. Patkin was blessed with a rubber face, which he contorted in countless ways. He wore a patchwork of different uniforms with a question mark on the back. Unlike Nick Altrock and Al Schacht, Patkin did most of his work in the minors (although Veeck also hired him to perform at Indians games, too). He was beloved in small towns throughout America, even playing himself in the 1988 film *Bull Durham.* He never missed a scheduled appearance, performing more than 4,000 times until he finally retired in 1993.

(C) (C) (C)

Yanks' manager Charlie Dressen had an ingenious way of catching curfew violators. At 1:00 A.M., he'd give the hotel elevator operator a new baseball and tell him to collect as many autographs as he could.

Defensive Standouts

The most underrated part of the game has its own set of superstars.

Luis Aparicio, SS

Aparicio's 2,583 games played is second all-time among shortstops (surpassed by Omar Vizquel in 2008). He defined slick glovework for the position until Ozzie Smith came along, and he still holds the AL career records for assists (8,016) and putouts (4,548) by a short-stop. When he first came to the big leagues, he played very shallow; when he moved back, people were astonished by his arm.

Johnny Bench, C

Bench put it all together: size, strength, quickness, and a powerful arm. He invented the art of one-handed catching, the perfect style with which to cut down the fleet basestealers of his era (although some old-timers will tell you that the style has ruined every other catcher since). Bench was named an All-Star 14 times, and he won ten consecutive Gold Gloves.

Hal Chase, 1B

Some say there was never a better fielder at first base. Smooth and handy, Chase was able to charge a bunt, snatch the ball, tag the man heading to first, and then make a strong throw to second or third to nail the advancing runner. In 1906, he had 22 putouts in a single game, tying a record that still stands. His Achilles' heel was errors, but many of his may have been intentional—"Prince Hal" was repeatedly accused of throwing games for money or trying to bribe others to do the same.

Roberto Clemente, OF

The Pirates right fielder could get to the ball and throw it as well as anyone had ever seen. And no one had ever seen it done with such ferocity, as though each ball hit his way was a personal threat. The list of great Clemente catches and throws is a long one; par-ticularly memorable was a play early in the 1971 World Series that turned the usually aggressive Orioles into timid baserunners.

Eddie Collins, 2B

Collins was the heart of one of baseball's first great infields—the "$100,000 Infield" of Connie Mack's Philadelphia Athletics. He may have been the most complete player of his era, and he played for a long time (1906–30). Nine times he led the American League in fielding percentage, and he's the all-time career leader in assists and chances by a second baseman.

Ray Dandridge, 3B

Because African Americans were banned from playing in the major leagues during his career, most fans never saw the artistry of Dandridge, a man with bowed legs, soft hands, and a superb arm. Roy Campanella once said, "I never saw anyone better as a fielder." In the late '30s, when Dandridge was playing third for the Newark Eagles, someone offered the opinion that the team's infielders would be worth a million dollars if they were white.

George Davis, SS

George Davis was one of baseball's unsung heroes of the turn of the 20th century. He started as an outfielder, but his hands and range were such that he was moved to shortstop. He was the star of the "Hitless Wonders" White Sox team that engineered one of the greatest upsets in World Series history—the toppling of the 116-game-winning Cubs in 1906.

Joe DiMaggio, OF

He was grace and elegance personified, and although others (including his brother Dom) put up better defensive stats, Joe DiMaggio patrolled the ominous spaces of Yankee Stadium with remarkable efficiency for a team that hardly ever seemed to lose. DiMaggio was careful to position himself for hitters' tendencies, and his arm was excellent. He occasionally neared perfection in his outfield play.

Buck Ewing, C

Although his name is largely forgotten now, Ewing was considered one of the greatest players of all time during his 1880–97 stint in the majors. Ewing was said to be the first catcher to throw from a crouch position and the first to back up other bases. He was also blessed with a sensational arm: He led his league in assists three times.

Keith Hernandez, 1B
Hernandez put together a string of 11 consecutive Gold Glove Awards (1978–88) because he was simply the best of his time. He holds the major-league record for most seasons leading first basemen in double plays (six). Hernandez, like Hal Chase, was known to charge to the third base line on bunts. In the "fielding runs" statistic that was created recently to determine how many runs are saved by an above-average fielder, Hernandez is the all-time leader among first basemen.

Andruw Jones, OF
While some outfielders are famous for their flashy catches, Jones makes the impossible look like a walk on the beach. From 1998 to 2007, he won ten consecutive Gold Glove Awards; no National Leaguer had done that since Ozzie Smith.

Jim Kaat, P
Even though he was a big guy at 6′4″ and 200-plus pounds, Kaat fielded his position like his idol, the tiny Bobby Shantz. No one was quicker off the mound to snag bunts or to cover first. His 16 Gold Gloves tie him with Brooks Robinson, behind Greg Maddux, for the second-most at any position.

Willie Mays, OF
Perhaps the most complete baseball player ever, Mays stood in center field and dared anyone to hit the ball to him. He could dive, leap, or slide for the tough ones, or use his trademark basket catch on the easy ones. His great catch in the 1954 World Series (one of the first such plays immortalized on film) was just as notable for the unbelievable throw he uncorked after the backward grab.

Bill Mazeroski, 2B

The Babe Ruth of defense, Mazeroski holds more defensive records than anyone else who has ever played. He holds major-league records for double plays by a second baseman, with 1,706 (Nellie Fox is a distant second, with 1,568), and double plays in a season, with 161 in 1966. Mazeroski led NL second sackers in double plays a record eight times, in chances a league-record eight times, and in assists a record nine times (including five in a row—another record).

Brooks Robinson, 3B

Nobody ever did it better at third than Brooks. He holds the highest lifetime fielding percentage among third sackers (.971) and is also the all-time leader in putouts (2,697), assists (6,205), and double plays (618) at the hot corner. No wonder he won 16 consecutive Gold Gloves and started in the All-Star Game 15 years in a row. His defensive work in the 1970 World Series is absolutely classic.

Ivan Rodriguez, C

"Pudge" Rodriguez redefined the idea of a catcher's arm. He had several seasons in which he threw out half of those who tried to steal against him (when around 40 percent is considered good for other catchers). His ability to remove the opposition's running game greatly helped his pitchers. He won ten Gold Gloves in a row, was bypassed for two seasons, then won another three.

Ozzie Smith, SS

"The Wizard" was one of the flashiest, most exciting shortstops ever. And he didn't miss the easy ones, either: He leads all shortstops in career assists. No other shortstop has led his league in assists (eight times) or chances (eight) more often. Smith's 1980 record of 621 assists smashed by 20 the previous mark, set by Glenn Wright in 1924.

Tris Speaker, OF

A lifetime .345 hitter, "Spoke" played the best outfield anyone had ever seen. Playing a shallow center, he turned an unassisted double play from the outfield a record six times (plus another in the 1912 World Series) in his career. No major-league outfielder ever threw out more runners or took part in more double plays. Only Willie Mays caught more fly balls.

Omar Vizquel, SS
When the last batter in Chris Bosio's 1993 no-hitter attempt grounded to Vizquel, the shortstop grabbed the ball barehanded and threw him out. Vizquel, who won nine consecutive Gold Gloves from 1993 to 2001, and 11 overall, has been delivering exceptional defense with a flair stylish enough to remind folks of Ozzie Smith, and he's been doing it since 1989.

Honus Wagner, SS
Wagner was so good at every position he played that he didn't become a full-time shortstop until he was almost 30 years old, but he still ranks as the best overall shortstop of all time. Built more like a barrel than an infielder, he was incredibly fast, and he had a powerful arm that could throw runners out from anywhere. He won eight batting titles in his career and fielded as well as he hit.

⚾ ⚾ ⚾

"I don't want to embarrass any other catcher by comparing them to Johnny Bench."

—Sparky Anderson, *50th Anniversary Hall of Fame Yearbook*

⚾ ⚾ ⚾

"He took great delight in fielding a base hit in right field with a man on first base and pausing. He'd just stand there, sometimes in deep right, and hold the ball saying, 'Go ahead to third.' Runners wouldn't dare go because Clemente nailed them every time."

—Maury Wills on Roberto Clemente, *On the Run*

Index

Contributing Writers

Paul Adomites has authored or coauthored six books, including *October's Game, The Golden Age of Baseball,* and *Babe Ruth: His Life and Times*. A former publications director for the Society for American Baseball Research (SABR), Paul founded the SABR *Review of Books* and published its successor, *The Cooperstown Review*. He is currently the book review editor for *Base Ball: A Journal of the Early Game*.

Bruce Markusen is the author of eight books, including *A Baseball Dynasty: Charlie Finley's Swingin' A's,* which was awarded the Seymour Medal from the Society for American Baseball Research (SABR). He also wrote *The Team That Changed Baseball: Roberto Clemente and the 1971 Pittsburgh Pirates, Tales From the Mets Dugout,* and *The Orlando Cepeda Story*. An employee of the National Baseball Hall of Fame and Museum from 1995 to 2004, Markusen currently authors MLB.com's "Cooperstown Confidential," found atbruce.mlblogs.com.

Matthew Silverman is the author of *Mets Essential,* the coauthor of *Meet the Mets,* and the coauthor (with Jon Springer) of *Mets by the Numbers*. He has been an associate editor for *The ESPN Baseball Encyclopedia* since 2004. Silverman served as principal editor for *Baseball: The Biographical Encyclopedia* and was managing editor for the sixth and seventh editions of *Total Baseball*. He has edited many other books, including *The Ultimate Red Sox Companion, Ted Williams: My Life in Pictures,* and two versions of *Total Mets*.

Jon Springer is an editor at a business publication in New York. He is a member of the Society for American Baseball Research (SABR) and the creator and author of "Mets by the Numbers" (www.mbtn.net).

Marty Strasen is an editor at www.TBO.com/*The Tampa Tribune* in Florida. He has authored or been a contributing writer on several sports books, including *Dark Horses & Underdogs* and *Reel Baseball: Baseball's Golden Era*.

Saul Wisnia is the author or coauthor of numerous books about baseball and other subjects, including *Prime Time Baseball Stars, Wit & Wisdom of Baseball, Babe Ruth: His Life and Times,* and *Best of Baseball*. A former sports and features correspondent for *The Washington Post,* Wisnia has also written for *The Boston Globe, Sports Illustrated,* the *Boston Herald, Red Sox Magazine,* and many other publications. He is a founding member of the Boston Braves Historical Association.